Culture, development and social theory

About the author

JOHN CLAMMER is currently Visiting Professor of Development Sociology at the United Nations University. Previously he taught development sociology, contemporary Asian studies and the sociology of art at Sophia University, Tokyo. He has taught, researched or been a visiting professor at the University of Hull, the National University of Singapore, the Australian National University and the universities of Buenos Aires, Kent, Essex, Oxford, Pondicherry, Handong (South Korea) and the Bauhaus Universität Weimar. His academic and practical interests range over development sociology, environmental sociology, urban sociology, the sociology of religion, post-colonialist indigenous social theory, social movements, economic anthropology and alternative and post-capitalist economies, the sociology of art and critical social theory, both Western and non-Western. His current research relates to solidarity economics, issues of art and society and the place of culture in development and in particular alternative forms of sustainable development. He is the author of numerous books, including most recently *Diaspora and Belief: Globalisation, Religion and Identity in Postcolonial Asia*.

Culture, development and social theory

Towards an integrated social development

JOHN CLAMMER

Zed Books

LONDON | NEW YORK

Culture, Development and Social Theory: Towards an Integrated Social Development
was first published in 2012 by
Zed Books Ltd, 7 Cynthia Street, London N1 9JF, UK
and Room 400, 175 Fifth Avenue, New York, NY 10010, USA

www.zedbooks.co.uk

FSC
www.fsc.org
MIX
Paper from
responsible sources
FSC® C013604

Designed and typeset in Monotype Bembo
by illuminati, Grosmont
Index by John Barker
Cover design: www.alice-marwick.co.uk
Printed and bound by CPI Group (UK) Ltd,
Croydon CRO 4YY

Distributed in the USA exclusively by Palgrave Macmillan, a division of
St Martin's Press, LLC, 175 Fifth Avenue, New York, NY 10010, USA

A catalogue record for this book is available from the British Library
Library of Congress Cataloging in Publication Data available

ISBN 978 1 78032 315 2 hb
ISBN 978 1 78032 314 5 pb

Contents

Acknowledgements

This book has grown over several years and has benefited greatly from the input of colleagues and audiences in a number of contexts. In particular I want to acknowledge the hospitality of the former National Centre for Development Studies at the Australian National University, where Chapters 2 and 3 were initially presented at workshops. A resulting earlier version of Chapter 2 was subsequently published under the title 'Culture, Development and Social Theory: On Cultural Studies and the Place of Culture in Development' in the *Asia-Pacific Journal of Anthropology* (vol. 6, no. 2, 2005). Chapter 8 was originally presented at the conference on 'War, Memory and Narrative' at the National Museum of Japanese History in February 2007, and I wish particularly to thank Professor Eyal Ben-Ari for his comments on the original version of the paper and to Mayumi Sekizawa for the invitation to the conference and her organizational skills in making it a success. An earlier version of Chapter 4 was written jointly with Marian Moya, whom I thank deeply for years of friendship, co-work, conversations and coffee, and was initially presented at a workshop convened by Paul Sillitoe at the Manchester Decennial Conference of the Association of Social Anthropologists on the subject of indigenous knowledge; we both thank Paul for his invitation to participate. Chapter 6 was originally presented in oral form at the 2010 Fireflies Dialogue at the Fireflies Intercultural

Centre, Bangalore, and I wish to express thanks to Siddhartha for the invitation to attend and for the members of the dialogue for their feedback and encouragement. A number of people have contributed in very practical ways to the realization of the book; in particular I want to single out Sakura Ono for her initial organization of the bibliography and her research assistance and friendship during the preparation of the manuscript, and Miyoko Ogishima for her tireless work in finalizing the bibliography and preparing the final version of the manuscript for publication. Thanks to you both this project has finally been brought to its publishable conclusion. I hope that its effects will justify your hard work and commitment. I also wish to extend my thanks to the two anonymous reviewers for Zed Books, whose comments have enabled me to sharpen my arguments and clarify a number of points that were obscure in the original manuscript.

PART I

On culture and development

Transforming the discourse of development: cultures, suffering and human futures

As the world enters the second decade of the twenty-first century, it is evident that, despite the widespread culture of denial that persists in sweeping our major common problems under the collective carpet, it is entering and has indeed already entered a period of unprecedented crisis. Unprecedented not only because of the scale of the problems, but equally because of the convergence of what were once seen to be, if considered problems at all, quite separate ones, and because the evidence is that the tools that we have used in the past to manage the crises that have beset human society are no longer adequate to the tasks in hand. Indeed, decades of technocratic, economistic and managerial 'development' policies and practices have signally failed to alleviate these problems, and may even be, as many critics have suggested, a substantial part of the problem rather than elements in its solution. Despite the lofty rhetoric of the UN Millennium Goals and despite evidence of pockets of improvement, mainly in East and Southeast Asia, the huge issues of poverty; ethnic, social and gender inequality; abuses of human rights; massive environmental degradation and global warming; unsustainable resource deple-tion; illiteracy and lack of access to education; woefully inadequate health care; and conflict and wars continue to plague the planet in undiminished ways. Some – rising inequalities between and within nations, conflict and ecological damage, for instance – have intensified and have been joined by their not entirely unpredictable by-products of terrorism, corruption, globalized crime, HIV/AIDS and other epidemics of international proportions, erratic weather patterns and growing water shortages.

Yet despite the demonstrable magnitude of these issues and their inevitable massive impact on both the human future and the future of nature as a good in itself and as the resource base on which all life depends, we occupy a curious moral and intellectual environment in which (short of the total denial of the existence of these problems or their seriousness – a syndrome that tragically does exist), they are largely banished to the very narrow specialization of 'development studies'. This curiously hybrid field has little intellectual status among the established academic disciplines and has few strong links to related subjects, such as ecology, conflict studies, cultural studies, philosophy or religious studies, but by far the strongest institutional links to the much contested and criticized subject of economics. But in reality the themes that conventionally appear under the rubric of 'development studies' do not constitute a specialized 'field' at all: in the present world situation it is the context within which all other disciplines and policy sciences should be exercised. The triviality and narcissism of much of the work that goes on in cultural studies, literary and art criticism, sociology and many other subjects is very apparent when they are placed side by side with the enormity of the human suffering and bio-ecological damage that are being inflicted daily on the world both by the pornography of 'underdevelopment' and by the violence of much of what passes for 'development' itself.

Yet libraries are filled with currently fashionable or now out-moded tomes of development theory reflecting the ever-changing repositioning of writers in a curious field in which yesterday's solutions become today's problems in an apparently never-ending spiral. From an honest scholarly point of view the question must arise as to why our interventions to change the world (even assuming that to be a legitimate vocation) are so often ineffective, unimaginative, bounded by a self-limiting discourse, or simply so short-term and self-serving. This we witnessed in the recent past, for example at the 2009 UN Copenhagen conference on climate change, or the 2010 CITES (the Convention on International Trade in Endangered Species of Wild Fauna and Flora), in which certain countries showed themselves totally unwilling to rein in their consumption of certain endangered species simply because those species were part of their traditional 'national diet'. Development theory – the attempt to make sense of the nature and dimensions of our crisis and to formulate a language of response – is itself in crisis, largely, as I shall argue in this book, because it has trapped itself in a self-contained discourse that has become separated from both the concrete experiences of human suffering and the suffering of nature. Similarly, development theory has to a large extent separated itself from many of the progressive ideas in the social sciences other than economics narrowly defined, including economic anthropology, cultural studies, social philosophy, philosophical anthropology and social/cultural theory, which illuminate the core issues that development theory purports to address, but are so far almost entirely absent from its vocabulary and discourse.

The necessity of bringing these together is the core argument of this book. For while the whole concept of 'development' has become rightly suspect as its destructive, environmentally unfriendly and socially marginalizing effects have become apparent, the problems that the concept was designed to address are still not only present but on the whole worsening. The voices of critique (e.g. Sachs 1995; Rahnema and Bawtree 2003) have rightly had a major and positive deconstructive role. But the question then becomes: where to go after deconstruction in positive and reconstructive ways? A number of approaches have of course been proposed – participatory development, human needs, sustainability, and perhaps most recently the discovery or rediscovery of 'culture' and indigenous knowledge. But each of these possesses its own philosophical and practical difficulties – human needs theory, for example, having been taxed with its tendency to essentialism, and 'sustainable development' with the charge that the very term is an oxymoron. The issue of indigenous knowledge, while clearly very well motivated, raises again the classical anthropological issues of appropriation, ownership of and participation in the benefits accruing from the exploitation of that knowledge. Likewise, many studies in 'culture and development' do not, paradoxically, deal in any concrete way with actual living examples of cultural expression, such as art, dance, music, material culture, theatre, cooking, architecture, fashion and so on, but either treat the term 'culture' as a synonym for gender or ethnicity, as an abstract category often used, as in classical sociology, as a residual explanation of last resort, or as a pragmatic element to be introduced to make more effective the 'delivery' of development goods or goals already decided on elsewhere. Fewer still take a critical view of culture as something that can impede as much as promote human fulfilment, happiness, creativity, satisfaction and a harmonious relationship with nature.

In this book I argue for some fresh approaches to development theory while keeping the notion of culture (to which I will return in detail in the subsequent chapter) central. At the core of the argument are a set of propositions about the relationships between culture and development. These can be summarized as follows.

The first is the closer incorporation of the existential issues central to all human life, and the suggestion, which will be worked out throughout the book, that the route to the elaboration of an existential paradigm for development theory is through confrontation with the nature, causes and dimensions of human suffering and the building of models for the alleviation of suffering based on what is essentially a philosophical rather than a technical investigation.

The second is that the analysis of the concept of 'development' itself is a philosophical and ethical as well as a political and economic enterprise. At the core of a truly humane conception of development are both notions of rights, needs, freedoms and entitlements, and those of hopes, futures, memories, happiness, creativity and imagination. Seen in this light, development theory becomes the contemporary incarnation of what used to be called philosophical anthropology.

Third, development does not simply involve politics, but more centrally *cultural politics*, which involves among other things the analysis of knowledge itself in the form of a kind of social epistemology: the examination of the gendered and social basis of knowledge, of its class, ethnic and cultural biases, and of the fact that in many cultures knowledge is not confined to the cognitive alone, but includes the sensuous and the emotional, and, very significantly, the relationship between humans and nature, a question only recently posed again in the West by the advent of deep ecology and the belated invention of environmental sociology. The fact that the mainstream social sciences have until now, when an unprecedented ecological crisis is upon us, ignored nature as a constituent part of human identity and of society itself reveals a profound cultural politics at work. The reintroduction of a central concern with nature into the Western social consciousness, first through the New Age movement and deep ecology and then through the subsequent rise of an activist environmental movement, the rediscovery of the non-anthropocentric ontologies of non-Western and Native American cosmologies, and the recovery of a connection between ecology and sociology, indicates a profound and hopeful shift in that cultural politics and a step beyond the necessary but anthropocentric gender and race preoccupations of what has passed as cultural politics up until now.

Fourth, a cultural approach to development involves a distinctive methodology, that of *listening*: the hearing of stories, the respecting of indigenous narratives, the recovery of forgotten voices and of the many suppressed histories and alternatives that are present in indigenous social thinking, and the production of organic intellectuals in music, art, religions and local spiritual traditions and ecological models, and that most ignored source of protest and utopias, indigenous literature. Finally, any culturally informed development theory must connect with debates and advances in a wider range of social sciences, especially cultural studies, postcolonial studies, globalization theory, feminist theory, social theory and developments within marginalized branches of cultural sociology such as the sociology of the arts.

Seen from these perspectives, development studies, far from being a sequestered technical discipline located in a distinct 'institute of development studies' located somewhere on the edge of a university campus, becomes a broad inquiry into the human condition, our place in nature, the historical processes through which we have reached our currently seriously dysfunctional social and ecological situation, and the resources of imagination and fresh thinking that can potentially lead us beyond our impasse. For whatever the critics of the concept of development might rightly say, it does nevertheless name the pressing issues of the day. These are the great ethical and practical questions of our generation. Furthermore, rather than approach these problems in a mood of pessimism and defeatism, a revitalized and constructive conception of development fuels our intellectual and moral excitement. For here are the truly non-trivial issues really worthy of serious commitment, the exploration of which spills over into and contributes to the renewal of other fields of human endeavour, including the practical search for social alternatives, a renewed form of social ecology that does not see humans and nature as basically opposed, a reorientation of science to basic human needs, new perspectives on conflict resolution, and sources of imagination and imagery for art, architecture, the theatre and literature.

Culture and the structures of development inquiry

More than a decade ago an 'impasse' was announced in development theory, arising from the exhaustion of the neo-Marxist model
that was then seen as virtually the only viable alternative to the
mainstream paradigms of growth, modernization and uni-directional
(industrial, consumerist and technological) development (Schuurman
1996). The problem, however, was not only that neo-Marxism was
largely exhausted, in part because of its failure and that of its parent
actually to change the world in a more socially just direction in the
face of deepening inequalities and rapidly accelerating capitalist-led
globalization (celebrated by the Right as signalling 'the end of
history'), but also that development theory in general seemed to be
going through a drought in which few critical let alone constructive
alternatives outside of Marxism seemed to be available. Instead a
succession of new methodologies essentially replaced creative theory:
'participation' and Rapid Rural Assessment, for example, in the
initial phase and latterly newer concepts such as governance, Millennium Goals, civil society, sustainable development and indigenous
knowledge. A reading of the World Bank's annual report or of the
parallel although ideologically different human development reports
of the UNDP provides a perfect barometer for tracking these shifting
fashions. But methodologies are not the equivalent of or a substitute
for theory, and while it can be argued that this theoretical loss of
nerve was due to a number of factors, including the professionalizing
of development and the proliferation of NGOs pursuing often very
limited and local goals, one main explanation in fact is the severing
of development thinking from creative work going on in other
fields, leading to an isolation from much of the most progressive
thinking on the key political, moral, ecological and justice issues of
the age. So while the mainstream social sciences have largely ignored
development, development specialists largely ignored new thinking
in the other social sciences except for economics and, to a limited

extent, sociology. And even with such development- related subfields such as development sociology, a similar process can be seen at work. Open almost any textbook in development sociology and the same discourse can be seen at work, not only in the conventional selection of the problems presented, but by the absence of any discussion of central cultural issues or linkages to major debates in other areas of sociology itself (for example, cultural sociology, urban sociology or the sociology of the family), or to anthropology, social history, cultural studies or ecology.

The place to begin in overcoming these absences is to look at the elements largely missing from or suppressed by mainstream development discourse. These include much of the subject matter of cultural studies – consumption, memory, the emotions and the sociology of the body, and the works of postmodern social theorists such as Baudrillard, who have drawn attention to the issues of value, death, subjectivities, ritual, sacrifice and the status of culture itself under a regime of postmodernism (Baudrillard 1993; Berry and Wernick 1992). Other exclusions encompass almost the entire subject matter of religious studies, ecology, identity politics and performativity (on the latter two, see Hetherington 1998), popular culture, actual cultural practices and production in the everyday sense of the word (dance, art, theatre, music, food and fashion), indigenous theories of the relationships between personal and social transformation, most of the extensive sociological work on the nature of modernity, social history, and, strangely enough, postcolonial theory. Development studies, paradoxically and ironically as it presents itself as the front line of engagement with the pressing social issues of the day, is often deeply anti-humanistic, for its real subjects, in all their existential depth, escape its grasp. The question then becomes how to put this dimension back.

Some attempts have been made to do so, mainly through the medium of reintroducing ethical debate into development discourse (Goulet 1995; Quarles van Ufford and Giri 2003) or by linking development and spirituality such that development comes to be seen as a personally and socially transformative process leading to greater sociality, levels of self-development and harmony, and studying this empirically by way of social movements that have some strong value system at their core (Zunes et al. 1999; Giri 2005). Both of these approaches have their virtues, but they need filling out in a number of directions which we will now consider. The resiting of development studies in a genuinely 'people centred' approach implies a sense of those people's existential needs, not just their 'empowerment'. Indigenous knowledge understood in its fullest sense includes these needs and their psychological and emotional dimensions, as well as their cognitive and political ones. As Stoller (1997) has shown, the phenomenology of local knowledges extends far beyond the rational. The now largely outmoded 'postmodern' turn in cultural theory, with its emphasis on deconstruction, fragmentation and pastiche, was clearly a luxurious outgrowth of the rich and overprivileged world, and its formulations sound at best ironical when applied to the larger part of the world where those same features are symptoms of tragedy not abundance. The political hollowness of postmodernism and its inability to confront in any meaningful way the deep structural problems of the contemporary world (Eagleton 2003) derive in large part from the decentring of values as a core element of any social vision worth having. Notions of justice, community, freedom, solidarity or beauty, together with ideals of peace, security and self-determination, a cooperative relationship between human rights and the rights of nature, or the notion of human responsibilities are rarely defined or discussed in mainstream development thinking, but are much more likely to be raised in 'peripheral' fields such as liberation theology (e.g. Boff 1997). While this is partly because of the absence of ethical analysis as a central theme in the social sciences, it is also due to the equally glaring absence of aesthetic and philosophical analysis and the absence of any systematic theory linking ecology, culture and development.

For it might well be argued that classical development, the outcomes of which we now see all around us in the form of environmental degradation, hyper-urbanization, resource depletion, growing inequalities, the social and economic exclusions of globalization, the hegemony of consumerist culture and the whole suite of problems that our pursuit of growth, industrialization and wealth has led to, has failed, and has failed not only empirically but also philosophically. When 'development ethics' has to assert itself and attempt to carve out a niche within development discourse, this is surely the sign of a major failure within development theory as a whole, which has long confused the political with the ethical. When nature is excluded from development discourse except as 'environmentalism' and as a purely instrumental factor and source of raw materials, and not addressed in its cultural, emotional, psychological, philosophical and religious dimensions, clearly a curious myopia is at work. When religion is excluded while in fact in most of the 'developing' world it is a central part of everyday life and certainly part of the colonial and postcolonial experience (Clammer 2009b), we are confronting a very limited discourse indeed. If these strictures sound a little harsh, the reader is simply invited to consult any of the standard texts in the sociology or anthropology of development, subjects which allegedly deal with the cultural and social aspects of development, or even those that specifically announce themselves as addressing the issue of culture and development (e.g. Grillo and Stirrat 1997; Webster 1986; Olivier de Sardan 2005; Long 2001; Gardner and Lewis 1996; Schech and Haggis 2000).

Paradoxically, even in the context of the sociology and anthropology of development, much of the social and, especially, cultural dimension gets lost. Critiques of the economism of developmentalism and of the neoliberal economics on which much of it is based are well and good, but without a systematic recovery of the genuinely non-economic aspects of life, or more accurately the fleshing out of what might be better termed 'social economics' – the study of the embeddedness of economic activity in social and cultural practices and values at which the now (at least in the development context) field of economic anthropology used to be rather good (Clammer 1985). Without such contextualization a socio-cultural approach to development itself will be only a partial tool, and it needs to be demonstrated that this dimension is not a mere luxury. The failure so far to do this is revealed in the marginalization of anthropologists, even in such development contexts as they are actually employed, in tiny numbers, such as the World Bank (Mosse 2004), revealing how in the policy world culture is not taken very seriously except as entertainment.

Yet anthropology potentially plays a key role in the reconstruction of development thinking and practice. Anthropology is the science of alternatives: not of science-fiction options, but of actually existing or historically recent working arrangements of social, cultural, economic and spiritual life. It has shown, for example, that beyond the state there are alternative models of political organization, although it has rarely exploited this knowledge for larger socially transformative purposes by linking it to wider socialist, anarchist, communal, alternative or even Third Way theorizing or practice (for a rare exception, see Graeber 2004). So while in principle anthropology leads the field in its accumulated knowledge of actual alternative social systems, even if it rarely exploits this knowledge in practice, development studies on the other hand frequently lacks real ethnography. Development policymakers generally refuse to take the time to undertake or consult detailed informed accounts of local socio-cultural conditions, and (as many anthropologists working in development agencies attest), if they listen at all, want rapid appraisal and a bullet point summary, and rarely want to be told that their proposed interventions are undesirable, will not work, or will simply generate yet more problems to be solved. The interface between the culturally informed social sciences and policymakers and implementers, whether official, multilateral or in NGOs, while extolled in rhetoric, is very shaky in practice.

Empirical research has shown that, even in situations of material deprivation, in the words of the Thai social scientist and activist Sulak Sivaraksa, 'the crucial dimensions of human life are not economic but existential. They are related to our needs for leisure, contemplation, love, community and self-realization' (Sulak 1992: 36). Writing of the (largely unknown outside of India) Oriya thinker, educationalist and philosopher Chitta Ranjan Das, the Indian sociologist Ananta Kumar Giri summarizes this mode of thinking as follows:

> By social change Das does not refer to the external indicators
> such as standard of living, but to transformation of consciousness,
> transformation of the quality and purpose of relationship among
> individuals in society. For Das, to talk of social change is to talk
> of change of base and the base here is not merely the base in the
> Marxian sense but what Das calls *anuragara bhumi* – the base of
> aspiration and desire … Das also believes that the object of true
> education and education of the future is to make us critics – critics
> of our desire, critics of the culture which contains many 'chains
> of illusions' for us, critics of the institutions which make human
> relationships unjust and degrading, and above all critics of power
> – power which claims to be a repository of virtue and the definer of
> truth. (Giri 2005: 253)

This summarizes very well both the existential basis of human needs and the critical and potentially emancipatory qualities of cultural analysis.

The trouble with culture

Simply to insert 'culture', however, in the hope that it will solve at a stroke the problems that confront our civilization is of course illusory, and Chapter 2 addresses the question of the meanings and competing definitions of culture at a moment when the very concept is itself being subjected to critique and itself represents a very contested zone as the social, economic and ecological contexts in which it is embedded themselves evolve. Culture has certainly

already returned to a more central place in social analysis, as signalled by the rapid rise of cultural studies as a discipline and the
vast outpouring of scholarly or quasi-scholarly writings addressing
some aspect of culture in relation to media, consumer capitalism,
consumption practices, fashion, popular culture, space, globalization,
the body and numerous other topics. What is now necessary is to
explore fresh facets of its meanings and strategic uses when it is
relocated methodologically in relation to problems of human and
ecological suffering, when it is understood as a critical as much as
a descriptive concept, when it is given some actual content and not
treated simply as an abstract category for explanation, and when it
is understood as a vehicle for hope and for exploring imaginatively
the possibilities of human existence (Harvey 2002). Certainly the
notion of culture in relation to development is not a new one, even
if it has been explored largely in terms of a vehicle for the more
effective delivery of development policies or goods, and indeed as
an aspect of business promotion (Skelton and Allen 1999), or as an
opportunity for applied anthropology to assert its relevance in relation to debates about human rights, marketization, aid, and issues of
multiculturalism and cultural diversity (Kikuchi 2004). At the same
time, in what are now widely regarded as outmoded versions of
modernization theory, culture was seen as an impediment to growth,
industrialization and development (Schech and Haggis 2000: 53).

   To complicate matters further, as is discussed in the following
chapter, a number of anthropologists have begun to argue that the
concept of culture is itself highly problematic, being hard to define,
used in contradictory ways in social and development discourse, and
sometimes too politicized to be of any analytical use (Kuper 1999;
Fox and King 2002). In the face of the information revolution and
the widespread dissemination of more and more technologically
based forms of popular culture, what in my view all this points to
is not the abandonment of the concept of culture, but its recognition
as a dynamic and contextually based idea, in which its political uses

– as in debates about multiculturalism, for example (Ivison 2010) – far from undermining its utility, demonstrate the strategic uses to which it is still widely put, and hence its salience in actual daily life, regardless of the problems anthropologists might have in finding a universal and waterproof definition.

These ideas indeed also point us in the direction of a redefinition of development itself, and one that takes us away in salutary ways from the hubris of so much top-down development. Despite appearances, development studies is a deeply undertheorized field and often represents intervention without any clear understanding of what the outcomes will be, despite decades of knowledge of the fact that policies always have unintended and unforeseeable outcomes in addition to, or instead of, the ones intended. As Roberto Calasso aptly puts it, 'Around us is an obstinate insistence on changing life, but without any specific notion of the facts of life' (Calasso 1995). Social theory, which should in principle be addressing these fundamental human issues, but mostly does not, may even itself become a source of alienation. Speaking of Japan, but in words that could equally apply to much of the world, Tatsuo Najita notes that during the much vaunted post-war reconstruction of the country 'Beneath the high growth there was a human experience that really did not coincide with the theory of modernization and rationalization being advanced by primarily Western social and historical scientists' (Najita 1989: 6). Indeed, and it is the quality of this human experience that should be the primary subject matter of development.

This human experience includes religion, the body and its pleasures and problems, the emotions, conceptions of selfhood, modes of expression (artistic, literary and in humble crafts such as cooking, embroidery, gardening and carpentry), bonds with nature in general and other animals in particular (pets being the obvious example), identity, sexuality, memory, cultural and personal relationships to death, work, the life cycle, fun and entertainment, and trauma and the crises of life, and the search for some sense of meaning in all these bidden or unbidden experiences. As Pierre Bourdieu among others has established (Bourdieu 1979), culture cannot be treated in an essentialized manner or as a static category, but is the primary human medium for strategizing life, and as such consists less of structures and institutions than of responses, adaptations, compromises, modifications, practices, performances, and the application of practical reason, agency, subversions and downright lies. Culture, then, is most certainly process, and in any particular empirical manifestation is always vulnerable and precarious and teeters on the edge of chaos and dissolution. It does not just exist in some abstract sense, but has to be constantly invented, defended, and its ever-evolving character and direction endlessly redefined. It is a permanently contested terrain not only because of its inherently fluid nature, but equally because what is often posited as a common culture is in fact divided internally along the classical sociological lines of class, gender and race. As postcolonial theory has so tellingly demonstrated, it is necessary to reinsert into theories of modernity (the progenitor of development theory), and its largely apolitical successor postmodernism, the dimensions of slavery, racism, sexism, forced uprooting, the cultural imposition of languages, architectures, costume and religions, migrations and the vast displacements and attendant suffering consequent upon colonialism as the first historical phase of 'development' and subsequently its successors, 'development' itself and latterly globalization.

The art rather than the 'science' of human and nature-centred development is the awareness of the constant interrelation of the macro and the micro, or of agency and structure. Actual existence on the ground and the attendant suffering of humans and nature need to be seen in a global context, for while one of the significant aspects of globalization is that it creates the breakdown of some structures of domination, it promotes the emergence of others. Globalization is a system that thrives on chaos, mostly generated by itself – the 'risk society' of which Ulrich Beck (1992), Piet Strydom (2002) and others have spoken – upon which it can impose new 'order' in the forms of the market and the institutional and political mechanisms created to promote and enforce this new order. The World Trade Organization (WTO) is a prime example of this trend, as are the neoconservative politics of all the major democracies including Britain, France, Japan and the USA. Deeply subversive of this new world order/new world chaos is the finding that what people desire and what the sustainability of our fragile planetary ecology and civilization requires liberation, rights/reciprocities/responsibilities, fulfilment, autonomy, community and meaning, rather than 'growth' and the disruptions imposed by the global expansion of marketization (Diener and Seligman 2004). The developer's definition of the good society and that sought by the often unwilling recipients of development are often very far apart. Among the glaring deficiencies of development theory has been its unwillingness to *listen* and to allow sensitivity rather than 'efficiency' to prevail. When it does, the results are inspiring, not least because of the centrality of the possession of genuine cultures to people's own perception of the fulfilled life and as the fundamental mode of their self-expression and mode of engagement with the world (Carmen 1996).

Culture, development and social transformation

If the definition of a fool is someone who does not learn from experience, then development studies must be among the most foolish of disciplines. The analysis of what James C. Scott calls 'great development failures' – meaning not only the failure despite huge technical knowledge and resources to achieve the large goals of poverty reduction, sustainability and the overall expansion of social justice at the international level, but also at the local level the persistent creation and enforcement of state-engendered universalist plans with little sensitivity to specific regional conditions or cultures – is very revealing. As Scott puts it, 'Such plans, designed to improve the human condition, have had melancholy results, in part because they have destroyed long standing patterns of community, work, and interaction with nature that have proven satisfactory and have replaced them with a "one-size-fits-all" formula that negates local adaptive knowledge' (Scott 1998: 37). In fact it is in the analysis of failures, in development as much as anywhere else in life, that the seeds of future wisdom are nurtured. But whereas 'evaluations' are certainly done of development policies and their implementation, few fundamental conclusions seem to be drawn from these, and certainly not conclusions that might subvert the development project as a whole. Much development activity is in fact deeply pernicious: it constantly announces hopes that will in the future arise from present sacrifices that are not then fulfilled, and then suggests that the failure is due simply to some technical problem that can be remedied by the next policy, rather than confronting the possibility that the whole enterprise is built on foundations of sand.

A simple but central example will illustrate this process. Assuming (and given the track record of conventional development to date this is a very big assumption) that massive poverty can be, if not abolished entirely, at least substantially eliminated by the dates set by the Millennium Goals, what then? Just as in many peacekeeping operations where there is no post-conflict policy in place, do we have any conception of a post-poverty policy? One, for example, that would not simply fuel consumption to the level where at-tainment of anything approaching a contemporary 'First World' standard of living would spell complete ecological disaster for the whole globe? While hopefully no one would disagree that a secure material base is a necessary prerequisite for any kind of civilized existence, we must also, as with the implementation of any policy, consider the long-term implications of what we are doing. In this particular case we must face some inevitable issues. The first is that the fulfilment of material needs in themselves, as we know, does not lead to happiness, but on the contrary can easily fuel a cycle of desire based on expanding wants, greed and consumerism with the knock-on effects that this has on the environment, social equity and human relationships in general once they become monetized. This consideration raises the critical but not often asked question of how to bring about substantial poverty alleviation without bringing in its wake massive corruption, overconsumption, socially destructive competition, the commoditization of art, health and even the human body, new forms of unemployment or underemployment, accelerating environmental destruction, overurbanization and the sicknesses of affluence that all too easily replace the sicknesses of malnutrition. The answer cannot lie in the reduction of poverty alone, but must reside in accompanying resocialization, education and cultural rather than material development, the last being the most neglected element of all in development studies. Culture *for* development certainly (this is the subject matter of much development or applied anthropology), but not the development *of* culture.

Indeed there is a paradox here: what will we do when we are all rich? I assume that we will all have the resources and leisure to engage in cultural activities, but there is a grave danger that we will for sure have leisure but no idea of what to do with it, and rather than generate our own culture will passively consume the commoditized, packaged, commercialized and standardized popular culture fed to us through television, advertising and the print media. This is assuming of course that we do not face a catastrophic ecological meltdown, in which case all these forms of cultural production might well be rendered obsolete. The point is, however, that, even given the latter scenario, a post-materialist society is not necessarily a culturally rich one, as material affluence can and often does coincide with an impoverished culture. None of these outcomes sounds much like the utopia that many of us thought that we were striving for. And in fact 'undoing' development implies, as much as raising material standards for the poor, also the recolonization or decolonization of the lifeworlds that have already been so ruthlessly colonized by corporate media and massified culture. For poverty is not only material deprivation: freedom of expression (in a non-political sense) and the enjoyment of a rich autonomous cultural life prove to be every bit as important as the expansion of material possessions.

A similar analysis could be applied to human rights. Rights are in fact not simply abstract legal categories, but are equally complex cultural constellations. They intersect with ethics by way of competing local and universal conceptions of value and so are, in fact, part of the very underdeveloped field of the anthropology of moralities. They also clearly intersect with legal norms, practices, assumptions and cultures, and so at that point can be examined from the viewpoint of legal and political anthropology. Any model of rights, and certainly one that grows from indigenous soil, is bound to reflect religious assumptions and notions of selfhood – Buddhist ones, for example, being markedly different from Christian ones. Rights do not exist in a static environment, but are faced constantly with emerging issues, such as those thrown up by medical ethics and new technologies, and the now central questions of the rights of humans in relation to the rights of nature. Broader cultural and philosophical positions also apply, such as individualism as opposed to communalism, the possibility of there being distinctive Asian values, the emergence of African philosophy as a vibrant expression of postcolonial identity and indigenous thinking, and the embeddedness of contemporary rights in the context of capitalism and the market in the rich countries (with legal cultures strongly defending the 'rights' of property and corporations), and, in the context of poverty, deprivation and social exclusion in the poor ones. In both cases we see the bureaucratization of society and the resulting phenomenon of what the anthropologist Michael Herzfeld has called the 'production of indifference' (Herzfeld 1992), which frames the practical political protection and implementation, or more usually the ignoring and denial, of rights and entitlements and the environmental hazards that have arisen from the anthropocentrism of most conceptions of human rights that privilege the human over the rest of nature. Some indeed would argue that the very conception of rights is contentious in the situation of societies where it is the majority who are excluded from the enjoyment of the rights to which they are entitled by virtue of their governments having become signatories long ago to the Universal Declaration of Human Rights, rights which are in fact only enjoyed by privileged minorities whose very privileges may well be derived from the suppression of the rights of the majority, and/or where human rights are the Trojan Horse through which new forms of neocolonialism are reintroduced (Esteva and Prakash 1998). Certainly the position that conceptions of rights are deeply influenced by culture cannot be gainsaid (Cowan et al. 2001), and, this being the case, we see again an instance where culture, far from being inserted into development as a distraction, in fact lies at the core of the ways in which both indigenous knowledge and more universalist discourses are framed and intersect – an issue that is taken up in more detail in Chapter 4 below.

So, if the cultural dimension fundamentally deepens development discourse, development issues politicize and give muscle to cultural theory: each without the other is one-dimensional. To speak of 'hybridity', for example, as is so often done in a celebratory tone in cultural studies, as a happy blending of cultures is naive at the least, when it is remembered that in many if not most cases that blending was forced on subject peoples by colonialism. The migration of cultures is the result of the migration of the peoples who carried those cultures: people in many cases forced into movement by slavery, poverty, colonization, political instability and persecution. In many cases variations on these themes are then re-enacted, even with less intensity, in the metropolitan countries of settlement, as many blacks in the United States, West Indians and South Asians in Britain, Moroccans, Algerians, Jews or Vietnamese in France, or Indonesians and Surinamese in the Netherlands will readily testify.

Behind these diverse phenomena lies the fact that the context of cultural production, reproduction and transmission has altered fundamentally under the regime of globalization. Inter- as much as intra-cultural processes are now foundational to the cultural and social geography of the world. Planetary and local processes constantly interact, as evidenced in music, fashion, cuisines, languages, film and many shared forms of popular culture. This requires a new modelling of our understanding of culture, as it is now a fact that it is the flows themselves as much as the points of transmission and reception that are significant, necessitating new methodologies for the study of non-localized cultural phenomena and the networks that transmit and link them. This changing spatial distribution of culture has political consequences, including the erosion of vulnerable local cultures and, in an increasingly commodified global environment, posing the question of the authenticity of cultural productions. Umberto Eco reports the existence of at least seven versions of Leonardo's *The Last Supper*, and the fact that some Americans who had seen both the original in Rome and one of the reproductions in California preferred the latter, the original having been 'too gloomy', and one of the facsimiles having the advantage of supplying Jesus with a moving arm so that he can raise his goblet of wine to his lips (Eco 1987).

The celebration of culture need not blind us to the dark side of modernity and the underside of globalization, and should also remind us that counter-knowledges emerge from both local and spatially mobile cultures and that it is in the theatre, art, music and cinema as much as on the barricades that resistance to new global hegemonies occurs. As the now neglected field of the sociology of knowledge used to teach us, the changing nature of society will be rapidly reflected in changing cultural forms. With the looming ecological crisis, cultural and social theory in the West has finally decided to take seriously the role of nature in the constitution of human societies and the impact of those societies on the environment. In Asian social theory (e.g. Clammer 1995) this was always so, and the belated recognition of society–nature interdependence in Western cultural and sociological thinking has raised some fundamental philosophical questions rarely pursued before in mainstream intellectual discourses, including that of the possibility of overcoming the mechanistic and anthropocentric paradigms that have been at the root of much Occidental thought at least since Descartes (e.g. Sessions 1995).

Recentring culture in relation to development, then, naturally reintroduces into that discourse a large range of issues and allows them to repossess their rightful status as central rather than peripheral matters of concern. These include, as we will see, the ethical and also the almost entirely neglected aesthetic dimensions of development. The globalization of culture poses the challenge of initiating both a planetary ethics and a dialogue between civilizations that far transcends the cynicism and myopia of the Huntington 'clash of civilizations' perspective, as understanding development as moral engagement is necessarily dialogical and must include the recognition and expansion of human dignity (Muzaffar 2005). It signals the need to place cultural policy at the centre of development policy, while being fully aware of the dangers of state appropriation of culture, on the one hand, and the distortion of natural cultures by capitalist commodification, on the other. Recognition of the role of culture also expands the range of concrete issues seen as falling under the rubric of 'development'. Social change, for example, involves the transformation of subjectivities, and the new social movements, usually the subject of a separate sociological specialization, prove in fact to be central to development sociology and development studies in general. Such social movements are transformative agencies in their own right and are often the settings in which creative social experimentation takes place: they are major sources of social and cultural creativity and are the arenas in which new forms of subjectivity, selfhood and agency are tried out. They are also often cultural in inspiration: for instance, whereas conventional social movements theory does not consider art movements to be part of their subject matter, in reality they are, and historically European art movements such as Expressionism, Surrealism and the Bauhaus have been highly significant agencies for changing sensibilities, linking culture and social transformation, and introducing new forms of cultural and gender politics. Similarly the currently much debated notion of civil society is not confined to the realm of NGOs, but very much includes the cultural institutions, organizations and processes that are the everyday medium of social existence.

This cultural medium is highly dynamic in nature. A very pertinent example is the Internet – of very recent invention and now enormously widespread. It is now recognized that the Internet is both a technology of freedom and democratic decentralization and also a new electronic medium for the redistribution of power. Not only are large gaps appearing between the electronically advantaged and the disadvantaged (the phenomenon that Saskia Sassen calls 'cyber-segmentation'), but the geographical dispersion allowed by electronic networks also allows corporations to create 'virtual centres' permitting control beyond the monitoring of governments, police or citizens (Sassen 1999). Development studies has often proved to be out of touch with research of this kind generated in the cultural sciences and consequently failing to anticipate social, economic, technological and cultural shifts that greatly influence the context of its work. Chaos theory, for example, indicates one way in which the contingency of risk can be incorporated into an understanding of development that both sees complexity as endemic and suggests that complexity itself contains dynamic patterns. Development theory has also in many cases reproduced consciously or otherwise the tragic mistake of the post-Adam Smith West: to allow economics, which Jeremy Rifkin rightly defines as the 'beneficiary' of culture, to become its progenitor, to colonize its host. Culture is where we have what he terms 'deep play', where intrinsic value is created; 'Deep play is always more basic to people's lives, and work has always been something that enables us to have survival in order to play' (Rifkin 2004: 1 39). The inversion of this fundamental relationship has turned *Homo ludens*, man the player (Huizinga 1970), into man the worker, perhaps the most significant distortion that civilization has ever experienced. The role of development is to restore this relationship to its proper proportions.

Structure of the book

These are large and complex questions and it is doubtful that a truly systematic study of them could be undertaken in a single volume. What is attempted in this book is a series of moves designed to clarify connections between culture and development, and to think through some fresh approaches to this dynamic relationship that bring into the debate fresh resources from cultural and social theory. This connects development theory to emerging methodologies for the analysis of complex systems, social as well as natural, such as chaos theory, and to topics that should be under the purview of the sociology and anthropology of development in particular, and yet are missing from any of the existing textbooks in these fields. These include peace and conflict resolution, 'natural economies' or the micro-economies that have long been the subject matter of economic anthropology, the natural corollary of risk society studies, namely the social and cultural responses to disasters and trauma, social movements, the connections between globalization and cultural policy in a development context, the understanding of social suffering as suggesting a model for the comprehensive analysis of and empathy with the disruptions, discontinuities and even violence of development, and the role of art.

The book continues with a synoptic examination of the relationships between culture, development and social theory, not least to clarify what is meant by the concept of culture itself. The next chapter then examines the relationship between the issues raised and considers the two practical questions of aid and cultural policy. This is followed by an examination of what is currently a major anthropological approach to the analysis of culture in the development context – notably the notion of indigenous knowledge – and explores from several angles the possibilities and pitfalls of this approach. The second part introduces two of the themes being recommended here for inclusion as central issues in development studies: the neglected field, both within contemporary anthropology and within development studies, of economic anthropology and its theoretical and practical usefulness; and the now central issue, given the extent and depth of the environmental crisis, of climate justice and its relationship to culture. The final part of the book explores four hitherto virtually untouched dimensions of development thinking: the relationship between models developed in medical anthropology and sociology for understanding narratives of illness and suffering and the potentially very valuable application of ideas derived from these models to development studies; the analysis of trauma and memory in the negotiation of the violence of development and the experiences of loss and displacement that it so often engenders; the aesthetics of development; and finally the role of the emotions in understanding the nature of culture and the social movements that attempt to transform society and reality in more humane and sustainable directions. These largely unexplored dimensions of development allow us to introduce new methodological, philosophical and ethical issues into development theory and allow the almost entirely absent field of the psychology of development to emerge as a significant, indeed vital, dimension of development thinking.

While these studies collectively will fill many of the gaps in current development thinking, and will complement those aspects of the cultural dimensions of development that are currently receiving more systematic treatment, such as gender studies, silences and absences still no doubt remain. Some of these would warrant a book in themselves, in particular the connections between culture, ecology and development, including both the impact of deep ecology on ways of thinking about human/nature relationships and the exploration from a development perspective of the growing literature on cultural conceptions of nature in specific ethnographic and geographical contexts (e.g. Bruun and Kalland 1995). Fortunately elsewhere the connections between culture and nature are being explored from a philosophical and political point of view (Soper 1995) and from the position of feminism (Eaton and Lorentzen 2003), and the interface between sociology, environment and development is now central to the newly emerged subdiscipline of environmental sociology (Bell 2004; Dickens 2004). In a parallel way, and often connected to these same questions of ecology, issues of spirituality have also re-entered wider development discourses, in some cases directly addressing the connection between spiritual traditions and nature (e.g. Gottlieb 2004) or extending the analysis of Latin American liberation theology to link environmental destruction and social justice (Boff 1997), or expanding the purported relations of spirituality and development to include even wider issues such as the economy, agriculture, social policy, peace, technology and the possibility of a post-patriarchal society (Griffin 1988). While some of these issues are touched on or implied in the current book, they are not all explored in detail even while their importance is acknowledged. Nevertheless it is hoped that the reader will take away from this book a broadened sense of what can and should constitute both the specific fields of the anthropology and sociology of development, and the larger and potentially world-shaping discourse of development theory as a whole.

Culture, history and development theory

Development theory has been a very ethnocentric enterprise throughout most of its history. Challenged around its edges, as it were, by movements and streams of thought and practice rarely if ever considered in mainstream development studies (Latin American liberation theology, Gandhian thought, 'Engaged' Buddhism and transformative movements that it has inspired such as the Sri Lankan Sarvodaya movement, to name but a few), it has largely persisted as the application of Western social thought and categories to the realities of Asian, African and Latin American societies. But whereas the most vocal critics of the whole development enterprise see this as an unmitigated evil, it also has another side. This is the prospect that contact between Western social theory and the 'otherness' of non-Western societies and cultures forces a profound and creative transformation onto that largely hegemonic mode of theorizing about the world. This transformation does not simply stop at the point of deconstructing its assumptions and epistemology, but equally provides a starting point for the reconstruction of theory which points it beyond the habitus of one historically conditioned and merely contingently hegemonic way of seeing the world (Clammer 1995, 2004).

Such a project necessitates what might be called an exercise in the sociology of knowledge: the clarification of basic concepts and the tracing of their roots to the social, historical and ideological conditions that gave rise to them. Nowhere is the need for this greater than in the field of development studies, where words are never neutral, and where there have been major shifts both in the world system and in our understanding of that world in the last two or three decades. One of these shifts has been in the understanding of what is meant by 'modernization'. Modernization is historically linked to the rather larger concept of modernity – the project begun during the Enlightenment in the West and subsequently universalized and exported, especially through the mechanism of colonialism, to most of the rest of the world. This 'Enlightenment project' has at its heart two impulses: on the one hand the political – the move-ment towards emancipation expressed in the French Revolution and in the subsequent revolutions and movements for freedom and enfranchisement that swept Europe in the eighteenth and nineteenth centuries; and on the other the epistemological – the promotion of a particular form of rationality and scientism that is still with us in the form of positivism in the social sciences and ideas of 'scientific management' in business, to name two of its principal manifestations. Marx is perhaps the paradigmatic figure who brought together, with profound effects, these two impulses in a single discipline. A great deal of development theory is still heir to this tradition.

But many would argue that the hegemony of this project is breaking down, both because of its historical failure to deliver the promised emancipation (Bauman 1999), and because fundamental shifts in its underlying economy have moved industry from Fordism to the flexible capital accumulation that has ushered in the age of postmodernity (Harvey 1989). The end of formal colonialism and the emergence of globalization, the efflorescence of ethnicism, identity politics and religious fundamentalisms, the end of the Cold War and the emergence instead of multiple regional conflicts, all signal a major shift in which technology has radically changed its characteristics and its corresponding social impact, as have the conditions of work and relations of production. At the same time ecological concerns have become central; new modes of communication are changing the nature and meaning of communities, relationships and perhaps even consciousness; indigenous knowledge systems are rediscovered and re-evaluated; and new political forms are beginning to emerge as old-style nationalism and national boundaries become increasingly irrelevant in a globalized, but still very unequal, world.

At the same time, many features of the old world order and world-views persist, and development studies has a highly ambivalent relationship to these old and new forces. On the one hand it frequently suffers from a kind of intellectual cultural lag, vigorously applying old-mind solutions to very new kinds of problems. On the other hand its constant evolution of new and apparently progressive terms such as 'sustainable development', 'human needs', 'participatory development', 'culture/values in development' are deeply ambiguous.

For while they can indeed signal a struggle against the economistic, positivistic and undemocratic paradigms of the past, they can also signal accommodation and compliance with those very models while hiding behind a seemingly progressive language. This double-edged character can be seen in notions like that of the postcolonial, which can indicate emancipation and the taking back of history and memory into indigenous hands, but can equally mask the quite possibly hierarchical, oppressive or patriarchal character of the pre-colonial social formations themselves. Nevertheless, these very basic and profound shifts in the nature of the world and the nature of nature force us to re-evaluate our whole development vocabulary and to create a language to characterize an emerging post-positivist world in which concerns with culture and ethics are again beginning to take centre stage.

In fact the ethical and cultural dimensions of any worthwhile development enterprise are central, and are closely linked to each other as, while there may be ethical universals, systems of practical morality are socially located and expressed in local cultural idioms. Decades ago the sociologist Peter Berger argued that all development policies must be measured in terms of their ethical and cultural impact, not simply in terms of technical efficiency or political expediency (Berger 1976). So equally must the utopian, in the best sense of the word, dimension be recovered. What we see ourselves as being and what we believe we can become are both vital components of development and also deeply cultural questions. The loss of interest in these questions signals not some wiser realism in the social sciences, but rather a loss of nerve and vision (Jacoby 1999, 2005). A critical and reconstructive sociology must permanently inform development thinking if the ultimate goal of development is to be life enhancement, a goal which implies of course the nurturing of culture.

The issue of conceptualizing good development, as with the related process of defining the good society, is in fact a philosophical rather than a technical or economistic question. It is the central issue of what used to be called philosophical anthropology, which includes the comparative and cross-cultural exploration of the characteristics of human beings as a species, including our emotional, artistic and religious make-up, our relationship to nature and to the world of material things, and, in the light of this analysis of our qualities, the definition of genuine needs and the empirical exploration of what people themselves believe to constitute their real fulfilment, their conceptions of justice and rights, and the means available to them to overcome their alienation from nature and from one another. Social theory informed by a strong sense of philosophy and of history then becomes the means through which the fundamental issues of human development are examined and reflected, provided that social and cultural theory can itself overcome, as Terry Eagleton so persuasively argues, its own evasions when it comes to matters of morality, values and justice (Eagleton 2003).

TWO

On cultural studies and
the place of culture in development

Mark J. Smith has rightly argued that changes in the meaning of the term 'culture' signify significant shifts in the broader ways in which we analyse society (Smith 2000). The weight given (or not) to such subjects as psychology, psychoanalysis, identity, textuality, ethnicity, gender or the body reveals paradigmatic or even hegemonic understandings of macroscopic social processes (and hence of political and economic ones too). This is as much true in the field of development studies as elsewhere, and the rediscovery of 'culture and development' as an approach to, or even a subfield within, development studies (e.g. Schech and Harris 2000) signifies such a shift.

As a response and reaction to the overwhelming economism of so much development discourse, this is a fundamentally healthy innovation, but is nevertheless one that requires careful examination en route to a nuanced consideration of what culture contributes to or even displaces from conventional development discourses. Simply 'adding culture' will advance constructive debate very little if it is not recognized that the 'cultural turn' in development studies is taking place at the very moment when the concept of culture itself is becoming increasingly problematized, especially within anthropology (Fox and King 2002), and, as with the notion of 'multiculturalism', also very much politicized. The debate is not simply an academic one: however useful and necessary are the attempts to deconstruct the notion of 'development' itself (e.g. Sachs 1995), the objective problems to which it refers – poverty, gross social inequalities, extensive viola-tion of human rights, hyper-urbanization, and the highly unequal distribution of the benefits of technological and productive advances and of the positive aspects of globalization – remain and intensify. Meanwhile new foci of debate such as sustainability, participation, governance and civil society have emerged into the conceptual and policy arenas, and conceptual debates invariably spill over into social practice. The repositioning of cultural considerations in relation to broader development discourse has implications, which we must seek to uncover as we attempt to clarify what it is that we understand by the term 'culture' and expose the scholarly and ideological baggage with which it is freighted.

Locating culture

We are all aware of the widespread perception of there being a wide-spread crisis in or of 'development' as a practice and as an ideology, and its practitioners are certainly aware of a crisis in development theory – of the ways in which the whole enterprise is conceptualized, understood and located in relation to other disciplines and practices. The 'great development failures' (Scott 1998: 37) and their environ-mental consequences have brought the whole project of growth, aid, poverty reduction and the export of democratization into serious question. At the same time, and closely connected to these failures, what has been called the 'impasse' in development theory (Schuur-man 1996) has left what should be, given the magnitude and human and ecological centrality of the issues that it addresses, the most crea-tive, relevant and imaginative area of social thought trapped within a narrow range of conventional options – Marxist, neo-Marxist or neoliberal for the most part – and very weak on alternatives or visionary thinking, and still mired in the economism so deplored in principle by its more sociological exponents. Not surprisingly there are not a few voices calling for the abandonment of the term 'development' altogether, arguing with some justification that it represents simply the latest phase of colonialism, this time packaged in the more user-friendly wrapping of 'globalization'.

But even if we do abandon the term, the problems to which it traditionally refers will not miraculously disappear with it. Consequently, for want of a better term (the alternatives such as 'human security' having never quite caught on), we need not abandon the concept of development so much as radically redefine it: to create a new lexicon for talking about and witnessing to the inequalities and distortions of the contemporary world and most, if not all, of the societies that it comprises. There are, of course, those who have attempted to do this – by way of anti-corporatism (Korten 1999; Starr 2000) or its variants (Theobald 1999), through varieties of basic needs and sustainability initiatives, a range of eco-socialist, mixed economy and technological liberationist models (Frankel 1987), social movements and civil society and through movements based on religions, such as Engaged Buddhism, Latin American liberation theology and attempts to define Islamic alternatives (on the latter, see Jomo 1993). It might even be argued that much of what passes for postmodernist thought, anti-foundational and apolitical as it usually is, actually represents a contemporary variety of utopian thinking.

Common to all these variegated approaches, however, is a central concern with culture. Not only is development seen as being as much a political process and a politically contested terrain as it is an economic one; it is also pre-eminently a social and cultural process. It is one that is based upon, transforms or destroys cultures, and radically affects the elements that make up those cultures – values, systems of belief, material artefacts, expressive and performative practices, modes of livelihood, kinship patterns and subjectivities.

Much of this we already knew – it was inherent in the older 'social change' paradigm in sociology associated with the modernization theory of the 1950s and 1960s, which, for all its functionalist overtones, was aware of culture but thought of it mostly as a negative or retarding factor (the peasant 'resistance to change' idea for example). So simply to reinsert culture into contemporary development debate, from which it has largely been driven out by the economists, is not enough for at least two reasons. The first is that in modernization theory culture, when not understood entirely negatively, was often the explanation of last resort rather than embraced as a primary and integral factor in understanding human, including economic, behaviour. The second is that without a more accurate and critical understanding of culture itself as rather more than simply the residue of other (primarily economic) explanations, no great advance towards a deepening understanding of development problems along cultural and sociological lines is going to be made. Indeed, without this preliminary step the reinsertion of culture into the development debate could even prove to be counterproductive, only confirming in the eyes of those who identify themselves as members of the 'hard' development 'sciences' (economics, management, policy sciences and environmental, agricultural and health sciences) the fuzziness and indeterminacy of a cultural approach and the validity of the exclusion from the core of development debate and policy the cultural sciences – anthropology, sociology and cultural studies. It consequently behoves the practitioners of those disciplines to clarify exactly what it is that they propose to contribute.

It was suggested above that a central paradox of re-emerging 'culture and development' debates is that culture is being reintroduced into development discourses at exactly the moment when the concept of culture itself is being problematized. Older notions of culture that can be found in almost any 'Introduction to Anthropology' textbook of the 1960s–1980s – of culture as a system, a functionalist whole, and one largely essentialized – with the world being divided into discrete 'cultures', echoes of which are still to be found in positions such as Huntington's 'clash of civilizations' thesis, have now largely been displaced by views that understand culture as process rather than system, as fragmented rather than holistic, and as negotiated and constructed rather than 'given', simply transmitted through unproblematic processes of socialization and acculturation (Friedman 1996). The so-called 'cultural turn' in the social sciences, within which the 'culture and development' move can be located, has recentred culture at the very moment when, under poststructuralist and postmodernist pressure, concepts themselves, including that of culture, are being decentred and relativized. To put culture back at the centre of development debates assumes that we can operate with a clear understanding of what culture can now be considered to be, and of how it articulates with other analytical levels of social conceptualization. This is indeed assuming that all levels of social analysis – the cultural, political, economic, social and psychological – are intellectual constructs that divide up what is actually a whole, a totality made up in reality of the intersection of all these elements.

The meanings of culture

Culture, I would suggest as a starting point, is a reflexive concept. Except as a totally abstract category, its definition is always contingent on its historical location, contemporary understandings of the relationship between culture and nature, the politics of the moment, the uses within social theory to which it is being put, and its own inherently local and grounded nature. Japanese understandings of culture, for example, assume a relational model in which the human person can only be apprehended as a node in a network of social and environmental forces and not as an atomistic individual, a position that places Japanese indigenous conceptions of culture rather closer to those of India or Melanesia than to the West (Clammer 1995;

Roland 1991). In a rather circular manner, culture itself is a cultural concept. Given this, it is possible to map a number of contemporary approaches to culture.

1. The idea of culture as process. This has a number of exponents, among whom might be numbered Jonathan Friedman with his notion of culture as a complex negotiation of identity now irretrievably embedded in globalization and linked intimately with consumption as the dominating form of so-called late capitalist societies (Friedman 1996). Likewise Arjun Appadurai, in also locating culture in the context of globalization and hence in the flows and hybridities that characterize that situation, additionally locates it in relation to modernity, the local environments in which global cultures are reproduced and modified, and ideas of scale and spatiality (Appadurai 1996). Building on this, Mike Featherstone elaborates on the ideas of the 'decentred' nature of contemporary culture, the significance of 'travelling cultures' and of the syncretisms and trans-social processes that now form our experience of culture, at least in the rich First World societies to which he refers and which he understands as being 'postmodern' (Featherstone 1997).

2. The rediscovery or recovery of 'indigenous knowledge'. The 'crisis of representation' stemming from the move from an objectivist to an interpretative approach in anthropology has led to a 'crisis of relevance'. It is largely in response to this that anthropologists, especially those working in the development field, have begun to search for ways in which their discipline can be applied without its simply becoming a tool of mainstream development planners. One solution has been to emphasize anthropology's ability, through the participatory application of the ethnographic method, to assist empowerment at the local level by acting as a midwife to the recovery by indigenous people themselves of the richness of their knowledge systems and of the potential application of

these to the solution of development problems locally and possibly elsewhere (Sillitoe 1998). While this is not the only approach taken by anthropologists who wish to rethink the somewhat problematic relationship of anthropology to development (e.g. Gardner and Lewis 1996), it is important because it relativizes knowledge in a significant political sense – by making knowledge (read 'culture') of the developed as valuable, if not more so, than the knowledge of the developers (Sillitoe et al. 2002).

3. Culture and political economy. Conventional development thinking has, of course, separated the economic from the cultural, hence the reaction marked by the 'culture and development' debate. However, as economic anthropologists have long been aware, the economy is not only embedded in culture, but is itself culture – a system of values, evaluations, processes of production, consumption and exchange, and of social arrangements predicated upon particular patterns of organizing these processes (Clammer 1985). The growing critiques of neoliberal economics as a failed system, both theoretically and in practice, have fuelled once again this approach, which I see as rapidly regaining significance as neoliberalism founders and as alternative approaches correspondingly strengthen.

These perspectives have an interesting relationship to the emerging literature on culture and development themes. The older literature (e.g. Dove 1988) took a relatively unproblematic approach to culture, understanding it essentially from the standard anthropological perspective of the time and then asking how it modified or even disrupted development programmes being largely imposed from the outside: a kind of pre-indigenous-knowledge approach calling on anthropology's traditional strengths in ethnography.

Later moves, however, have gone primarily in one of two directions. The first has been to bring culture and development together without seriously problematizing the concept of culture itself, but instead largely replacing it with a vocabulary of globalization, feminism, human rights and nation-building, while concealing this lacuna behind the pose of being 'critical' (as with Schech and Haggis 2000). The other approach has been to take a more everyday definition of culture – as comprising literature, theatre, art and so forth – and then examine how autonomous forms of such enterprises might be developed and how such development might transform political cultures and understandings of the real workings of economies and their underlying and concealed ideologies by decolonizing the minds and expanding the creation and ownership of knowledge on the part of the indigenes. Such approaches (e.g. Carmen 1996), while they have close connections to older community development movements, are even more closely linked to ideas of participatory development, not as an adjunct to interventions from the outside but as a source of renewing the 'soil of cultures' from which true autonomy grows (Esteva and Prakash 1998). The interface here increasingly becomes one with alternative or even 'post-development' movements, rather than with the simple harnessing of culture to the locomotive of conventional interventionist development (Munck and O'Hearn 1999).

While this brief discussion is far from exhaustive, two issues stand out. The first is that much of the most interesting input is coming from cultural studies, as much as it is from anthropology, the social science that used to consider itself the specialist in the study of culture. Cultural studies furthermore is beginning to break out of its Western-oriented preoccupations (Chen 1995). But so far cultural studies and development studies have hardly spoken to each other. Exploration of the potentialities of this interface is an important task, and one that we will outline here. The second is that the concept of culture being utilized in existing culture and development debates is still inadequate to grasp the full depth of the issues involved, which are in fact deeply existential ones disguised by the term 'development'. If Amartya Sen has argued that 'development is freedom' (Sen 1999), I am here going to argue that 'development is meaning'.

From a development studies perspective, and when confronted with the realities of poverty, inequality, ecological degradation, conflict and violations of human rights, a great deal of work in cultural studies appears narcissistic, focused on issues of popular culture such as bodybuilding and beauty contests, game shows, television soap operas, comics, and the like: on 'lifestyle politics' rather than on emancipatory politics, and to a great extent pre-occupied with a peculiarly Western notion of the self and of the body and of their needs and wants (Scott and Morgan 1993). To a large degree these criticisms are correct, but not entirely so since many of the preoccupations of cultural studies do illuminate central aspects of the human experience, including the emotions, the body, entertainment and sexuality, which have been occluded by the overly positivistic approaches to the phenomenology of everyday life (the exceptions being, apart from North American ethnomethodology, mainly French, e.g. Lefebvre 1971; de Certeau 1984). Yet in fact such foundational issues as the emotions, embodiment and conceptions of the self are central to a holistic conception of development, and their exclusion is a major factor in the failure of so many develop-ment policies. The rise of civil society and of social movements in contesting the meaning of development, and the shift by even such an organization as the World Bank towards at least a rhetoric of participation and values, signal the dawning of the recognition of the silences of development theory, silences that we can now begin to address more systematically.

These silences are in part revealed by the movements that have taken place around the edges of mainstream development studies and that provide an implicit critique of its absences. These include a growing concern with the 'politics of meaning' (Lerner 1996), with the recentring of values in social discourse (Clammer 1996; Fekete 1987), with the moral dimensions of social movements (Jasper 1997), with the revived study of ethics in sociology and anthropology (Smart 1999; Howell 1997; Etzioni 1988), with trenchant critiques of modernity (the very phase of history and mode of thought of which development is a reflection and an expression) in the works of such sociologists as Zygmunt Bauman (1995, 1999), with the whole large area of postcolonial studies, and increasingly with the emergence of deep ecology and other forms of radical environmentalism, and the appearance of environmental sociology as a new sub-discipline parallel to and in close dialogue with the sociology of development.

It would be simplistic to interpret these movements as just re-actions to the economism of conventional development studies: they also represent a reaction to, or even a reflection of, modernity and constitute individually and collectively attempts to redefine development along what are explicitly cultural lines – as attempts to define the good life, the desirable forms of society, and the possible mechanisms for achieving it. This list also excludes other important trends: utopian and futuristic forms of thinking, New Age and new religious movements, and what Jan Nederveen Pieterse among others calls 'alternative development' and 'post-development' movements and thinking, most of which also place cultural concerns and notions of human fulfilment at their core (Nederveen Pieterse 2001; Rahnema and Bawtree 2003).

Nederveen Pieterse in fact places ideas of culture so centrally in his arguments about the nature of development theory that it is worth turning briefly to an examination of his thesis. His synoptic view of current development thinking begins with the prioritizing of culture as one of the main foundations for alternative or critical approaches to development (2001: xi). To do this adequately a work-able concept of culture must be deployed. In his view this has several elements: locating culture within the context of globalization, and understanding that it is hybrid, historically layered, contains internal diversities and has both temporal and spatial dimensions (2001: 1, 70). In Nederveen Pieterse's view, the importance of the culture and development movement is that it prioritizes agency over structure, and hence draws attention to enablement and choices, to the strategies and resistances that elsewhere Pierre Bourdieu understands as being the voluntarist nature of culture itself (Bourdieu 1979). 'Participation' in such a view becomes not just a new methodology for getting things done more efficiently, but the essence of a cultural approach to development. People always 'participate' in their own lives: what is significant is their mode of incorporation into the possible forms of autonomous (or otherwise) decision-making and individual and communal empowerment. Such an approach has both practical and theoretical implications. At the level of practice, it means that in any discussion of civil society, culture is one of the inevitable components (Nederveen Pieterse 2001: 10), and at the level of theory the broad turn in the social sciences towards constructivism, hermeneutics, semiotics, discourse analysis and agency applies as much to the study of development discourses as it does to any other level of cultural production (2001: 11, 28). 'Development' does not float above or outside of discourse: it is a specific language game that like, say, theological language, has attempted to define its specific discursive strategies as privileged, while in fact being as much subject to deconstruction as any other world-view.

Given these considerations, how is culture to be reinserted into development? Here Nederveen Pieterse has a number of pertinent points to make, including the observation that if any effective progress is to be made in the culture and development debate, it must first be recognized that culture is an arena of struggle (2001: 60). It is not, that is to say, simply some abstract category, neutral in its political and ethical implications. Culture has been and will be used in the pursuit of nationalistic goals (Kusno 2000) and in the construction of civilizational agendas, and not only of the Huntington variety (Nandy 1999). The uses of culture in postcolonial discourse are likewise not innocent, often embodying not only nationalism but also myths of uniqueness and new forms of ethnocentrism, and at its worst a narrow localism in which appeals to tribalism and 'tradition' are disguised under the idiom of 'indigenization'. If I am reading

Nederveen Pieterse correctly, he is arguing rather that only a critical understanding of culture is informative in relation to development thinking. A notion of culture that fulfils this primary condition becomes immensely enabling as it potentially provides the basis for alternative understandings of development, not least because it problematizes the idea of development itself by introducing the often unasked question of the goal of development, places development discourse beyond both ethnocentrism (the localizing and indigenizing Scylla) and Eurocentrism (the universalizing Charybdis), and it enables the relativizing and reflexive advances in development anthropology, in particular the turn to indigenous knowledges, to be incorporated significantly into mainstream development thinking.

It is not, then, just a question of 'add culture and stir', in much the same way that feminist arguments have pointed out the fallacy of just 'add gender and stir'. What is at stake is the much more fundamental move of re-problematizing the very notion of development from the perspective of the values and practices embodied in human cultures and lifeworlds, the holistic decolonization of which, to modify Habermas's celebrated phrase, becomes the objective of development. In the course of this many elements of culture itself might have to be rejected, rethought or renegotiated. If development is freedom, as Sen suggests, or if it is better understood as meaning, then alternative understandings of development are crucial.

Cultural studies and development theory

The 'cultural turn' in the social sciences has shifted attention from anthropology to the newer discipline of cultural studies, and indeed at the moment when anthropology itself is being interrogated on its colonial past, its modes of representation of the 'Other' and its recent attempt to appropriate the field of indigenous knowledge as one of its special areas of expertise. With this dilution or expansion of the space or identity of cultural specialists – people who do not necessarily create culture, but spend their time studying what others have created, and whom Featherstone has labelled 'cultural intermediaries' such as academics, book and film reviewers, critics, art historians and cultural journalists (Featherstone 1997) – the centre of gravity of scholarly activity has shifted. If cultural studies has now grown into a full-scale discipline and is now a main location for the study of culture, it is necessary to explore its potential relationship to development studies, a relationship that might prove to be very creative for both sides of the equation.

I would suggest that the 'cultural turn' is signalled by a shift of interest from structure to agency and from explanation to hermeneutics. While this turn has its significant weaknesses (very evident in many self-proclaimed forms of postmodernism), principally in that its political contribution or implications are obscure, and that its eschewing of structural analysis greatly weakens its ability to formulate a systematic critique of large-scale social processes such as capitalism or globalization, it also has significant strengths. First among these is that cultural studies addresses implicitly the silences and absences of conventional development theory.

What are these silences and absences? First, I would say, is its ignorance and neglect of psychology, and its general occluding of the fact that social change (read 'development' or 'social transformation') involves as its central element the reconstruction of subjectivities. In relation to this we immediately encounter a paradox: that while 'development' can be seen as a central plank in the modernist project, development theory itself has not for the most part assimilated or even entered into sustained debate with either the large body of literature in social theory about the nature of modernity (Giddens 1990), or its significant failure to deliver on its promises of emancipation and plenty (Bauman 1999). To a great and alarming extent development studies has remained as a self-contained discourse except in relation to economics, a tragic lapse given its vital positioning vis-à-vis the great moral questions of the day.

While cultural studies itself, in the form at least of its post-modernist and deconstructivist framing, has not much addressed these moral issues either (although its more sympathetic commentators are increasingly aware of this lacuna – e.g. Bauman 1995), a generous reading of cultural studies quickly reveals a vision of human reality closer to that of actual experience than found in the work of even most development sociologists. As suggested above, all social change involves a reconstruction of subjectivities and with them new conceptions of self, identity, gender, nature and the supernatural. As old categories of self-understanding are dissolved so new ones are created. Old ontologies are recast and with them conceptions of rights, justice, freedom and happiness (Clammer et al. 2004).

Central to such shifts in subjectivity are shifts in the organization of desire, whether for things and the pursuit of identity through consumption, or in the reordering of feelings and emotions (Zeldin 1995; Clammer 2000), and with them the charged and changing significance of memory and nostalgia and of the ways in which narratives of person, identity and history are constructed and reconstructed. The surge of recent literature on memory in the social sciences is symptomatic of this, as is the equally large efflorescence of interest in the body and the growing interest in the sociology and anthropology of the self and of the emotions. With this has come a renewed interest in human spatiality as well as temporality, an expanded interest in the visual aspects of culture in addition to the more classical written forms, media studies, sociological interest in public spaces and renewed forms of urban sociology and anthropology drawing on semiotics, landscape architecture, ecology and feminism, and fresh appreciations of the impact of technology on social and cultural organization. Critical approaches to culture, the understanding of culture as process and the expanding of the range of cultural studies coincide, and the potential impact of this on development studies is considerable and even revolutionary.

In essence this revolution consists of the formulation of a new philosophical anthropology, one that attempts to capture the wholeness of human beings while refusing to reduce them to abstract categories. It implies a notion of human beings as culturally 'in process' – as unfinished and permanently mutating; as having a complex and symbiotic relationship to nature; as sexual, embodied, emotional; as having personal histories constructed subjectively out of narratives of struggle; as suffering; as having spiritual aspirations; as constantly constructing the future and reconstructing the past out of hope, desires and intentions; as being at least in part the agents of their own destinies; and as mortal, having life trajectories that involve ageing, transformations in the passage from one life phase to the next and ultimately individual death. The main failure of conventional development thinking has been to ignore the existential qualities of human life. An economistic, oversocialized and much too rationalized conception of the human person can never capture the reality of actual lifeworlds. These lifeworlds involve joys as much as they do struggle, the latter dimension being belatedly reflected in the social sciences by the introduction of the idea of 'social suffering' (Kleinman et al. 1997). Any adequate conception of either culture or development must include these elements, for without their inclusion both are seriously impoverished. The contribution of cultural studies has been to put them back on the intellectual map. The task remains to relate them more systematically to development studies, to bring together the hermeneutics of the cultural approach with the political-economy and politically informed approaches of the best development theory. The 'impasse' in development theory has arisen from its failure to seek new models in unexpected places and to be deaf to those that fall outside of its own conventionally constructed paradigm.

Culture represents the constant creation of meaning, in particular to render valid disordered experiences (illness, disasters, poverty) precisely into *cultural* experiences. This is done to a great extent through storytelling, myth, ritual and the domestication of those experiences, many of which are in fact traumatic. Culture, then, should be thought of as narrative rather than as structure, and not in the deconstructionist sense of a 'text' outside of which there is no other reality, but in the sense of an ever-evolving and constantly edited response to a very insistent reality constantly impinging on the human subject. This model both accounts for the ambiguities and inconsistencies of actual lived experience and culture, and signals the dangers of an over-abstract and disembodied conception of culture: the very form of explanation that rapidly leads to a culturalist rather than a genuinely cultural mode of explanation.

Reasserting culture

The 'cultural turn' that has finally reached development thinking from the other social sciences is a positive move if it helps to ward off the baleful effects of economism. By reinserting real people, individuals with emotions, memories, stories and values, who suffer and seek meaning in their suffering and who seek continually to expand their capacities and range of experiences, 'development' begins to take on its real meaning. To do so is both to introduce the existential into the field of development and to create a sound basis for alternatives to the conventional mainstream. For culture is not irrelevant to the construction of social theory and ideology. Postmodernism in its eagerness to deconstruct master narratives has also rejected the idea that there can indeed be such things as human nature and hence human needs. The anti-humanism of a cohort of thinkers, of whom Lévi-Strauss, Foucault and Althusser are exemplars, has made the very idea of the human subject unstable or even untenable. While paradoxically structuralism, rather like the deep grammar of Chomsky, requires and posits a relatively stable human subject, one subject to transformations, but transformations deriving from a basic universal pattern. There is a careful course to be steered here between essentializing and illegitimate universalizing (rightly both thoroughly critiqued by the deconstructionists) and the assertion of a post-structuralist new foundationalism in which basic needs, rights, freedoms, spaces for cultural and psychological fulfilment, emotional growth and at least a minimum level of material satisfaction are recognized as the grounds of human unity and of responsible development.

A potential means to address this conflict of paradigms is by way of the analysis undertaken by Marilyn Strathern in her analysis of selfhood and society in New Guinea (Strathern 1988). There she suggests that society is a provisional accomplishment rather than functional reproduction, and that as a consequence it is necessary to move away from older anthropological preoccupations with codes and systems to the study of practical enactments and improvisations. In such a model both the concepts of 'society' and 'culture' as essentialised or rigid notions are destabilized, and so their status as universals, systems or units of comparison are radically undermined. As a result certain characteristic assumptions of much social science analysis – for example, in social psychology the idea that society and individual stand in tension with each other and that their relationship needs 'explaining' – are likewise displaced and rendered unnecessary.

In what is effectively a commentary on Strathern, Nick Thomas points out that if all this is true, then what we have previously thought of as groups, cultures or collectivities are in fact not social aggregates, but what he calls 'images of unity' (Thomas 1997: 257). He goes on to comment:

> Strathern's category of 'collectivity' is relevant to contemporary nationhood precisely because nations are prejudiced by economic and cultural globalization that undermines their sovereignty and ideological particularity. Collectivity is not the same as society; it is not a continuing field or container of relationships, but rather an expression of a kind of unity or difference that may be belied by other expressions and affiliations. Particular forms of collectivity are

therefore likely to be imagined episodically, even though they may exist implicitly, as memories, potentialities and sources of tension, at other times. (Thomas 1997: 258)

Culture, then, is accomplished or potential accomplishment – a field of potentialities the realization of which follows complex and only partly determined paths. Both rituals and artefacts are for Thomas 'ways of imagining a collectivity that may not otherwise be invoked', not as the reflection or expression of 'society' but as rhetorical efforts (Thomas 1997: 259).

In much the same way that the notion of self organizes and gives a sense of continuity to what may in fact be fleeting and constantly evolving and relational attributes of being an individual (Battaglia 1999), so 'culture' similarly organizes the processes of collective identity formation and affirmation into what appear to be patterns, and as appearing as such become so through repetition and socialization processes.

Such an 'open' approach also implies a certain humbleness that contrasts with the hubris of much development thinking: its development decades, five-year plans and millennium goals. It recognizes the limits of explanation in the social sciences: the fact that as scholars of such fields of religion and suicide have had to recognize, there are areas of human action that lie beyond their categories and that cannot be 'explained' except by the crudest and most tentative models. Invoking culture exposes us to these mysteries and reveals that development studies often operates at the most superficial levels of human experience and desire and penetrates little into the most fundamental problems of human existence. But at the same time all this opens up possibilities. If culture is a process, dynamic, negotiated and constantly under construction, then the future is open. It is certainly full of the same risks for all of us – accelerating ecological degradation, retreat into fundamentalisms, the severe disruptions created by globalization, among many others. It is here that we realize that the cultural turn is not just a theoretical one, but is intensely political as well. It is no accident that the 'politics of identity', 'lifestyle politics', 'cultural politics', the 'politics of recognition' and multiculturalism, to say nothing of feminism, postcolonialism and new forms of religious revivalism now dominate the landscape of political discourse, a very different agenda from the class struggle and the attempts to define a New Left of a generation ago. Paradoxically again, with the theoretical decentring of the human subject, culture reasserts itself in unexpected forms and the human subject just refuses to go away. This suggests, of course, that under the conditions of globalization it is up to us not to simply accept culture as a given or an imposed reality, but rather to determine what kinds of culture we desire to promote human fulfilment and ecological justice.

Beyond path dependency: theoretical and practical implications

Such a view of culture and of its relationship to development has certain implications, for social and development theory on the one hand and for strategies of practical application on the other. The concept of culture has been transformed under the impact of globalization in diverse ways. While the hybridity of actually existing cultures has to be recognized, it is also true that globalization triggers the search for the authentic or the indigenous (the 'local') and forces, or should do, our explanatory framework to encompass but then move beyond a language of postcolonialism and Eurocentricity into a fresh paradigm. This should be one where the multicentred nature of the world is grasped and with it the complex, subtle and contradictory flows of cultures in which representations do not flow only in one direction, but are refracted, mirrored, partial and kaleidoscopic. Society and cultures in fact operate on principles closer to chaos theory than they do to the structural and classificatory axioms of conventional social science. Globalization should in principle liberate alternative epistemologies, and with them alternative anthropologies. That it in practice tends to impose hegemonic intellectual structures is one of the reasons why it so often has to be struggled against and indeed subverted by the elaboration of those alternatives. If, again, to co-opt Habermas's celebrated term, the negative expression of modernity is the colonization of the lifeworlds of people, then alternative development becomes the decolonization of those same lifeworlds, the liberation of everyday life from necessity into meaning and freedom.

The decolonization of the lifeworld, while it involves personal transformations implicit in the restoration of culture, empowerment, autonomy and the rediscovery of sociability (Murphy 1999; Carmen 1996), also involves social transformations – liberatory structures and institutions within which the decolonized mind and lifestyles can flourish – and changes in the methodology and mode of thinking of development studies itself towards a concept of the open future. This implies culture understood as the 'not yet', or 'in progress', in which the search for new models, new forms of social knowledge, and visions of integrated development in which social, economic, cultural, political, spiritual and environmental elements are holistically related. Development studies then becomes, in the best sense of the term, futurology. The violence of development needs to be confronted in the same spirit in which the violence of colonialism has been confronted, and both placed within the framework of the violence of modernity, to which there are indeed alternatives if we seek them.

It is here that the notion of participation once again enters the picture, as it is through participation – that is, autonomous management of one's life-space – that new forms of liberatory thinking and practice emerge. Civil society also means civil culture. As Boris Frankel has argued, in attempts to think through what might constitute a post-industrial society, culture becomes not something that simply exists prior to the individual and the collectivity, but is the constructive process of redefining both the private and the public spheres, re-examining the relationship between them, and planning how to get from 'here to there' – from our current dysfunctional society to a more humanized state of social being (Frankel 1987). Frankel also recognizes squarely that culture is a field of conflict, of competing social visions and deep contradictions, with old religions, identities and traditions struggling with emerging new ones, and rightly notes that any future society would have to manage these tensions: there is no 'end of history'. The unintended consequences of all social plans and policies are themselves part of the inevitable cultural dynamics of all societies in change.

As social movements theorists such as Alberto Melucci have recognized, the boundary between the cultural and the political in the examination of the nature of such movements is very porous (Melucci 1989). In his view, cultural processes are totally implicated in the conduct of politics in general and so-called 'life politics' in particular. Social movements involve reflexive actions in which collectivities reorient themselves in terms of values and strategies within an existing field of constraints and opportunities, aimed ultimately at breaking what Buechler (2000: 179) calls the 'compatibility' of the dominant or hegemonic system. In Melucci's model, social activism is largely a response to intolerable forms of social control, many now based on the manipulation of symbolic and cultural capital, new forms of surveillance, and the control of information. Resistance to such control, even when it takes cultural forms, is a political act, a challenge to prevailing systems of power. These, as we now well know, are themselves embedded in discourse, and in the taken-for-granted structures of everyday life where inequalities and domination are constantly and subtly reproduced.

While it is easy to trivialize the role of culture in resistance (which I prefer to think of as the struggle to achieve autonomous 'spaces'), as in some of the literature on commodification of society in late capitalism which sees shopping as resistance, or makes the assumption that 'anti-corporate' bands or artists are really outside of the nexus of commercialization, it is nevertheless true that cultural practices do provide a place where agency can be expressed, even if in the gaps and interstices of 'the system' (Starr 2000: 34–7). As the urban sociologist Sharon Zukin has argued, while culture always needs to be tied to political economy, 'Focusing attention on cultural practices and cultural categories has had the great virtue of enriching an experiental understanding of social justice' (Zukin 1996: 224). This is an idea extended at length by Edward Soja in an essay in the same volume in which he reconfigures the relationship between justice, culture and subjectivities in such a way that the historical (rather than the political economy) nature of social experience is recentred, and in which culture is seen as expressed in spatiality (Soja 1996). The relationships between space, time, identity and justice are thus remapped, and all are seen as constituting the sphere that Melucci would presumably call 'cultural politics': the point at which cultural and political struggles become effectively indistinguishable. Here culture and governance merge and the field of development anthropology is the disciplinary point at which anthropology (the 'science of culture'?) becomes 'part of the practice of governmental-ity' (Moore 2000: 196). This is exactly why culture has reentered debates on citizenship (Ong 2000), peace-keeping and peace-building, the naming and addressing of 'cultures of terror', poverty, capac-ity-building, NGO mobilization and effectiveness, democratization, corruption and a host of other locations that take culture out of the realm of conventional cultural studies and into that of politics. Development thinking is nothing if not political, and however fluid the notion of culture might be, it is the means through which agency is characteristically exercised upon the world, and the way in which notions of the self are integrated around relatively stable categories of understanding. It links the individual to patterns of meaning, and condenses that meaning in such a way that it can become the vehicle for political intervention. Transformations of subjectivity at the level of the individual are mirrored sooner or later in the desire to create transformations in society and culture at large.

A closing meditation on 'spaces of hope'

One of the most important works of social theory to have appeared in recent years, in my view, is David Harvey's *Spaces of Hope* (Harvey 2002). The book is an extended meditation on the geography of late capitalism and globalization, the possibility of a refurbished socialism, and the recovery of the idea of the utopian project as a necessary step to carry us into a future worth inhabiting in the face of the massive economic, ecological and political crises that we all now face. Harvey's argument is too complex and subtle for it to be easily summarized in its fullness, but here I would like to draw out a few central ideas that I think frame and speak to the issues that we have been discussing in this chapter.

The first of these is the idea that to grasp in any way the fullness and richness of the concept of culture, it is necessary to confront the power of the human imagination. For Harvey the key element in any future political project is the preparing of our imaginations for alternative futures, and the liberation of them, in so far as we are able, from the existing material and institutional conditions which so fence them in. His question is not whether such imagination exists (his book itself shows that it clearly does), but whether we are prepared for radical change and able to undertake the work of cultural reconstruction necessary to achieve it.

The second is the idea, derived directly from Marx, of our 'species being' and the confronting directly of what such a notion implies for the nature of our political and cultural projects. This involves, among other things, examining seriously but without falling into geneticism or the ideologically charged waters of the more reactionary forms of sociobiology, the biological and physical basis of human nature and our ecological location as creatures within nature, not above or outside it. As Harvey puts it:

> We are a species on earth like any other, endowed, like any other, with specific powers that are put to use to modify environments in ways that are conducive to our own sustenance and reproduction. ... This conception defines the 'nature imposed conditions of our existence.' We are sensory beings in a metabolic relation to the world around us. We modify that world and in so doing change ourselves through our activities and labors. Like all other species, we have some species-specific capacities and powers, arguably the most important of which are our ability to alter and adapt our forms of social organization (to create, for example, divisions of labor, class struggles, and institutions), to build a long historical memory through language, to accumulate knowledge and understandings that are collectively available to us as guides to future action, to reflect on what we have done and do in ways that permit learning from experience (not only our own but also that of others), and, by virtue of our particular dexterities, to build all kinds of adjuncts (e.g. tools, technologies, organizational forms, and communications systems) to enhance our capacities to see, hear, and feel way beyond the physiological limitations given by our own bodily constitution. ... The argument for seeing human nature in relative terms, as something in the course of construction, is not without weight and foundation, But it also points to a connection between the concept of 'species being' and 'species potential.' (Harvey 2002: 207–8)

The various contemporary sociologies of the body and of nature are elsewhere making the same point, and indeed elsewhere in his book Harvey does discuss in some detail the relationship between the physical body and the body politic, a missing term in almost all discussions of development.

Third, Harvey notes that culture accumulates. We do not construct our culture anew in every generation, but we do build on, even while rejecting many aspects of, our particular history. And history is now both expanded and relativized by globalization, which in a sense now makes everybody's history available to all of us. Culture does indeed represent openness, but it is also necessary to remember that in making cultural choices – for example, by quite literally building something – we are foreclosing on other possibilities, and it is fact within this field of foreclosures imposed on us by previous generations that we live much of our lives. Fourth, Harvey suggests that what deep ecology, socialism (and, he might well have added, Buddhism) teach us in an intellectual environment dominated by ideas of difference is the need to understand the self in relation to the other, to search for the 'Great Self' that surpasses difference in a larger unity, as philosophers in the tradition running through Buber and Levinas have long recognized.

Finally, following in the steps of such neglected thinkers as Ernst Bloch and his principle of the future as the 'not yet', that which can be brought into being, Harvey argues for the vitality of the utopian impulse as that which keeps the future open, inspires the imagination and provides the raw material out of which actual futures are constructed, and constructed moreover to a great extent out of our cultural choices. I think that he is right, and that development studies is the art and science of conceiving and bringing into being that future, the one we want, not the one imposed on us.

THREE

Aid, culture and context

A common hazard in the social sciences is 'old mind' thinking applied to new problems or to old problems when the context or environment of those problems has changed. This is nowhere more true than in debates about 'development' in general and specifically about the contentious issue of aid within that broader discourse. The apparent intractability of many of the central problems of development, poverty being the most glaring, is indicative of this. For when considering the issue of aid – its nature, desirability or maintenance as a policy – the same critical questions need to be asked that can be directed at any other central institution, in this case of what has become probably the central platform of the development 'industry'. For most of us are probably familiar with the principal arguments about the desirability of aid as a solution to the pressing global issues of poverty, inequality and social exclusion in the light of its often negative effects – the creation of dependency, indebtedness, corruption, non-absorbability, and socially and culturally destructive side effects. Some consequently argue against aid in principle – for example, the recent controversial book by Dambisa Moyo (2009) – while others, who would certainly see aid as a tool of intervention in humanitarian emergencies, centre their arguments on the *efficiency* of aid and its assessable usefulness in concrete and local situations and the problems of avoiding the corruption and socio-economic distortions to which it can so easily give rise (Roodman 2007). But in few cases is the issue of aid linked in any systematic way with culture: with the practical issue of the role of culture in promoting the absorbing of aid and the characteristic issues of corruption that it tends to generate; with the impact of large amounts of foreign aid on indigenous cultures and social structures; or with aid directed not to economic growth or infrastructure, but to the development of culture itself.

In large part the 'problem' of aid arises from the fact that the environment (quite literally indeed when 'environment' is read as 'ecology') in which aid has been given has changed since aid was first conceived of as a development policy, and continues to change rapidly in the context of globalization and its manifold effects. Our initial task, then, should be to attempt to clarify what these changes are, how they affect the aid environment, and the extent to which that environment is increasingly made up of actors concerned not only with being donors or recipients of aid but with proactively renegotiating the very meaning of 'development' and with the processes through which it is being delivered and the wider ideological contexts within which it can be thought – again globalization, but also, in more critical terms, neocolonialism. Initially, then, I will approach the cultural rethinking of aid through the identification of four layers of discourse, which I will call, respectively, language, environment, actors and solutions.

Language

It would be quite possible to write a history of development, or at least of development thinking, through a close examination of the shifts that have characterized its discourse, and indeed this has to some extent been done (e.g. Sachs 1995; Preston 1996). If one conventionally begins with Harry S. Truman's 1949 definition of development as the directed process of rescuing the underdeveloped (economically and politically) nations – that is, the members of the 'Third World' not yet absorbed into the expanding socialist bloc – from their poverty, postcolonial degradation and lack of democratic institutions, it is possible to trace an evolving vocabulary. This has variously encompassed notions of progress, growth, democratization, trickle-down, human needs, participation, empowerment, human rights, and most recently indigenous knowledge, civil society, sustainability and ecology. This at least has been the language of the capitalist-donor sector: the language of the socialist bloc naturally tending towards a vocabulary of postcolonialism, peasant empowerment, anti-capitalism and revolution. The general thrust of these shifts has been slowly away from top-down, donor-driven, externally defined conceptions of development towards increasing democratization of development discourse and practice (even within the language of the World Bank), the recognition of political, sociological and cultural factors as well as purely economic ones, and towards a holism in which environment, gender, empowerment and spirituality have been recognized as intrinsically linked, and very importantly, to a widening of a pool of actors concerned less with 'being developed' than with participating in the very definition of that development, its goals and the appropriate policies for its effective realization. As suggested, even the World Bank belatedly recognized in its 2000 *World Development Report* (World Bank 2000) that trickle-down does not happen, that development without participation is a charade, and that the era in which the multilaterals, national donor agencies, civil society and even business could be thought of as separate and non-communicating actors (or as actors only communicating with hostility and mutual incomprehension) is now well and truly over.

Not only are these actual shifts on the ground of major importance for the conception of aid and the means by which it is delivered and to whom, but so is the language. For the language itself is a bearer of ideology; most significantly in this context the shifts in vocabulary, with all the fuzziness, unclarities and inconsistencies that continue to plague the language of development – think, for example, of the problems of defining or agreeing on the meaning of a term as apparently simple as 'sustainability' – signal major changes in which the subject of development is being thought. This is no irrelevancy as it is thinking that in its practical and policy expressions affects the lives of billions. As suggested in the previous chapter, the language in use reflects what is thinkable and considered possible – whether this opens up liberatory and progressive possibilities or whether an outmoded form of discourse serves to help keep the majority in the iron cage of poverty while the minority luxuriate in the velvet cage of affluence and overconsumption.

Environment

Shifts in language reflect, signal or even create changes in the objective environment within which development practices, including aid, operate. There are many elements in this emerging or already emerged environment – the now central place of ecological issues, a growing concern with the significance of cultural values, the unignorable role of gender, and the concern with the impact of any current policies on future generations. But in particular I would argue that there are two key factors that must be absorbed into development debates if we are to move creatively forward beyond the 'impasse' announced not so long ago by thinkers still for the most part operating from old-mind paradigms – notably a classical view of modernity, a pre-postmodern understanding of the nature of capitalism, and a clinging to classical socialism as the only counterweight to capitalist growth theory while simultaneously admitting that the Marxist paradigm had itself failed (Booth 1985). This impasse, including – with the exception of a very few early eco-socialists such as Murray Bookchin (1982) – the failure to take into account any ecological, cultural or sociological factors and the extraordinarily undemocratic conceptions of development found among some leading proponents, was in fact really a crisis of the Left, in this case an old Left unwilling to address four issues that I would regard as essential: globalization, chaos theory, ecology and culture.

Globalization, of course, means many things to many people; while for some it is a process to be celebrated and accelerated, for others it is most certainly a worldwide phenomenon to be decried, opposed and where possible reversed (the literature is now huge, but for some sensible accounts, see Greider 1997; Hay and Marsh 2000; Khondker 2000). As a condition or maybe *the* condition of contemporary life, whatever the perspective, it is unavoidable. But in the context of aid, some of its key characteristics need to be identified. The first of these is that globalization is highly uneven in its effects, and in many ways it parallels, reproduces or mimics a number of processes, including Dore's concept of the 'late development effect', the simultaneous coexistence of differing modes of production within the same society as identified by the investigations of neo-Marxist economic anthropology (Clammer 1978), the uneven penetration of capitalism as theorized in many versions of dependency theory and its uneven geographical and human rights impact (Harvey 2002). Second, as we now all know, the global interacts dialectically with the local, influencing and being influenced by it and reproducing itself not only through its transnational structural effects, but also in and through specific local conditions. Third, globalization is by no means only an economic phenomenon, but is also profoundly cultural (Featherstone 1997). This is not only to say that globalization simply impacts 'traditional' cultures, but also that the very meaning of tradition changes under conditions of globalization. The hybridities, travelling cultures and creoles so beloved of cultural studies are not just a passing phenomenon, but are now part of the global landscape and will remain so for the foreseeable future. But why are these three dimensions of globalization relevant in our discussion of aid?

A primary reason is that the sociology of aid is every bit as important as the economics or politics of aid. Its absorbability, socially and culturally transformative effects, impact on local meaning systems, patterns of gender relations and structure of local employment and work practices are all aspects of the sociology of aid at the same time as these sociological elements are themselves in a process of dynamic transformation or dissolution under the regime of globalization. Likewise it has to be recognized that the structural qualities of globalization make specific aid interventions problematic. Do they in fact make any (positive) difference? Here let me quote the distinguished urban anthropologist Aidan Southall at some length. Writing of the destruction of communities, the penetration of commodification and massified popular culture, and the domination of narrowly capitalist values over all other possible ones, Southall says:

> The prospect is so horrible that most of the time we refuse to
> face it; we go on optimistically and euphemistically talking about
> development, as many of us are paid to do. Is there any escape? Can
> we hope for any revolution with positive results? Nothing in past
> history seems to give grounds for any such hope. But population
> projections for the twenty-first century show impossibly large,
> explosive concentrations of destitute poor throughout the Third
> World. They will be likely to overthrow elites cooperating with
> the capitalist world in their exploitation. Yet, this may only lead to
> more authoritarian military-backed regimes.... Or will increasing
> sensitivity to such danger lead to a real transfer of surplus from
> North to South? So far, we have bilateral and international famine
> relief, Bob Geldof and Oxfam, splendid outpourings of the human
> spirit, which never come near to tackling the real problem. The
> advanced capitalist countries will not spend enough in finance or
> understanding to transform the Third World societies, still less will
> they leave them alone. This is the context in which we have to try
> to apply our anthropology. (Southall 1992: 300)

While I think that Southall is something of a pessimist for reasons that I will shortly explain, without anywhere using the world 'globalization' he has certainly put his finger on the central problem: the structural constraints, most of them in fact political rather than economic, of the context in which any aid interventions are currently required to operate.

One of these reasons, perhaps a little unexpectedly, is the topic of chaos theory in the social sciences and in the context of development in particular. The human lifeworld is inherently complex. Globalization intensifies that complexity by constantly introducing new elements, new relationships between those elements and the speed with which they change. Policy, on the other hand, is usually simple and the evaluations of its effects rarely multidimensional, which is why it so often does not work or has entirely unintended side effects. Complexity theory, which is what we might call the social-science cousin of mathematical and natural science chaos theory, suggests that the full outcome of a policy can never be known or predicted, that small causes can have large, unintended and unexpected effects, and that human stubbornness and recalcitrance (i.e. what we usually call 'culture') inevitably supplies its own subtle feedback responses to policy interventions (a practice that often takes the form of resistance). While this might lead to despair on the part of policymakers (and certainly in the development context a little humility is a good thing), it need not necessarily do so. For a due recognition of the nature of complexity and its empirical manifestations can lead to policy undergoing its own revolution: its becoming negotiation not imposition. This possibility may become clearer when we consider the things that Southall has left out of his account.

Actors

The depression that anti-globalization activists are often prey to is I suspect because they feel alone in the world. They should, however, take heart. One of the most profound changes in both the international and domestic social environments has been the emergence of numerous new actors or the revitalization of old ones almost unimaginable not much more than a decade ago. States, businesses and the multilateral institutions are no longer the only powers on the global stage and their influence has been, if not displaced, at least seriously modified by the emergence of all those diverse elements that make up civil society: NGOs of all sizes, NPOs, CSOs, social movements, people's movements, communes, co-operatives, new religious movements and even sectors rarely taken seriously by sociologists, such as the New Age movement, now fill the landscape (Hawken 2008; Bornstein 2005). Of vastly differing levels of expertise, funding, purpose, constituencies and professionalism, they have collectively transformed the range of development or counter-development possibilities. Many are in the South, some of which form important links between the South and the North, and others work in the North on both their own local problems and attempting to transform public attitudes and the actions of their own governments on global and development issues. So significant have they become that states, big business and the multilaterals have all begun to talk with these CSOs, to consult with them in many cases on policy and delivery as powerful actors in their own right, and in many cases as the authors of significant alternative development initiatives, often from a low resource base, in situations where massive and officially funded aid projects have failed.

Such social movements are a vital component in the contemporary aid environment. They matter not just because they are there, but, as we will further explore in the final chapter, because they are the sources of new local knowledges and praxis, representing as they do social experiments in progress. So here I would set myself directly against those theorists who have argued that social movements are irrelevant in the development landscape because they so often 'fail' (e.g. Schuurman 1996; Rigg 1997). Often they do not, and even when they do failures (as are common among official development projects) are instructive in pointing out where analysis or application have gone wrong. Even when they are relatively weak actors it may be not that they are fundamentally flawed, but that a little help (advice, technical expertise, education) would expedite their role as change agents and help them expand the dimensions of transparency and internal democracy that they sometimes lack. For above all they represent local voices, and the current fad among development anthropologists for privileging local or indigenous knowledge has not yet fully caught up with the fact that such knowledge is dynamic and emergent and by no means resides only in the 'traditional' sectors of a society, even supposing that any such even exist any more. If slogans of participatory development are to be turned into reality, it may well be that, as many donor agencies are now beginning to recognize, that the most effective investments are to be made in civil society organizations rather than those of the state, especially in contexts where it is the failure of the state that is the primary source of development problems.

Solutions

With the rise of alternative voices and of proliferating actors, and with them new definitions of the development process, new solutions are emerging in many places, especially in local contexts, although unfortunately most of this vast body of development wisdom is not systematically documented or shared. Indigenous knowledge has always been the source of innovative and ingenious solutions to problems agricultural, environmental, technical and social. From what might be termed 'alternative' development circles a plethora of extraordinarily interesting solutions in education, health-care appropriate technology, energy, micro-finance, agriculture, ecologically adapted architecture, new economic networks and community building has emerged (see, for example, the documentation in McKibben 2007; Wines 2008; Maheshvarananda 2003; Bakshi 2007), as well as theoretical work in such areas as non-Marxist socialism, Gandhian initiatives, postmaterialist values, postmodernism, post-Fordist production systems and new urban possibilities (e.g. Korten

1999; Theobald 1999). The problem for many of these initiatives is not the quality of their ideas, but rather that of scaling up from the local to large-scale solutions, and of finding ways to overcome the structural domination of the world-system mechanisms that Southall and others have identified. Equally important in such movements are the identification and overcoming of their own internal prejudices and inequalities. For example, the now increasingly well known Indian Swadhyaya movement, which is developing highly innovative approaches to poverty alleviation through agricultural practices, forestry and local handicraft production, has had to confront head-on the profound influence of caste and rural social structures embedded in its own culture as well as in the surrounding society that work against its positive influences introduced into Indian rural society (Srivastava 1998). These diverse attempts to formulate and implement innovative and appropriate solutions to the pressing global problems indicate a vast grassroots movement of initiatives, experience, wisdom and creative thinking and practice at work.

It doesn't need to be stressed, I trust, that these four dimensions or considerations fundamentally affect the ways in which aid is understood and administered. They also raise a number of other urgent questions, paramount among which is the changing nature of the whole political environment suggested by the emergence of civil society actors in such a major and visible way. Classically this has been raised in the form of the questions of the relationship between the state and civil society, and that of whether, in a post-nationalist age (i.e. a globalized one) governments still really rule. This is a legitimate dimension of the question of governance, but certainly not the only one. Jean Baudrillard has suggested, for example, that the fundamental problem of governance must nowadays involve an analysis of the media. Where massification of society occurs, with its attendant commoditization and media saturation, paradoxically individualism flourishes and there is an implosion of meaning in which the social disappears (Baudrillard 1983). In such a context politicians and the population at large are simply no longer talking to each other, or rather perhaps both are talking, but nobody is listening. The crisis of democracy in such a view is not that of the creation of representative institutions, but the fact that they no longer work as they once did because commodity culture has essentially depoliticized the population. Even power is no longer to be found in conventional politics, but in the media, business and perhaps diffused in some Foucauldian fashion among the various sectors of civil society. This theory is in many ways similar to that of Anthony Giddens, who has argued that the big political shift is not from socialism to capitalism, but across the board of political systems from what he terms 'emancipatory politics' (concerned with freedom, rights, labour issues and the like) to 'lifestyle politics' (concerned primarily with individual benefits and with little concern for the wider social entity) (Giddens 1990). In fact a closer examination of the widespread activism of social movements and large gatherings such as the World Social Forum suggests that emancipatory politics is alive and well, but that it has changed its character. With the demise of the old left and its apparent hegemony over revolutionary and transformative possibilities, the emancipatory agenda of the new movements is often expressed in forms that may not initially appear to be political in the traditional sense at all – as culturally revivalist, spiritual, anti-modernist, ecological, New Age, or precisely to do with the creation or preservation of lifestyles that are not commoditized ones.

The major implication of this for governance is not that politics has disappeared, but that it has in many cases radically changed its form and meaning. The 'global associational revolution' identified by Lester Salamon (1994) not only diversifies the range of political actors, but also suggests a shift in the location of power from institutions to networks. There are several secondary-level implications to this, one of the most important of which is the emergence of new understandings of democracy and of the concept of citizenship, no longer confined to the right to vote, but representing a kind of vastly scaled-up version of the classical Greek model. The focus shifts, in other words, from the periodic right to elect 'leaders' to represent public interests, to the expectation of direct participation and consultation whenever issues arise that bear directly on the lifeworlds of those affected (Hudson and Slaughter 2007). One aspect of the 'global revolution' has been not only the sheer expansion of the voluntary sector but also, more significantly, the recognition that local issues now almost invariably have global import. This is a factor long understood in environmental sectors, but now spreading rapidly to include such issues as human rights, war crimes, weapons trafficking, migrant labour conditions, and the rights of children. As we look back at the evolving vocabulary of development studies, we see this clearly signalled in the languages of feminism, deep ecology, conscientization, participation, empowerment and autonomy that have now become part of its lexicon but have largely entered it from outside, primarily from new social movements operating separately from or even opposed to mainstream development practices. Grasping this reinforces the claim that we should take very seriously the social praxis and social theory expressed in social movements, and also the special status of indigenous knowledge, provided that we encourage the producers and consumers of such knowledge to take the same critical and reflexive stance towards it as we hopefully take towards our own (local too, despite its universalist pretensions) knowledge.

Culture, globalization and aid

Globalization and the environmental effects that it has set in train are the two major macro-social processes of the era in which we live. It is, as we now know, a double-edged phenomenon, promoting a hitherto unknown unity at some levels, while generating new forms of exclusion, marginalization and cultural erosion at others. Culture itself, then, is not simply an autonomous entity floating separately from the other sectors of social and environmental life. In fact culture and our sense of reality change with and are shaped by the larger economic and social forces that frame our individual lives. Yet in much of the 'developed' and in increasing sectors of the developing world, production of things is being displaced by the production of culture and of images. As a result, as Baudrillard suggests, the media – widely globalized television networks, international news agencies, cable services, Internet providers, newspaper chains, publishing houses, film companies, international advertising agencies, CD and DVD distributors, and the easy accessibility of the technology to access these diverse but often integrated resources – increasingly shape our imaginaries and our subjectivities. Our sense of self, individual and collective identities, perceptions, the categories by which we divide up the world, our sense of space and time and the nature of our relationships are now increasingly mediated by electronic means.

These phenomena, which have variously been described as a move from production to consumption, from an economy of the production of things to that of images that the sociologists Lash and Urry (1991) call 'economies of signs and space', or as 'postmodernity' with its attendant 'space–time compression', blurring of genres and pastiche-like characteristics (Harvey 1989), are of profound cultural significance, for they imply a number of things. These include new forms of culture such as the genres of fusion musics that draw on numerous musical traditions to create novel blends no longer specific to any one cultural area, hybrid forms of culture where one tradition has assimilated or adapted forms originating elsewhere and has to some degree indigenized them – Disneyland, tango, coffee and departmental stores in Japan, for example (Tobin 1992) – and widespread cultural sharing and multidirectional cultural exchanges (Bollywood movies, the curry-eating English or New York yuppy sushi eaters), and the international reach of the UK and US popular music industries (Hesmondhalgh 1998). We could in fact multiply examples of the interplay between culture and globalization almost indefinitely. As John Tomlinson puts it, 'Globalization lies at the heart of modern culture; cultural practices lie at the heart of globalization' (Tomlinson 2000: 1).

The 'problem' of culture from the perspective of globalization is often taken to be that of the erosion of local cultures and whether it is possible to maintain their authenticity and vitality in the face of the homogenizing tendencies of global cultural forces – the phenomenon of 'McDonaldization' (Ritzer 1996), the assimilation of local cultures into a single bland, homogenized, standardized and nutrition-free form that suppresses local creativity, innovation and variety. But in fact many studies suggest that far from globalization simply creating an international monoculture, it actually triggers reaction at the local level and as such is a self-limiting phenomenon where culture is concerned: integration at one level (say the economic) stimulates increasing diversity at others (in local cultural expressions, artistic activity, native cuisines and so forth) as people seek to stem the loss of local autonomy that globalization seeks to impose. As we have seen, the world is teeming with local social movements, ecological initiatives, co-operatives, a spreading organic food movement among both producers and consumers, direct marketing networks, citizens' movements and numerous other social and cultural initiatives (Smart 1999; Starr 2000).

The context in which aid is 'delivered' is thus a complex one, shaped by a globalization that is itself driven largely by the dynamics of consumer capitalism, the hegemony of which is resisted by many local cultural and social movements. The basic framework of aid, including the broader ideological environment in which it operates, remains, despite the language of altruism frequently used by aid agencies, international and local capitalism; and, as we have seen so frequently from the policies of the World Bank and the IMF, its purpose is often to open markets, increase consumption and promote certain forms of industrialization rather than deliver essentials to the very poorest segments of the targeted countries. Aid policies consequently do not operate in a vacuum, but at the interface of links and conflict between the international development agencies, civil society and business (Ichikawa and Clammer 2002). Curiously, too, aid is rarely directed at *cultural development*, but almost always exclusively to infrastructure, economics and industrialization, leaving culture to fend for itself as best it can. Aid as a consequence tends to promote globalization rather than critique it or provide alternative resources and models to a 'developing' society. While we are now very aware of the highly uneven impact of globalization economically, it is rarely assessed in terms of its impact on access to cultural resources (Smiers 2003). Given the highly unequal access to the Internet and to communications networks (there are more telephone lines in Manhattan than in the whole of sub-Saharan Africa excluding South Africa; Ghana has less than one computer per 100 people compared with 35 per hundred in the USA), there are massive imbalances in access to educational resources, knowledge, databases and accessible cultural heritage (if, for example, we count the number of museums and art galleries per capita). As Ray Kiely suggests, 'the information superhighway has passed by most of the world's population and is likely to do so for the foreseeable future' (Kiely 1998a: 5). But we can reasonably argue that just as global justice requires economic justice, so too it demands cultural justice, and the highly unequal flows of cultural power triggered and intensified by globalization require as much attention, and perhaps appropriate forms of aid, as any of the other effects of globalization and international capitalism.

But this is not a simple process: if in principle we could agree that cultural development is as important as economic development, we would have to face the fact that today cultures are increasingly hybrid: they draw on each other and transform, assimilate and reflect back what they have borrowed. In a globalizing world this tendency is accelerated and intensified at all levels of culture, including religions which spread out of their original heartlands into culturally quite remote areas: Buddhism is now growing fast in the West and the Japanese 'new religion' Soka Gakkai is spreading rapidly in Southeast Asia, for example (Clammer 2009b). Culture indeed has many facets, including art, theatre, dance, fashion, cuisines, architecture, games, religion and popular culture, and these exist in a dynamic interplay with each other and their counterparts in 'other' cultures, except that in a sense there are no longer 'other cultures' in an increasingly shared cultural world in which hybridity is the norm. The intensifying cultural effects of globalization ensure that contemporary culture is not a museum but a crucible. It is no longer possible to have an essentialist conception of culture (Brah and Coombes 2000). It is in understanding these cultural dynamics in relation to development and globalization that, as suggested in the previous chapter, cultural studies, cultural sociology and anthropology have an important but still undervalued role to play.

Out of all of this emerge at least two insights. The first is the need for a conception of global cultural citizenship as a much broadened version of traditional political notions of citizenship, and for development to include the development of culture as much as of the economic sphere. The second is that this economic sphere, whatever specific form it takes, has cultural consequences. In a recent study of globalization in Southeast Asia (Yamashita and Eades 2003), for example, tourism emerges as one of the major forces transforming local cultures in both positive and negative ways – by revitalizing local traditions and forms of art and by introducing a monetized economy into spaces formerly dominated by barter or exchange systems. A large sector of tourism is now cultural tourism – a broadening experience for the tourists no doubt, but with effects on the local economies, values and ecology, to say nothing of the wear and tear on the monuments themselves, Angkor Wat being a very good case in point. Indeed in that very case, promoting cultural tourism to revitalize a war-ravaged local economy is a positive idea, provided that its effects on local social structure and culture are taken into account. Yet development policy and cultural policy are rarely integrated. At its best cultural policy will seek to find a balance between the global – the preservation and accessibility of civilizational heritage sites of significance to all of us – and the integrity and autonomy of the local communities. When this works well, local economic and social life is revitalized (Shuman 2000). When it fails, numerous problems are created. For example, in the creation of an archaeological 'culture park' around the famous monument of Borobudur in East Java, large numbers of local farmers were displaced from their ancestral lands and driven from an area where they had lived for generations. Significantly, then, a discourse is appearing in which the necessity of linking development issues to cultural issues is emerging and in which the notion of human rights is being expanded to include cultural rights as well as political ones (Cowen et al. 2001). To be serious about culture is to put it at the centre of debates about development and globalization, not at the periphery, and to recognize that true and integral human development takes us beyond the necessity of a world in which basic material security and well-being are mandatory to one in which culture is central: the enhancement of expression and performativity, the freedom to seek self-realization and meaning, the welcoming and nurturing of creativity, the expansion of our imaginations and imaginaries, and the achievement of a situation in which we can explore the riches of our collective heritages and our individual subjectivities in freedom.

Aid refigured in the context of culture

The notion of aid, instead of being seen as a technical issue in which the main concerns are its effective delivery and the political considerations that inevitably surround it, thus needs to be reconfigured in a cultural context. This has two main dimensions. On the one hand, aid has cultural impacts as well as economic ones, and notions such as dependency, much employed by the critics of aid, apply as much or more to culture as they do to other forms of relationship between the donor and recipient. On the other hand, the development *of* culture is rarely seen as being a priority in aid or other forms of development projects. Yet culture, as the bearer of subjectivities, meaning systems, values, and creative and expressive practices, lies at the heart of life and especially of definitions of the good life. The connections between conventional development and culture are real and controversial, for these connections are the source of commoditization; the expansion of consumer culture as a way of life; the aping of the cultural forms of the donor societies; the promotion of education based on metropolitan models, however inappropriate these may be for local conditions; and the stimulation of migration to those metropolitan countries on the part of those who believe that they will find both higher standards of living and higher levels of culture in those societies than in their own. This in turn promotes brain drain (Argentina, for example, having more of its locally trained PhDs outside of the country than within, and the Philippines having more of its medically trained doctors and a higher percentage of its nurses residing outside of the country than within).

The current world situation is one in which new interfaces have appeared between the multilaterals, business and civil society and between the multilaterals and the NGOs (Heyzer et al. 1995; Clayton 1996). These interfaces have emerged in a context in which there is a widespread perception of the failure of the state, and indeed of the failure of 'development', especially in the poorest countries and those riven with social, ecological and ethnic problems. Decades of conventional development have not only failed to solve these problems, but in many cases have exacerbated them, a process often intensified by the pressures of globalization, especially those aspects of it that are just marketization by another name. A fundamental line of enquiry for development studies if it is to have any intellectual legitimacy or morally defensible future is to address squarely the question of why this is so. The answers will be painful in that they radically question the validity of much mainstream (which effectively means Western) academic 'knowledge', much of which in fact turns out on closer inspection to be ideology in disguise, and of the policy interventions that have been made on the basis of that knowledge/ ideology. As the hegemony of the historically central knowledge systems are called into question, the voices from the periphery begin to move to centre stage as it is increasingly recognized that their local knowledges may embody wisdom absent from the technocratic centre. Aid itself is a belief system. Unfortunately for the rest of the world, it is a belief system that – in common with, and sometimes accompanied by, its associated religions – the centre, often for good and unselfish motives but often from politically driven ones, has sought to impose on the periphery.

But the context in which this was originally possible (the post-World War II and Cold War period) has now changed beyond recognition. New actors have appeared with agendas very different from those of governments and donors, neither of which has any longer a practical monopoly on the definition of development. In an increasingly post-nationalist world, the hegemony and legitimacy of both governments and the multilaterals is being eroded by the emergence of civil society organizations and social movements. While this hardly means that governments are about to wither away, it does imply a changing balance of power domestically and inter-nationally, a growing plurality of actors, new forms of participation, growing demands for transparency of international financial, political and military transactions, the internationalization of human rights, ecological issues, and a growing chorus of voices trying to define, promote or oppose 'development'.

Yet at the same time it behoves us to be realistic about the dimensions, coherence and effectiveness of civil society organizations. The 'global associational revolution' is indeed happening, and is I think one of the major historic shifts of our times. It is, however, currently self-limiting in many ways: fragmented, protean, often suffering from as much of a lack of transparency, accountability and internal democracy as the institutions that it criticizes, and often without it being clear what constituencies CSOs speak for who or they truly represent. But these issues are now all on the table and many NGOs are acutely aware of the problems. And what they largely signal, I would argue, is not at root a set of technical or managerial questions, but rather a challenge to our imaginations. We do not yet fully know how to 'think' this 'post-development' world or how to grapple with the nature or possibilities of governance in a post-nationalist or even post-political environment, one in which even as new possibilities seem to expand, so do the problems that they need to confront. We truly live, in Ulrich Beck's now celebrated term, in a 'risk society' (Beck 1992).

But this risk, we should remember, is largely the creation of our own civilizational choices and the systemic crises that we ourselves have created (global warming being an obvious example), together with the fact that we are collectively very unclear as to our own long-term goals. Are they growth, or are they social, economic, political and environmental justice on a global scale? Is the purpose of development the generation of material abundance for the greatest number, or is it, as Amartya Sen suggests, ultimately about the expansion of freedom (Sen 1999)? We tend, when confronted with such large questions, to hide behind equally big words – 'globalization', 'progress', 'growth', 'postmodernism' and the like, when what is really at stake is the generation of provable methods for understanding the complexity and contradictory nature of the real world, one in which globalization and localization exist together, and in which decentralization and participation operate on some levels and increasing state control, militarization and corporate concentration operate on others. As Southall suggests, a common response to crisis is not cool analysis and more participatory decision-making, but a reversion to authoritarianism and militarism, both being forces still very much alive in the contemporary world. But, strangely, although change is the medium in which we live, our ability to analyse it or direct it constructively is still the methodologically weakest dimension of the social sciences. Change happens, but learning to direct it in positive social and ecological directions is increasingly the big issue. Aid, as a mechanism designed to accomplish just that, must then necessarily be located within the parameters of our knowledge of how to create, and not just suffer, social transformations. Given the dimensions of the current ecological crisis, if we fail to do this we may as a species have no future.

To return concretely to the issue of aid, there are those who argue that the new century has ushered in changes in the nature of development cooperation that can no longer be ignored: the scale and seeming intractability of so many basic development problems, challenges to the legitimacy of the state, the difficulty of knowing whether aid and other forms of policy intervention have 'worked', unclarity about the notion of 'good governance' as an indicator of development 'success' and so forth. As Goran Hyden argues (2001), expectations are high in relation to prospects for positive results, leading to burn-out, donor fatigue and general cynicism about the possibility of ever creating real change when those expectations are not met. If, for example, development success is not apparently related to the level of aid, then why continue to give it? If the neoliberal globalization model favours trade over aid, should we not just relax our development efforts and celebrate with the likes of Francis Fukuyama the supremacy of the market?

On the whole I think not. Hyden suggests indeed that inter-dependence calls for more development cooperation, not less, especially as major problems, most notably poverty and environmental deterioration, are in many respects increasing not decreasing in extent and intensity, shared public goods such as the environment are at risk, but yet solidarity and cooperation among people are in many cases increasing across boundaries as the references cited above to Hawken (2008), Bornstein (2005) and Salamon (1994) attest. In these respects I think that Hayden is right and the menu of solutions that he suggests are interesting and valuable. These include geographical concentration of aid on the poorest countries, greater emphasis on humanitarian assistance, return to a focus on state capacity, more institutionalized cooperation between North and South, insulating disbursement of funds from political patronage, securing the personal safety of aid workers in the field, restoring public confidence in the usefulness of aid, ensuring that development cooperation is demand-driven, getting development bureaucrats to be more innovative and flexible, and enhanced emphasis on rights. These are all individually excellent goals, but the question is whether they go far enough. The subsequent chapters of this book suggest some of the ways in which they need deeper cultural and existential contextualization. As we have suggested in this chapter, aid as a specific and major example of development policy has necessarily to be also located within the larger changing environment within which it operates.

This environment includes an awareness of the profound but complex and even contradictory effects of globalization, of the ramifying networks of actors concerned with social transformation and the protection of the environment as an absolute priority in those transformative processes, the competing definitions of development now emerging and with them a range of alternative solutions often quite outside of the paradigm of conventional development thinking. Governance in the traditional sense of the collective management of communal resources will continue to be central to these concerns regardless of what specific empirical form they take. This is where the primary cultural challenge takes place, for here we enter the realm of the imagination. The bottom lines of development are the alleviation of human suffering and the protection of the environment that supports all human life and makes it possible (quite apart from the issue of the intrinsic rights of nature). Ultimately all thinking on development and development cooperation must come back to these existential realities and must seek solutions consistent with the broadest definitions of human needs, with the huge body of indigenous wisdom that has long existed to address these primary questions, and with absolute honesty in addressing our failures to achieve globally even the minimum developmental goals. The failures are highly instructive as they are the necessary stepping stones to recognition of the true magnitude of the problems, to the poverty of many of the conventional approaches that have hitherto been tried, and as a stimulus to the human imagination, so rich in its technological and cultural achievements and yet still so inadequate in its hardly developed thinking, outside the realm of science fiction, about the future and its unavoidable challenges. To open up creative avenues for generating and exploring such possibilities should be the role of a truly liberatory social science. Critical sociology has flourished, but a transformative and future-oriented sociology is still weak. Just as the environmental philosopher Arne Naess drew a distinction between shallow and deep environmentalism and recommended the latter as the source of solutions to our ecological crisis (Naess 1995), so too do we need a deep sociology as opposed to a shallow one: one concerned with the inner workings of the human self as well as with its external collective manifestations (Clammer 2009a). Aid, as a main pillar of conventional development thinking and practice, is an ideal starting point for demonstrating both the wider cultural and the sociological contextualization of all attempts at policy intervention, and of the need for the inner dimensions or what might even be called the 'psychology of development' to be made manifest. To be a recipient of aid, however well intentioned, is not simply to be helped in some material way. For, on the one hand, it is the source of the temptation to corruption and to dependency and to accepting so-called 'structural adjustments' that may have widely negative effects on many sectors of the recipient society. On the other hand, it is an invitation to changes in lifestyle, subjectivities and culture that will have inevitable effects, including in so many cases the erosion of the cultural integrity upon which pre-development solutions to social, economic and environmental challenges were successfully based for generations.

FOUR

Liberating development from itself:
the politics of indigenous knowledge

Development anthropology, as the subject supposed to address the problems raised in the previous chapters, has always faced a two-sided challenge: that of legitimating itself as a respectable subdiscipline within a more theoretically inclined anthropology, and that of representing itself as a useful source of knowledge in or to the wider field of development studies, a set of practices and ideas largely dominated by economists. Among its emergent responses to these challenges has been the recent move to argue that anthropologists, by dint of their close acquaintance with the ethnographic and the microscopic minutiae of culture, are uniquely positioned to offer themselves as experts in 'indigenous knowledge' (Sillitoe 1998). This knowledge, a variant in fact of what used to be called 'ethnoscience', or, in the dialectical understanding of globalization as the interplay of the global and the local, as 'local knowledge', purportedly contributes to the development process by revealing the cultural orientations and epistemological frameworks of the people undergoing 'development' and makes that development more effective by harnessing such local knowledge and deploying it strategically in relation to development tasks.

This view, however, is fraught with difficulties, philosophical, political and ethical, and a central argument of this chapter is that if the notion of indigenous knowledge (IK) is to be useful at all, it must be defined in relation to these issues, and, perhaps more controversially, liberated from its captivity within the assumptions of characteristically Western anthropology. Outside of that framework and seen as genuine epistemological alternatives, indigenous knowledge might appear as a powerful tool for autonomous social transformation. Within it, however, it is more likely to become yet another pawn in the ongoing game of epistemological hegemony-seeking, characteristic of wide swathes of the social and natural sciences with their universalizing (and consequently homogenizing) ambitions.

Notions of indigenous knowledge are hardly new in anthropology as they have always been inherent in the nature of ethnographic knowledge. What has given the concept new life has been a complex of forces including globalization, which has not only provoked a corresponding interest in the local and of the interplay between the global and the local but has also triggered an intense interest in the cultural consequences of that globalization. Culture, of course, at least until the emergence of cultural studies as a recognizable discipline, is supposed to be the special preserve of anthropologists (Featherstone 1993; Robertson 1995). Likewise changes within development thinking and practice, and in particular the emergence of participation, participatory development and the increased importance of NGOs and social movements, have made the acquisition of local knowledge suddenly more germane than it was under the regime of primarily economistic thinking, a trend reinforced by the parallel (re)discovery within development sociology of a 'culture and development' approach (e.g. Schech and Haggis 2000), although this with perhaps more emphasis on indigenous social structures and institutions than on culture or knowledge as such.

Anthropology and development have both entered one of their own periodic and perhaps endemic cycles of crisis. The former is uncertain about its role in a postcolonial world and the basis from which, as a historically compromised discipline, it can hope to proffer advice to a troubled world. The latter is under attack both for its failures to deliver on its grandiose promises and for the allegations that behind its philanthropic front it is in fact a vehicle of Western neocolonialism, a promoter of the negative aspects of globalization and a supporter of the forced homogenization of cultures and values. As such it is widely perceived as an agent of destruction rather than of positive social transformation, and has consequently triggered anti-development movements and calls for us all to enter not so much a space of alternative development as a post-development world in which the McDonaldizing effects of conventional development are transcended (for an analysis of these trends, see Nederveen Pieterse 2001). Into this minefield of competing and often antagonistic positions has come IK. But is it a solution, or is it part of what was in the past called the 'impasse' in development theory, a blockage that has still not been overcome? To answer this question we will turn to a deconstruction and then hopefully a reconstruction of the idea of IK in order to see if a route can indeed be charted out of the dilemmas of development theory and development anthropology.

Critical approaches to indigenous knowledge

In his introduction to a collection of essays on the anthropology of development (Sillitoe et al. 2002), Paul Sillitoe argues that (yet another) 'revolution' has occurred in anthropology with the discovery of the continuity between participant observation (what anthropologists have always done) and participatory development, the new paradigm of grassroots, bottom-up development now espoused even by such institutions as the World Bank, not out of a sudden enthusiasm for democratization, but because they have finally noticed that the landscape of top-down development is littered with very expensive failures. Working with a largely unproblematized (and certainly undefined) conception of 'development', Sillitoe goes on to argue that this is a new opening for anthropology to demonstrate its public relevance (or, quite frankly, to cash in on the opportunities suddenly available to it by involving itself in development consultancy) through stressing its expertise in the discovery and utilization of indigenous knowledge. He goes on to provide a working definition of IK and to propose some methodologies for discovering it. Anyone would hopefully accept that this is an ethically laudable aim – to give voice to the 'developees' who may be having all sorts of social changes imposed on them from without and in the absence of their own input. But, equally clearly, this position needs some deconstructing since there are at least four major critical and unaddressed problems here.

The first is the unproblematized conception of what is understood to be 'development'. What if ethnographic investigation of a particular people's IK throws up the fact that their knowledge and certainly their morality are directly antithetical to the imposed development scheme, or proposes a vision of the desired future and of the means to get there radically at variance with the received notions of the developers? What will the anthropologist do then, become a convert to and an advocate of that 'progress rejecting' position? Or will he or she try to persuade the natives that their knowledge, interesting as it no doubt is from an ethnographic perspective, is just too old-fashioned and out of step with a globalizing world to be workable, and so should be abandoned or modified? Perhaps this knowledge can be recorded according to the strictest canons of professional methods and ethics, and then stored in the archives of anthropology and used as fascinating illustrative material in a textbook or in 'Anthropology 101' while being in practice bracketed away when it comes to the negotiation of the actual development path being imposed on that people? A key implication of IK in relation to development should be that all local knowledges are equal, theirs as well as ours – an implication explicitly rejected by Sillitoe (Sillitoe 2002: 12). Although he recognizes that in principle IK might challenge conventional conceptions of development, he nevertheless works entirely from within that conventional paradigm, assuming that at most IK, where it is not useful to them, might simply irritate funding and development agencies or lead to demands for some kind of 'endogenous development'. But this is a failure of the anthropological imagination. IK by its very nature may in principle radically challenge or even reject entirely the very notion of 'development', an implication grasped by some commentators who are outside of anthropology itself, but deeply committed to socially just development alternatives (e.g. Quinn 1999; Mies and Bennholdt-Thomsen 1999).

A second problem with IK now circulating is that it is a romantic concept. In opposing, as it widely does, 'our' scientific knowledge with 'their' local – and by implication deficient – knowledge (they are after all 'underdeveloped' presumably because their IK did not serve them well in that respect), there is a severe danger of overlooking the increasingly hybrid and globalized nature of all knowledge and its constant and accelerating circulation, appropriation and inter-penetration. In its rush to link participant observation to participatory development by way of IK, development anthropology is in danger of overlooking other advances in development thinking and practice that are equally important, such as the renewed emphasis on gender and development and the associated fact that knowledge itself may be gendered. It may equally well be classist: the hierarchical nature of many communities suggests that knowledge, or certainly access to it or the ability to deploy it effectively, is related to positioning within the social structure. Despite pleas for interdisciplinarity, anthropological approaches to IK show that this goal is by no means achieved. While classical European sociology traditionally placed the sociology of knowledge at its centre, anthropology has not done so in the same reflexive manner. For anthropology, knowledge appears to be an object of study; for sociology, it poses the question of how the very subject 'sociology' is constituted. This raises the fundamental issue in the philosophy of the social sciences of the social conditions under which things may be known, including social knowledge itself, which is not epistemologically privileged in any way. This issue seems only to have dawned on anthropology with the 'crisis of representation' debates and the problems of authority, writing and legitimation thrown up by postmodernism and deconstruction, but these issues do not seem to have deeply impacted development anthropology. In fact all knowledge is political; this is as true of IK as of any other kind, and as such IK represents not simply fresh epistemological options, but also, as we know at least since Foucault, power relations as well.

If we have, then, a problem with the romanticizing of IK and its definition not as knowledge *sui generis* but against or in opposition or contrast to Anglo-Saxon forms of hegemonic knowledge, we have a further problem with its relationship to anthropology. If the notion of development itself is left largely undefined in the new development anthropology, so, strangely, is the notion of anthropology. The assumption in current IK thinking is that the nature of anthropology is unproblematic as it is allegedly a 'scientific' discipline, and as such a universal one. These are large claims, especially in face of the critiques of anthropology that have surfaced within and without the discipline for several decades now. We know now that a convincing argument can be made that historically anthropology is a child of colonialism, and certainly of the nineteenth-century spreading of the political and economic hegemony of the West. Since Boas and Malinowski 'we' have studied 'them', but the attention has not been much reciprocated, although there is evidence that some of 'them' studied their own internal or colonized others, as with the rise of ethnography in Japan and its application to the study of, in particular, Korea (Kawada 1993; Atkins 2010). As Marshall Sahlins has eloquently suggested, anthropology is part of the 'native cosmology' of the West, a form of local knowledge, itself informed by certain limited and culture-bound notions of truth, representation, data and feeling (Sahlins 1996). Unfortunately many of its practitioners confuse this form of IK with the absolute and the universal. The patronizing assumption of IK is that anthropology is somehow specially privileged as the vehicle for discovering and representing this knowledge. In fact, logically the whole notion of IK radically relativizes the possibility of there being *an* anthropology, and poses the alternative possibility of there being in principle *many* anthropologies, including those which radically interrogate the West, its practices, social organization, culture and epistemological and ontological assumptions (Clammer et al. 2004). If indeed the native cosmology of the West has produced its version of anthropology (and other sciences, social sciences, arts and humanities too), among its many fruits, so too other cosmologies explicitly or implicitly contain their own anthropologies. The paradox is, of course, that the relativizers of culture have rarely applied that relativizing to their own knowledge or its production practices, even if they might apply it to their own culture in other respects, for example by way of ethnographies of communities or minorities within that culture. IK implies a critique of anthropology itself, not simply its 'application' within a new paradigm of development thinking.

Finally there is, of course, the issue of appropriation. As many have become aware, IK poses its own ethical dilemmas, despite or because of its desire to promote participatory development. Among the most important of these is that of the appropriation of such knowledge for personal, military or commercial use, or, in more legal language, the issue of intellectual property rights. This issue connects very directly to human rights, cultural autonomy, the question of commercial enterprises making profit out of indigenous resources without due recompense, and, dare we say it, the propensity of anthropologists to build careers and reputations on the expropriation and publication of other people's IK, often in locally inaccessible languages or media. Of course one can argue that all knowledge is part of the heritage of humankind and as such should be shared, a good argument if indeed it was to be applied equally and fairly. In fact, as we know, it is not, and the capitalist corporation that will jealously guard through patents and other legal devices its own products, discoveries and processes may well be the same organization ruthlessly exploiting indigenous resources and knowledges. Accessing IK raises these issues in a very stark form. If a major purpose of development anthropology is to discover and reveal such knowledge, who indeed will control it or has the rights to its benefits (Gupta 1991; Brush and Stabinsky 1996)? Anthropology would be naive to assume that its own self-conception of moral purity is shared by those (including local elites) who might benefit financially and in other ways from the exploitation of the knowledge that it so painstakingly and professionally uncovers. Once again we find ourselves confronted not with epistemological questions but with political ones. The way forward for an authentic IK approach lies in a combination of an awareness of its political nature (a characteristic it shares with all knowledge), its practice of what Linda Tuhiwai Smith (1999) calls 'decolonizing methodologies', and an awareness of the radical potential of IK to destabilize not only development but also anthropology.

This last point requires some elaboration. Globalization, through revealing and making accessible a plurality of knowledges, should carry with it the seeds of alternative anthropologies. Anthropology as taught in university departments is the product of a specific historical process in which the economic, political and epistemo-logical hegemony of the West was assured. This situation no longer obtains, and a fundamental implication of IK is the possibility of other anthropologies, that is to say indigenous accounts of local cultures and, by extension, the application of the methodologies and cosmological assumptions so generated to the analysis of other cultures and societies, including of course those of the West. While

IK is attractive to Western anthropology and development practice because it is 'useful', it is not regarded as a source of radically alternative world-views that might challenge both that utilitarian view of knowledge and the systems of knowledge production and reproduction (in this case anthropology) that claim the right to investigate other systems without being so investigated in return.

Thus, while one might easily imagine an anthropology of Buddhism (which indeed exists), it is harder – to put it mildly – for Western anthropologists to imagine a Buddhist anthropology. This would be a system of knowledge radically at variance with Western conceptions of reality and causality, which, if applied to the analysis of such Western epistemologies, might show them to be parochial, philosophically narrow, and possibly the source of Western civilization's dire disregard for the environment that ultimately sustains it, and of much of its greed, consumerism, brutality and violence (Loy 2003; Jones 2003; Keown et al. 1998). A major and unexplored implication of the IK debate is the suppressed presence of other anthropologies, a presence or potentiality that radically relativizes the local Western variety, and creates the possibility too of radically different conceptions of development. This has uncomfortable implications for various vested interests as it denies the legitimacy of many imposed development plans while simultaneously situating Western anthropology as a local form of knowledge that has expanded for historical and political reasons that have little to do with its limited epistemological legitimacy. Prevailing views of IK as merely 'useful' in an externally imposed development process have the effect of neutralizing local anthropologies rather than encouraging their emergence. For some, this is a possibility too radical to contemplate, even though, given the conditions of contemporary globalization, even such local anthropologies would almost certainly be hybridized and conditioned by market and other forces.

In almost any social situation, although they may not have the analytical tools to structure and interpret that knowledge, locals are usually better informed than even the most sensitive foreign anthropologist. In situations where a developed indigenous anthropology does indeed exist (India, Mexico, Brazil and Japan, for example), the native anthropologists possess the local knowledge, access to and credibility within the community, as well as the ability to create new forms of dialogue between the local and the foreign anthropologists, and not just between foreign anthropologists and local 'informants' (Kuwayama 2004). Under these conditions it is even the case that we might need a new label for such practices and question whether they should really be called 'anthropology' at all, since the suspicion now arises that anthropology as it stands is too committed to the study of the 'Other' and the 'Otherization of the world' as its main professional orientation. The concept of alternative anthropologies would, rather, be tied to the notion of 'Us-ization' and the swapping of reflections leading not just to the recovery of existing IK but also to the generation of new knowledge and subjects of knowledge which equally both challenge and change the existing world-views of the dialogue partners and may generate new approaches to practical problem-solving and suffering alleviation that allow IK to emerge not only as a response to global/modernizing pressures, but also as a reflection of genuine indigenous desires. As Posey has rightly noted (2002), many indigenous peoples are already and have long been engaged in such cross-cultural and political projects. In Ellen's words, 'Anthropologists, lawyers, development practitioners, environmental NGOs and political activists, having created IK in a particular form, now find that the indigenous are wreaking their righteous revenge, not only in claiming it back but by deploying the concept in ways often not anticipated by the non-indigenous' (Ellen 2002: 253). In fact, indigenous people are not really 'claiming back' IK (they are already in possession of it); rather, they are appropriating the *concept* of IK as the only way for local people to reappropriate that which has been appropriated, and to use it, in some cases, against the appropriators themselves (Merry 1997).

The problem of knowledge

Yet before we reach the point of the uses of knowledge, a kind of philosophical house-cleaning is required. Anthropologists have always had problems with the idea of knowledge, classically having preferred to talk about culture or one or another of its components such as myth or religion. This allowed them to talk about not what other cultures *knew* (a position that would commit the anthropologist to an unambiguous position in respect of the truth claims of native informants' statements), but rather about what they *believed*, a fuzzy position that not only skirts the philosophical problems inherent in the concept of belief but also avoids the embarrassment of the anthropologist having to commit to those beliefs. Many will remember the debates that swirled around Evans-Pritchard's *Witchcraft, Oracles, and Magic among the Azande*, which raised exactly this problem, posed in the form of a debate about rationality. In the Zande case, Evans-Pritchard's interpretative problem was that to believe in the system of causality embodied in Zande witchcraft (that personal misfortune is the result of specific malignancy directed towards one on the part of another person who possesses malign supernatural powers – a witch in other words) is to lose all objectivity and thus be unable to render a coherent anthropological account in terms acceptable to a 'scientific' Western reader. But if one does not believe, then one is denied access to the inner logic and subjective states of that system of belief. Evans-Pritchard's solution was to fall back on the validity of Western science, from which point of view Zande causality is interesting, but false. IK raises a similar problem: if it is valid knowledge, then it is subversive of hegemonic knowledge and commits the anthropologist to the acknowledgement of its truth claims, even if those claims contradict standard Western epistemological assumptions. But is the anthropologist generally prepared to go this far? Not to do so is in practice to admit that IK is in fact inferior knowledge; to do so is to commit the anthropologist to a position of radical advocacy for that form of knowledge and its anti-hegemonic and potentially socially transformative implications.

Much of the recent interest in IK can better be seen as an episode in the sociology of anthropology rather than as a real innovation. IK is hardly new from the point of view of ethnography, and anthropologists had little role in formulating the principles of participation and grassroots development to which many of its more applied practitioners now pay at least lip service. Rather, it is largely a strategic repositioning by anthropologists to take advantage of developments taking place outside of their discipline and not led by it. This puffing up of the role of anthropology is naive unless better rooted, on the one hand, in a more sophisticated understanding of knowledge, and, on the other, in emerging understandings of the nature of culture.

Many of the theoretical and methodological tools to deepen this rooting already exist, in the work of Pierre Bourdieu, for example (Bourdieu 1979), and in the work of those ethnographers who have examined the complexity of knowledge systems as strategic and perpetually modified devices rather than as structures in a Lévi-Straussian sense, or as the residues of a functionalist holism. Let us here examine just one example of an ethnographic approach to knowledge, in this instance Michael Lambek's study of the Muslim-dominated island of Mayotte, situated in the western Indian Ocean between the mainland African coastline of Tanzania and Madagascar (Lambek 1993).

In his analysis of what might be termed 'folk Islam', or a local expression of a universal religion in dialogue with indigenous ideas of sorcery and spirit possession, Lambek comes to the conclusion that such IK constitutes neither a system nor a structure, but is in fact a set of discourses, not all of them compatible, in constant circulation and with their own interpenetrating modes of reproduction and survival, each permeating and being reciprocally influenced by social practices, and all embedded in a nexus of power relations. Different forms of knowledge, some oral, some textual, circulate in the same social and physical space, each promoted by local experts – spirit mediums, Islamic scholars, diviners and so on – and consumed in varying degrees and to different depths by the local citizenry. All of these categories in practice overlap and interpenetrate: the spirit medium is also a Muslim and may be a client of a local herbalist. Each 'discipline' or regime of knowledge provides a space for the exercise of power, authority and competence for those who can utilize that particular set of resources, but equally sets limitations on action, no one body of knowledge being universal or fully inclusive of all the others. Furthermore, Lambek raises the question, first posed by the social phenomenologist Alfred Schutz, of the extent to which the social investigator has the role or the right not only to interpret, but also to critique. If, to use the example which seems to have become the most fashionable one, a culture practises female circumcision or other forms of genital mutilation, should this practice be passed over as another interesting ethnographic fact, or does it commit the investigator to a critical position and action on the issue? Such questions are unavoidable sooner or later in any IK discourse, but have not so far been centrally addressed in that context.

While not wishing to give it any special priority among a range of other exemplary ethnographies, Lambek's nuanced study, while itself not engaging fully with the philosophical issues surrounding the subtle relations between knowledge, belief, culture, practice and ideology, does very well illustrate the problems of discussing knowledge at all in a coherent manner. In common with any culture, Mayotte residents deal daily with a complex universe of knowledge consisting of, among other forms, textual (Quranic) knowledge, oral histories, prophetic versus secular forms of knowledge, forms embodied in discourses of spirit possession, everyday knowledge related to farming, fishing, child-rearing, sex, diet, or the weather. Some knowledge is considered highly objectified, some as essentially embodied or tacit. Knowledge, then, 'has no essence to be described', but is a contested domain of currently acceptable beliefs (Lambek 1993: 8). It is connected to power and morality and is constantly influenced by new ideas entering the realm of any particular regime of IK, some participants of which will resist, others welcome, and still others synthesize or hybridize (or simply misunderstand) such fresh inputs.

Two major issues, then, arise from Lambek's ethnography. One is the highly complex and shifting nature of 'knowledge', including IK, which does not have any privileged simplicity or clarity in this respect. The other is the social location of knowledge. Whether or not one fully agrees with Lambek's fashionable social constructivist approach, he does make it abundantly clear that it is not knowledge as such, but *access* to knowledge that confers status and power, and that the acquisition of knowledge and seeking means of access are processes that never socially stop. This point is even more relevant in a globalizing environment where knowledges interpenetrate and where the validity of a local variety, and hence of the experts who practise it, can be called into question at any time by the discovery of alternative and competing possibilities. Knowledge, then, is always contextualized, is socially distributed (and distributed unequally), is linked intimately to the local political economy (Lambek 1993: 95), is a major element in determining the social structure of local communities (84), and it is transmitted selectively since its possession confers authority (144). Lambek then succeeds in seriously problematizing the unity of local knowledge, claims of consistency by or for cultural systems, and attempts to locate the study of knowledge outside of the social context and political economy within which it is embedded. His anti-essentializing argument also has another final twist to it: that the ethnographer, posing in the final, polished monograph written in a metropolitan language quite possibly totally inaccessible to the original informants and larded with the latest French theory, is in fact, as Elizabeth Bowen brilliantly demonstrated several decades ago (Bowen 1956), actually rather like a child – no expert at all in the local knowledge system, constrained by language ability, and socially positioned and fashioned by her/his own culture as is everybody else, at best an initiate rather than a technologically overloaded expert. This is a humbling message for IK evangelists. Similar issues and a set of equally nuanced views on the complex and contested nature of local knowledge can be found in a range of other ethnographies of knowledge (e.g. Keck 1998), although theorists of IK seem on the whole reluctant to draw on such evidence.

If the philosophical problems of knowledge are one side of the IK problem, the other side is the political, and in particular the politics of culture. In some recent debates about culture the question has arisen of the apparent inability of anthropologists to define their central working concept. This weakness has led in the direction of anti-essentialism, to notions of hybridity, and to the rejection of structuralist models, and has even led some to propose with varying degrees of conviction that anthropology can dispense with the concept of culture altogether; see, for example, the collection edited by Fox and King, *Anthropology beyond Culture* (2002). While granting that the standard textbook definitions of culture are hard to sustain in the face of the actual complexity and messiness of human activity, the more mainstream anthropologists represented in the Fox and King volume tend to the position that since we cannot agree on a definition of culture, then the concept itself is either meaningless or a function of the research questions being asked, whereas the more politically inclined contributors or those who have found that their fieldwork site raises unavoidable political and ethical questions (South Africa, Guatemala, Ecuador) come to a more qualified answer. The reason for this divergence is not hard to see. For the latter, while the concept of culture, rather like that of the 'self', may or may not exist, it is constantly evoked strategically by those in positions of political and ethnic conflict, who are facing racism, post-colonial injustice or discriminated minority status or who are seeking to incorporate a more universal language of human rights and of the 'politics of recognition' into their particular struggles. In this zone of discourse, while we can find self-essentializing or self-Orientalizing at work, we also see crucial issues of identity, rights, memory, and social and spatial boundaries being exercised using the very concept that the anthropologists are fast abandoning. As this is true of the concept of culture, so too it is of knowledge, a word which in IK circles is apparently usually used as a synonym for the former.

In fact the conflictual nature of knowledge, or rather perhaps of the relations between knowledge 'systems', is paramount. All 'development' is in a sense a form of violence, and violence is perpetrated by some people on other people, or on nature. The romantic idea of the homogeneous community as the object of anthropological study evaporates once it is recognized that all communities contain social differences, or what Ellen (2002) insists on calling 'social position' (i.e. class?), and that, as Marx recognized a century and a half ago, such positions influence what is considered to be knowledge and how it is used socially. Conflict is a fundamental factor in the production of IK and in the imposition of development itself, whether seen from the perspective of the developers or the developees. New knowledge is formed out of conflictual situations, and the unveiling of such conflict not only demands that prejudices, power relations and inequalities be exposed, but also has potentially creative functions, since the liberation of tensions within a group provides a pathway towards solutions. This factor also bears on the ethical dimensions of knowledge. While we may not usually need to resort to such extreme examples, how would IK theory deal with such cases as torture, in which torturers received systematic training and were imparted know-how on effective methods and techniques (for which there are well-documented cases from Latin America, from Northern Ireland and from US treatment of prisoners at its Guantánamo Bay facility in Cuba). Are such cases to be included in our definition of IK? While methodological tolerance is obviously a virtue in determining what is knowledge, extreme relativization jeopardizes the necessary ethical margins of what we might consider legitimate knowledge, rather than forms that ought to be banned or suppressed.

The politics of knowledge

The elements linking the various levels of the IK debate must, then, be a philosophically inclined politics and a political economy of knowledge. Interestingly, despite its holistic claims, anthropology largely ignores developments in its sister discipline of sociology, and in this context the sociology of knowledge. This classical field of sociology has long explored the social conditions of knowledge production and distribution, and of the power relations that structure these fields, whether they be scientific, artistic, literary or medical, and whether they are organized through literacy, numeracy, educational institutions in general or by less formal but powerful socio-cultural mechanisms such as the media. We need to understand this nexus of power and knowledge not only from the perspective of Foucault (1980) but also through a larger range of comparative examples, and from the perspective of the analysis of the generation of the hegemonic knowledges of the kind that most attracted Foucault, and that of local knowledges operating beyond, in the gaps of, or in opposition to, such grand narratives. Seen from this perspective IK is potentially anthropology's postmodernism, but with a necessary political slant.

This idea can be stated in this abstract way, but also can be explored through a number of specific case studies of knowledge-in-production. These are necessary not only to demonstrate the political nature of IK, but also because much IK thinking, in not sufficiently separating knowledge from ideology, tends to treat all knowledge as *ethically* equal, since the logic of IK works against the possibility of the anthropologist (except perhaps the indigenous one?) from exercising a critical function. Furthermore, while most practical applications of IK have been in the fields of agriculture, medicine and ecological management, few have looked at the application of IK to economics or political organization, and even fewer have taken up the religious dimension of much IK. In societies pervaded by religion, the boundary between knowledge and belief is blurred, and indeed it is telling that in Lambek's discussion of local knowledge, the focus is in fact on religion or quasi-religious forms of local Islam, spirit mediumship and sorcery, although he does not tie any of these to development implications in his investigation. Religion is, of course, something of an embarrassment to IK, since it suggests forms of knowledge at radical variance with both standard science and the cosmologies held by many Western-trained anthropologists. The result is an anthropological approach to religion that attempts to explain it in a methodological impoverishment that diminishes or erases the transformative power of religious ideas by subordinating them to a taken-for-granted epistemology in which religion is 'interesting' but not accredited with any explanatory or transformative primacy (Clammer 2010a). This is partly the result of an over-Cartesian emphasis on the cognitive aspects of knowledge to the detriment of the emotive, tacit and embodied aspects (Clammer 2002), and partly due to a wider methodological inability to manage or accord any epistemological reality to what Stoller in his important but neglected work (1997) calls the 'sensuous' aspects of human beings' interaction with their environments, social as well as physical, in which rationality itself, the key notion in Western epistemologies, is reframed in embodied terms.

Towards a strategic theory of indigenous knowledge

IK, then, cannot be a simple tool, a manual for the recovery and utilization of that which can be recorded and handed out to development practitioners going into the field, or to World Bank executives sitting securely in their North American office suites. It is, like all knowledge, contested, unevenly distributed, often hidden from the outsider, contradictory, something in the process of being constructed rather than an end state already achieved, and deeply embedded in local political and economic processes and structures. Such local knowledges may well be used within a community to control or annoy its members by those who manage or have access to particularly powerful local variants, such as bureaucratic procedures (Herzfeld 1992). Certain implications flow from this which development anthropology will ignore at its peril, and certainly at the risk of its irrelevance. These include the fact that that all IK is political; that the juxtaposition of IK with Western hegemonic 'scientific' knowledge to the detriment of the former is illegitimate and a sure sign of epistemological hubris (Harding 1997); that there is usually a major gap between the actual nature of IK, much of it embodied in poetry, myth, art, religion and ritual, and what development practitioners want from it – usually a set of tools to expedite the fulfilment of already and externally determined goals. It must also be recognized that IK cannot be equated only with cognitive forms of knowledge, but must also be sought in forms alien to most Western philosophy – in somatic, emotional, spiritual and embodied and performative modes. The primary role of anthropology in relation to IK is not to set about 'applying' local knowledges, but first of all to attend to anthropology's primary task of attempting to understand and communicate these forms of knowledge and the epistemological and ontological assumptions on which they are based for their own sake.

These primary implications also entail further ones, since the centrality of the analysis of differing knowledge 'modes' (rather than 'systems') within the anthropology of knowledge, and most certainly the study of IK, points anthropology away from its oversocialized conception of the human individual to the broader ecological, onto-logical and epistemological frameworks that shape and nurture selves within particular social systems. IK implies, as we have suggested, radically differing conceptions of 'development' in which notions of culture play a central role and are themselves shaped within specific social formations and by the historical contingencies that have moulded them. The concomitant possibility, a positive heaven for the writer of science fiction or futuristic analyses, is that of there being many alternative anthropologies based on assumptions at variance with those of hegemonic Western anthropology and its philosophical underpinnings.

Globalization, usually seen as a homogenizing principle, in fact has exactly the opposite implication. By bringing local cultures into unprecedented contact with each other, it liberates a huge number of alternative systems of thought, culture, belief and social organization into a shared universe. While it has radical implications for knowledge (by bringing differing knowledges into interpenetrating relationships with one another), it also has radical implications for social, cultural and ecological practice by bringing myriad actual and tested adaptations and strategic formulations (i.e. actually existing or historical cultures) into the realm of the universally possible by revealing the range of experiments in human life in nature that have in fact already been tried. It also provides a basis for cultural critique, an area from which anthropologists have mostly shied away given the commitment on the part of many of them to some form of cultural relativity. If IK is to be understood, as de Sousa Santos suggests (1999), as emancipatory knowledge, then all knowledge formations, including the two primary civilization-shaping forms of the West, economics and science, are also to be judged primarily by their emancipatory potential rather than by their logical consistency. For those in a position of suffering, the precise condition in which many of the 'underdeveloped' live daily, knowledge is praxis, and arises from struggle not leisurely reflection in the study. The realization of this must commit the anthropological observer to the position that Gustavo Esteva and Madhu Suri Prakash call 'epistemological humility' (1998: 202) in the face of this massive suffering, rarely shared by the academic observer. This humility leads not to cultural relativity or to the relativizing of all truth claims, but to the recognition that any culture is the organization of meaning around a particular centre, contingent but actual for its participants. Not only is that particular configuration 'real' to those participants; it is also from the recognition of the diversity and multiplicity of such centres that dialogue between human groups can occur.

What is perhaps easily forgotten in IK debates taking place within the discourse of anthropology is that debates about knowledge are now central to the contemporary intellectual universe generally, particularly in the light of the challenges posed by postmodernism, on the one hand, and postcolonialism, on the other. If in the first, claims to authority have been radically decentred, knowledges relativized, and the power relations inherent in any universe of discourse – including that of development (Gardner and Lewis 1996) – exposed, in the latter indigenous philosophies have emerged and taken centre stage as critiques of Western reason and of the social and institutional practices that have given rise to and reinforced and spread, often through violence, particular regimes of knowledge along with the political regimes that contain and promote them (Eze 1997).

Such recognitions, many of them informed by developments in philosophy proper, need to be placed alongside both evolving understandings of the nature of anthropology in relation to development, and internal critiques of development practice. In the former instance, for example, numerous case studies have revealed that, despite all the rhetoric, people often do not participate in development processes even when they have the opportunity to do so, or when they do such participation is in fact just formal and is in any case politically and socially stratified and certainly not as open as its proponents like to pretend or hope (Pottier 1997; Nyamwaya 1997). Even when it is, an imposed rhetoric of participation and empowerment in fact 'sets definite limits on peoples' participation. It does not give them the power to define development for themselves' (Woost 1997). IK in itself, without addressing the socio-economic and political stratification of knowledge, cannot rise above these limitations. When it does, however, and when it is rooted in local histories, indigenous agricultural knowledge and practices, and respects local social structures, it affords the possibility of providing a rich, sustainable and culturally rooted basis for endogenous development to occur, as an expanding literature now attests (Subramaniam and Pisupati 2010; Haverkort et al. 2003; World Watch Institute 2011).

What exactly is the paradigm shift?

Anthropological interest in IK as applied to development problems represents a belated recognition of a major paradigm shift in development thinking, at least at the level of rhetoric if not always at the level of practice. Even the World Bank has discovered 'participation', and with it the significance of NGOs and of civil society institutions as mediators between the planners in the multilateral institutions and the grassroots, although again with the strategic motive of better 'delivering' aid and accomplishing the structural adjustments and erosion of sovereignty that always accompany World Bank interventions (World Bank 2000). This, of course, is not a serious engagement with IK. For that to occur several intellectual and ethical steps need to be taken. The first of these, as Raff Carmen cogently argues (1996), is recognition of the links between the ownership and creation of knowledge, genuine participation in the application of that knowledge, and cultural autonomy, leading to what he terms 'autonomous development'. The second is the recognition that knowledge does not appear in a vacuum: it is socially generated and politically structured, and arises from praxis. This implies that those agencies engaged in the production of such knowledge are themselves part of the 'field' of IK and not just external observers of someone else's knowledge. Such agencies may include indigenous intellectuals and even universities, but are most likely to involve social movements, the location where practical knowledge for social transformation is usually being generated and tested.

The study of social movements, largely absent from anthropology and largely overformalized in sociology, is a necessary basis for understanding the social production of knowledge that is being used to critique or promote empirical instances of social change (for a good compendium of cases, see Peet and Watts 1998). There are important socio-epistemological factors here too. Amory Starr, for example, argues that social movements – in her case studies anti-corporate and anti-globalization ones – are the sources of new social imaginaries, promote new forms of democracy (which in turn become avenues for the creation of yet newer knowledge and patterns of social, cultural and gender possibilities), and are the source of what she tellingly calls 'moral epistemologies' beyond the purely cognitive and the iron cage of rationality alone (Starr 2000: esp. pp. 154–5, 188). The siting of knowledge, as much as its formal characteristics or potentialities for action, is as critical to the understanding of IK as it is to any other form of knowledge. Indeed without this socio-political situating there is already evidence that the analysis of IK becomes overformalized and reduced to exactly the methodology of the hegemonic, 'scientific' mode of knowledge that it in fact calls into question, and becomes a system of vectors, charts and diagrams that precisely deny its dynamic, unstable and emancipatory qualities (as many of the essays in Sillitoe et al. 2002 sadly reveal). The ever-present danger of the co-option of IK is lessened when its social roots are clear, and for that very reason cannot be successfully transplanted outside of the integral context in which it emerged.

A chronic problem for anthropology is its unwitting role in the reproduction of modernism, ironically so since the very subject matter that it uncovers ethnographically subverts that very project and the universalisms upon which it is based. Part of the reason for this is its continuing Cartesianism, which leads to, among other things, an interest in, but not a willingness to adopt, alternative knowledge systems based on different foundations. It remains consequently deeply Eurocentric. To transcend this requires the generation of new theory for contemporary real-life situations. At the current juncture, issues of knowledge, epistemology and ontology are intimately tied up with the whole meaning of 'development'. As a result an increasing number of anthropologists are willing to adopt 'applied' status, especially as traditional academic sources of employment shrink. But as they have done so the context itself has changed to an environment in which globalization, the 'risk society' and what Zygmunt Bauman calls 'liquid modernity' (2000) have pointed the social sciences away from the overriding concern that has prevailed since Durkheim via Talcott Parsons at least as far as structuralism to a more postmodern concern with pluralism and the recognition that perhaps chaos theory better describes the world, both social and natural, than old-style sociological theory. In this situation, IK should point towards the recovery of forms of emancipatory knowledge that not only speak to and from the indigenes who have generated and live by it, but for all of us, since hegemonic knowledge systems have clearly failed to deliver the 'development', progress and happiness that they so falsely promised. To reiterate a point made earlier, globalization should not homogenize knowledge, but pluralize it by making available as a universal resource a vast variety of alternatives that can be learned from and that can suggest new possibilities of emancipation, new subjectivities in better accord with our ecological situation as one species among many, answers to the pressing problems of sustainable living, and fresh means of approaching our common existential condition. This is surely the heritage of anthropology, but for that heritage to be realized there has to be a shift of paradigm within anthropology itself. If all knowledge is local, then there can be not only one anthropology, but many, and some of these alternatives may well interrogate the Western original as much as they may interrogate the meaning of 'development', and point to some radical solutions in doing so.

Six theses on indigenous knowledge

1. IK is always political and conflictive. It is an arena of political, economic, social, cultural and even judicial struggle (Melkevik 2004) between and within local populations and between those populations and outsiders who may be seen as coming to extract and appropriate that knowledge and profit from it. Development practitioners, governments and corporations, and, at one time at least, missionaries fall into this category. Anthropologists can be on one side or the other, or are busy struggling to maintain a 'neutral' middle position, and this ambiguity requires reflection on the role of the anthropologist not just as a 'scientist', but as a participant in any arena of struggle. For in reality the issue of IK is one of struggle and not simply of 'research' as each participant attempts to take possession not only of material resources, but also of the symbolic resources contained in or surrounding IK. Paradoxically, IK as a *concept* probably means little to local people, for whom it is simply their everyday and unreflective practice, while the same knowledge may be of immense interest to laboratories, governments, corporations and environmentalists. Awareness of the dangers of appropriation by these agencies or simply interest on the part of outsiders naturally incites indigenes to seek ways to benefit from that knowledge, or even to take it hostage, once they realize its value, probably in market terms, outside their own original cosmological frame.

2. The context of IK and the analysis of that context is crucial. Context is in many cases confused with text. When IK is seen in Barthes' or postmodernist terms as a 'text' separated from the actual power relations that connect the local with the global, the political

aspects of the issue remain insufficiently transparent. Roy Ellen expresses his understanding of context in the following terms:

> There is really no end to the amount of context that might be provided and the difficulties faced in describing context in ways that are consistent and intelligible ... there can be no doubt that much knowledge is successfully modularized, decontextualized and transferred, for example to the labs of pharmaceutical companies, as well as via local diffusion between 'indigenous populations'. (Ellen 2002: 250)

Ellen, however, understands 'context' as a gathering or collection of visible elements to be detected on the local stage and thoroughly described – in other words the classical ethnographic enterprise. But context should also be conceived as the sphere where the global and the local are included and interrelate, and where the local social structure, itself entailing power relations at the levels of both the intra-social and the inter-social, is central. This complex web of interrelations and interweavings cannot be understood and analysed only by detecting and describing its elements, as most components are not visibly given. Indeed to attempt to enumerate all the elements 'inside' a society would itself be an act of decontextualization, since to do so would be to extract the local society from global forces, today the fundamental source of change and transformation. In effect, without global forces there would be no need for 'development'.

In the same paragraph, Ellen speaks of 'biopiracy', which in itself cannot be explained without taking into account the socio-political context of global society and its political economy. Likewise he raises another significant point when he spotlights the necessity of a 'sophisticated analysis' of the organizations (funding bodies, project sponsors, etc.) professionally involved in development activities. Although he is apparently not thinking of this necessity as a way of uncovering mechanisms of overt or covert control, the remark is important because the tendency in development analyses, with but few exceptions, has been to consider only one side of the developer–developee equation, namely of course the latter. The unilateral focus on the weaker side of the pair is concomitant with the ideological separation of the local society from the global arena. In fact the consideration of the total process also sheds much-needed light on the often asked but rarely answered question of why development projects so often fail, and what factors enter into the success of those that can be regarded as 'succeeding'.

What might be termed 'non-traditional' IK (for example, knowledge gained from modern-style schooling but then contextualized and assimilated into the local situation) may be a reaction or response to changes or new models of reality imposed from outside, an outside however that in a globalized world is also often inside too. If this is the case, exposure to such external pressures and stimuli stimulates creativity within the local, and new manifestations or innovative transformations of the traditional IK emerge as a result. However, an uncomfortable implication of this is that such creativity is not necessarily the manifestation of the true potentialities of local people, but is a forced response to modernity, an attempt to solve urgent problems foisted on the community by the very process of development itself.

3. 'To give voice'. It is widely said that indigenous people should be empowered to make their own decisions and to control their own resources, and indeed that this is an ethical obligation, however frequently violated in practice by external collaborators. Nevertheless, the historical process of the original deprivation of those very resources requires a change in the form of the statement. Rather than to facilitate control of resources, the current historical move should be the restitution of those resources. While many call our attention to the 'shoulds', fewer voices indicate the 'hows' of this empowerment or re-empowerment process, especially given the vested interests of donors, development agencies and local governments. Why are these agencies entitled to 'empower'? The question is again posed in

asymmetrical terms as a move from someone who 'owns' the power and graciously agrees to devolve some of it upon recipients who can only obtain it from that source. The language of donor/recipient, of the acting agent and the passive beneficiaries, reproduces the very epistemological and political inequality that IK sets out to remedy. Without a rupture in such a structure or relationships IK is neutralized as a transformative agent, since its subservience is still implied in the language of development discourse. No one in fact gives the developer or the anthropologist the right or the mission to 'give voice'. The Other already has a voice. The problem is that this voice is silenced, drowned out or only listened to in a romanticized way, and even when heard is rarely acted upon, since to do so would radically shift the whole balance of the donor/recipient charity logic of the development process and of the anthropology that supports it, or seeks to do so.

4. A constant problem with IK discourse is that IK is reified – seen, that is, as an object, thing or product, generated within people's heads. This Cartesian or utilitarian conception of knowledge regards it as essentially encompassing only the useful, that which can be applied. The practical applicability of knowledge is the categorical criterion for deciding if something is really IK or not. But, as I have argued elsewhere (Clammer 2002), knowledge has many other dimensions (art, rationality's framing within the emotions, sensuous knowledge), but these levels are discounted both because they are harder to 'verify' by positivist methods, and because the ways in which development 'problems' are posed make it difficult for practitioners to see their 'utility', although such dimensions may in reality constitute the greater part of a holistically conceived IK. Given the multiple mirrors through which 'reality' reflects and refracts itself, IK may be seen as a construct itself, a hermeneutic tool utilized in different ways by both the indigene and the analyst. Reality is chaotic and never fully understood. The increasing hybridization

and syncretization of cultures makes it even harder to find any 'pure' culture uninfluenced by others. IK itself represents attempts to construct systems and codes of meaning and intervention in the world, and as such should be seen as an engagement in the process nature of knowledge production, modification and self-reflection and not as some kind of cultural essence that can be defined and described.

5. IK not only implies the possibility of alternative anthropologies, but also suggests the necessity for currently hegemonic Western anthropology to listen to the voices not only of native 'informants' but also of native anthropologists. An extensive set of anthropological discourses, derived from but by no means identical to their Western parent, exist in India, Japan, Latin America, Southeast Asia and elsewhere. The reluctance of many Latin American anthropologists even to speak of 'development' reflects a perception that it is little more than a perverse excuse to legitimate and reinforce exploitation and oppression. In India and Japan anthropology operates not only as the study of the Other, but equally as the study of themselves from within highly hierarchical societies. Evans-Pritchard's problem with the Azande was that although he found their system of ideas fascinating, he could not possibly believe in it. But what if we can and do? What does it do to our notion of anthropology if we take IK to be not just a subject of knowledge appropriation, but as valid information about how the world works and how we should relate to it? This whole issue must in any case be seen in globalized terms. There is a strong tendency in development studies to take a unidirectional approach where the global unilaterally feeds on the local. Daniel Mato, a Venezuelan researcher, brings forward a very interesting counter-example, however. Felipe Tsenkush, a prominent leader of the Shuar people of Ecuador, explained to him how it is becoming more and more complicated to be an indigenous leader today, since they first had to learn the language and the laws of the

'conquerors', then they had to learn to travel by plane, to send a fax, and now they are supposed to be familiar with Internet usage and email, and to be able to negotiate and interact on a global level (Mato 2001). This is an eloquent example as it reflects the ways in which IK is not an artefact but a process in which local societies get acquainted with global knowledge and techniques in order to resist and control as far as possible the expropriation of local resources, both material and symbolic. The indigenes become translators of codes, and it is in this process of translation that the essence of IK lies.

6. IK, then, is in danger of becoming a discourse, a construction of Western anthropology. It should, however, be a conversation, since conversation carries within it the possibility of mutual conversion, insight and enlightenment.

PART II

Expanding the boundaries of development discourse: two illustrations

Reframing social economics: economic anthropology, post-development and alternative economics

Despite the appearance of the field generally known as 'applied anthropology', one of the least exploited resources for development studies, especially in its alternative or more radical forms, has been economic anthropology. Given that much of conventional development studies is fixated on economics this is odd, as economic anthropology is the empirical and theoretical study of actually existing alternative economic systems. Economic anthropology is neither science fiction nor utopianism; it does not purport to describe or create new forms of communal or intentional communities. It describes through ethnography and analyses through anthropological theory real forms of economic practice and their relationship to their environment and the forms of social and cultural organization that are congruent with the mode of economic organization. As such economic anthropology is potentially a uniquely valuable resource not only for development practitioners seeking culturally viable ways of insinuating development policies, but perhaps even more importantly for those seeking alternatives to current forms of globalized capitalism, more ecologically responsible modes of being in the world, and forms of sociality that overcome the fragmentation and alienation of so much contemporary life. The whole question of alternative lifestyles would indeed be greatly enriched by dialogue with economic anthropology, while at a theoretical level the sub-discipline might well provide powerful tools for the critique of conventional neoclassical economic thought.

The starting point of this argument is the provisionality of neo-classical economic thought. Here I am referring not so much to theoretical critiques of conventional economic thought (by Marx-ists for example), as to its cultural provisionality. By this I mean, following Marshall Sahlins's lead in his celebrated Sidney Mintz lecture (Sahlins 1996), that, rather than describing a universally true set of processes and relationships, neoclassical economics is in fact an ideology and as such a key element in the cosmology of the West in particular, and of capitalist societies in general, and as such a cornerstone of local conceptions of identity, value, progress and the nature of politics within that particular historically conditioned culture, which, for contingent reasons (colonialism, the spread of its technology and conceptions of science, and its ability to con-centrate manufacturing processes being among the main ones), has become temporarily hegemonic. As the previous chapter has argued, globalization (as the latest and perhaps 'highest' expression of the neoliberal project and its political and intellectual fellow travellers) is paradoxical: it in principle throws open to all of us a huge range of local knowledges and practices (social, cultural, sexual, aesthetic, architectural, scientific, economic), yet in practice these alternative modes of being/knowing are subordinated to the hegemonic culture of capitalism and its commoditized practices and social relations, driving out, destroying or relegating to the realms of fantasy the possibility of alternatives. To question neoliberalism ideally requires not only theoretical critiques and evidence of the environmental, social and psychic damage that it occasions, but also an empirical point of reference – the existence, that is, of alternative forms of economy and attendant socio-cultural organization that call its premisses into question and suggest that, were it not for certain turns of world history, things could have been, and might again become, very different.

These issues have profound implications for the self-understanding of the West and its increasingly shaky foundations, given the accelerating environmental catastrophe that is largely of its own making, and (at the time of writing) the rapidly deepening economic and financial crisis that the world is plunging into, which again can be attributed directly to the dysfunctional economic system generated by the same region of the world and in particular its major and most self-congratulatory capitalist state – the USA. But perhaps even more importantly, since they did not invent or propagate it, neoliberalism has huge implications for 'developing' societies. These, seeking ways out of poverty and dependency, are largely forced, to a great extent because of the absence of other available models, onto a path that eventually creates even greater problems of debt, resource depletion, ecological collapse, social inequality and semi-integration into a highly unequal globalized system of trade and aid on top of the already fundamental problems that they are already facing. Many minds have, of course, addressed these issues and many remedies have been suggested – reform of the WTO, new theories of poverty alleviation, the socialist alternative, import substitution, to name only a few. This chapter will not, however, rehearse these proposals but will suggest another line of approach altogether: that there are in fact resources for rethinking and retheorizing economic life along radically non-neoliberal principles, and that two of these resources exist in the form of economic anthropology, on the one hand, and alternative attempts to reconceptualize the economy among a small but profoundly interesting group of contemporary socio-economic theorists, on the other. In the course of the chapter we will also attempt to bring these two together, hopefully sparking an even more potentially stimulating and alternative-provoking dialogue.

Background to the debate

There are many possible, and anthropologically actual, forms of economic life. Exchange may be common to all of them, but the 'market' as understood in neoliberal terms is only one form. It is obviously possible to have economies without markets, and recent rethinking by sociologists and anthropologists, as well as sceptical economists, of the relationships, actual or potential, between economy and society have suggested many variations of the role that markets or marketized relationships might take (Friedland and Robertson 1990). Given the ethnographic variety of actual economic systems, this in itself provides an argument for the relevance of economic anthropology. But someone will immediately argue that these ethnographically known 'alternatives' can only work for very small-scale societies and cannot possibly survive scaling up to larger or already industrialized ones. This line of argument, however, seems to me to represent a failure of the imagination rather than an empirically demonstrated position. The idea that alternatives *a priori* cannot work is itself an ideological viewpoint and, in assuming that the neoliberal model represents the only possible reality, overlooks the historical contingency of neoclassical economics and the economic system it derives from and sustains and the fact that it was itself for a long time a contested and far from widely accepted theory even in the West, where it was far from certain for a long time that capitalism would eventually triumph (Hirschman 1981). It also overlooks the existence of extensive, historically deep and very efficient, but non-capitalist, systems of trade and exchange in Asia and North Africa long pre-dating the current economic era (Frank 1998).

But, most damagingly, in offering itself as the only realistic version of economic theory and practice (socialism being allegedly dead), neoliberalism as a totalizing system cannot account for the problems, failures, crises and contradictions (and, seen from the viewpoint of many of its victims, the downright injustices and absurdities) of the neoliberal market model itself. The god has clearly failed, but the theological interpretation is that this is merely the result of momentary lapses of attention and absent-mindedness, temporary readjustments in an otherwise perfectly functioning system, not an argument for atheism, or at least for changing one's economic religion. This leaves the landscape of social possibilities extremely impoverished and suggests that neoliberalism is a reality-draining not a reality-enhancing system of thought, a totalitarian (alternative-excluding) system promising, as such systems usually do, to enhance freedom – freedom in this case being in the last analysis simply the freedom to consume what the system itself produces, while concealing the actual but hidden ecological and social costs of that (temporary) freedom.

So far, then, the manifest failures of the neoliberal model have for the most part (except by Marxist critics) been dealt with by simply shifting around the elements within the model – interest rates, floating exchange rates, or seemingly radical but what are in fact intra-model suggestions such as the proposed 'Tobin Tax' on international capital transactions. The so-called 'Third Way' of Tony Blair and his intellectual mentor Anthony Giddens (1998) is again only a reformist, neo-Fabian adjustment policy designed to offset some of the more socially damaging effects of the neoliberal model, in particular by attempting to retain the key social gains of the earlier welfare state model while holding on to and actually advancing its capitalist core. In the development field the sudden recent efforts by the World Bank to put a humane face on its entirely neoliberal, pro-market structural adjustment policies represent another example of attempts to maintain the dominant ideology while concealing its actual long-term negative effects, including ecological unsustainability and widening social inequalities. Any scientific paradigm subject to such failures would have long ago been abandoned as fatally flawed and consigned to the museum of historical curiosities.

If the practice has been so damaging, its underlying explanatory framework – the academic discipline of economics – has fared little better, being inconsistent, non-predictive and only operative at all on the basis of a set of 'assumptions', including the exclusion of cultural factors such as choice, values and motivation, and the bracketing of 'externalities' such as ecological resources and the actual costs of waste disposal and the effects of by-products.

Yet since the decline of socialism in the West and the rapid de facto marketization of the remaining formally socialist societies such as China and Vietnam, the assumption has become widespread that there is no viable economic alternative to capitalism of a neoliberal kind and the forms of social, political and cultural life that it engenders. This view was indeed most vocally expressed by Margaret Thatcher in her infamous statement to that effect – 'There is no alternative'. But to claim this, leaving aside what it says about an extremely short-term historical imagination, lack of comparative cultural awareness and blindness to the environmental consequences of continuing to pursue our present path, overlooks at least four other possibilities. These are as follows. First, the possibility and indeed reality of the revival of modified forms of socialism (for example, the German PDS, the former leader of which is at the time of writing Germany's (female) chancellor, or of neo-socialism such as the eco-socialism of the European Green parties. Second, the possibility of forms of capitalism not following the neoliberal model and underpinned by very different forms of social theory and cultural practice, such as the Japanese form and the 'relationalism' that activates it and inspires much of its corporate practice – to the extent that some observers have even suggested that Japan is actually a socialist society hiding behind a facade of capitalism, as suggested by such practices as overmanning, lifetime employment, personnel transfer to subsidiaries rather than downsizing, and so forth. Third, the comparative lessons of economic anthropology, primarily that a huge range of economic formations are empirically possible and exist or have existed, and that in understanding any total society the articulation of economic factors with social practices is vital, and the recognition of the fact that both are rooted in culture. Finally, there is a substantial body of existing social theory and theories of post-industrial society that present themselves specifically as alternatives to capitalism. Here I will focus primarily on the last two, and on the potentially important although little explored relationships between them.

Alternative economic thinking

Although it is often described, in an uncomplimentary way, as 'utopian', it seems in fact evident that engagement with issues raised by authors who have attempted to articulate visions of possible worlds that do not correspond to the reality assumptions of the neoliberal model are crucial for at least three reasons. One is that alternatives by their very nature stimulate the imagination and even critical reaction to them clarifies assumptions and ideological positions very vividly. It is for this reason that Russell Jacoby has bemoaned the decline of utopian thought (Jacoby 1999). A second is that examination of alternative proposals poses in very practical terms issues of workability, scaling-up, gaps in economic theory and, above all, the crucial question of mutually linking in positive (humane and ecology respecting) ways economy, culture and society. While these issues have been raised in the past by attempts to clarify anthropologically the notion of 'political economy' (Clammer 1985), they are raised afresh in very practical ways by those who would attempt to spell out socio-economic alternatives or to define what a post-capitalist society might look like (e.g. Korten 1999). Finally it creates the possibility of an intellectually and potentially practically creative project – the forging of a dialogue between discussions of economic alternatives, whether in 'utopian', culturally different or development studies form, on the one hand, and economic anthropology on the other. In what follows I will attempt to show how economic anthropology can prove to be a vital fertilizing element in fresh thinking about economic alternatives, and in turn can itself be revitalized by a more central concern with industrial/post-industrial societies, and by being forced to think more clearly about its own social purposes as being not merely ethnographic and academic, but also a potent plat-form for social transformation. Economic anthropology can in fact provide, if turned in that direction, a powerful tool for developing a culturally informed critique of the neoliberal model from outside of the sphere of conventional economics as usually understood, and a resource and database for the attempt to articulate post-capitalist alternatives that are rooted in actual ethnographic experience (for broader discussion of economic anthropology in general and its relationship to development in particular, see respectively Narotzky 1997; Gardner and Lewis 1996).

There is empirically a diversity of forms of economic life. These, however, derive not only from purely material factors, or from the abstract working of economic 'laws', but from social practices embedded in ontologies and cosmologies. This can be seen clearly in the analysis of institutions: an institution is always the embodiment of both ideological factors and particular economic forces 'crystal-lized', as it were, in that particular institution and its mode of social reproduction, and this is as true of a lineage as it is of a firm. An essential move is, then, to re-examine the possible links between social practices and economic forms. For example, the conflation of economic life and market exchange in mainstream Western economic theory creates a culturally specific language of self-understanding. While this may be conceptually valid within the terms of the capitalist/consumerist system, it is inadequate within any bigger or more comparative framework and cannot provide the foundation for thinking about alternatives or social futures outside of the market paradigm, and in particular makes any coherent or theoretically based critique of globalization impossible. Not only, then, does the apparently 'common sense' language of the conventional equating of market and society have to be transcended, it also has to be shown how the moral language of critique of the neoliberal model and its main consequence – globalization – can be recouched in an alternative economic language. These moves are essential if the pseudo-economics (or perhaps, more accurately, the ideological economics) of the neoliberal model is to be deconstructed and supplanted, in part by showing how its assumptions about human beings are invalid as well as pointing to its practical consequences. This is a task at which anthropology has, as Carrier and Miller (2000) rightly point out, largely failed despite its moral claims to speak for the cultural Other and of its existing ethnographic knowledge about the existence of social practices that do not correspond to those assumed as normative by the neoliberals. These include gift-giving and contexts in which consumption can become resistance rather than a, quite literal, buying-in to the dominant order.

The neoliberal model, then, is one historically specific and ideologically motivated (suggesting that it reflects the interests of certain social groups who profit from it) form of economic activity and mode of explanation of behaviour in the world.

The reasons for its 'success' can be analysed historically and sociologically and have little to do with its objective 'truth'. Rather, it has largely created the reality that it purports to represent (Carrier and Miller 1998). The sources not only of critique but also of constructive possibilities can, however, be sought in a number of other places: existing critiques of neoliberalism, especially those tending towards a cultural, ecological or ethical point of view (e.g. Etzioni 1988; Friedland and Robertson 1990; Kovel 2002); epistemological challenges coming from deep ecology; religious sources (liberation theologies, alternative Islamic economic thinking, Engaged Buddhism); feminist perspectives (e.g. Ferber and Nelson 1993); new social movements; economic anthropology and articulated economic alternatives; and in particular what Boris Frankel calls the 'post-industrial utopians' (Frankel 1987).

But before examining some of these possibilities in more detail, let us first articulate a basic insight of anthropology: that, in a sense, anything is possible, any number of a huge range of economic possibilities can work, provided that they are rooted in cultural practice, biological needs and a viable cosmology, create a real sense of self-worth and are ecologically sustainable. While the notion that economics *constitutes* culture largely through the process of commodification, as in the neoliberal world-view, would seem absurd to the members of many societies, the organic symbiosis between the economic and other aspects of culture is a critical constant in all societies. The key issues then become, first, theorizing the nature of this fit in societies actual or potential not based on the neoliberal model, and second, the 'scaling up' of small-scale economic experiments, not only of an anthropological nature but also as found in the form of co-operatives, communes, innovative development schemes and the like. While I would certainly accept that there can be 'resistance from within' to neoliberalism, either through such devices as malingering, petty theft, sabotage and other such deviant activities, or through certain patterns of consumption or non-consumption that may constitute at least partially counter-hegemonic definitions of an alternative identity, I would argue that such activities do not constitute a challenge to the neoliberal system itself. Given the ecological and other dysfunctional problems of consumption as a lifestyle, it is not surprising that alternative conceptions of the economy almost always focus on low consumption, non-commodified consumption or post-materialist approaches on the grounds that ecological sustainability is the essential foundation, both physically and morally, of any 'post-economics'.

In the light of these preliminary considerations, I will now turn to an examination of some aspects of alternative economic thinking, not in order simply to survey or catalogue such possibilities, but rather to identify the critical issues that they give rise to, and to link these to debates in economic anthropology. This should provide at least some preliminary pointers to what might be involved in attempting to generate an alternative economics, one that avoids the massive stresses that the neoliberal model has imposed on the world, and that instead places the fulfilment of human needs and rights (culturally as well as materially) and ecological sustainability at its centre.

Articulating alternatives

The anthropology of utopias is an almost non-existent field. So too, relatively speaking, are anthropologies of intentional communities and of social movements, a field that has largely been ceded to the sociologists. These are rather critical omissions, since the anthropological analysis of what might be (as distinct from simple futurology), based on a sound ethnographic analysis of what is and has been, would be a powerful tool for exploring what is possible. Of all the human sciences, anthropology is best suited for doing this by way of its inherent project of what Henrietta Moore calls a 'critical politics of difference', a space defined by anthropology's engagement between itself and Others, a space that anthropology should never attempt to vacate because to do so 'would be to give up on the possibility of a critical politics and a critical ethics linked to an understanding of the way the world currently is and to the multifarious ways in which people are living out their lives' (Moore 2000: 6). This space is related to, but also different from, the effects of the deconstructionist/postmodern project, which, while having many positive results (the abolition of essentialism for example), has proved to be very weak in terms of articulating politically or economically constructive alternatives, and so by itself does not provide a vehicle for social transformation. In particular its conflation of aesthetics and ethics has proved very unhelpful in hard-pressed developing countries, however attractive it might sound in the yuppie salons of the intelligentsia of Western Europe. The centrality of ethics to the disciplinary practice of anthropology is rarely contested, but a simple return to responsible ethnography cannot be enough in a world in crisis. The question that builds on the issues that Moore raises is that of how to link anthropology to these existing or emerging issues without repeating the errors of postmodernism. If neither simple activism nor ethnographic quietism is the way, the answer must lie in translating critical politics and critical ethics into a concrete social programme.

In their discussion of the thesis that modern economics is built on the discovery of the paradoxical fact that private vices (greed and ambition for example) lead to public virtues (growth and competition for instance), Carrier and Miller suggest that 'Anthropology's most important strength against economics is its claim that it can rearticulate models of economic processes with the lives of economic agents' (Carrier and Miller 2000: 25). This is located in the context of the argument, with which I fully agree, that contemporary Western subjectivities are shaped primarily by economic considerations (progress, happiness and satisfaction being all largely defined in economic terms), and that the discipline of economics (not economic life as such) is a 'virtual science' – one that creates what it purports to describe rather than discovering it in the actual processes of social interaction and human/environment interaction. But their main methodological move is then to suggest that the key question is the 'articulation between the microscopic and the macroscopic' (Carrier and Miller 2000: 27) leading to a way out of our current theoretical impasse, since it is 'for anthropologists to achieve what economists have not, a re-articulation of the private and the public through a clear understanding and portrayal of the consequences of each of these for the other' (43). To keep the macro in mind when discussing the micro is an excellent idea, but I would suggest that this be done in ways rather different from those suggested by Carrier and Miller. To identify this difference is important because it clarifies a choice of directions that subsequent analysis can take.

The essential problem with the private/public distinction is that it assumes their separation and an identifiable boundary between them. Analytically, in any society this boundary is in practice difficult to find, and from a communitarian, socialist and from most utopian perspectives is a distinction that is to be negated. It may indeed be that by assuming and reinforcing in numerous subtle ways just this distinction, neoclassical economics has generated a range of subjectivities highly functional to the neoliberal model (it is in effect its 'operating system'), and does in fact (although Carrier and Miller play this down) contain a theory of motivations, status-seeking and consumption. It is, in other words, itself an 'anthropology', not the negation of what academic anthropologists think that they are doing. It is not, then, the public/private distinction that is important in itself; rather, it is the uncovering of the anthropologies inherent in economic models, which shape patterns of subjectivity and social practice. The articulation of alternatives to this hegemonic model is not simply the creation of utopian or even science fiction versions, but the showing in concrete ways of how possible reformulations of the mutual relationships between social practices and economic activity might eventuate in new economic models. Traditionally this issue has been approached from what is in fact a philosophical anthropology – a language of 'human nature' assuming that, from the neoclassical side, humans are basically greedy, selfish and lazy, but that these vices (which are not in fact private at all, but are universally distributed across society and determine the working of all institutions, not only economic ones) can be channelled by structural devices to benefit those who can manipulate these forces. From the 'alternative' side (of which exemplars would be, although of rather different ideological positions, Herbert Marcuse and E.F. Schumacher) the assumption on the contrary is that human nature is essentially altruistic, cooperative and well-intentioned, but has been distorted by the creation of false needs and the objective conditions of work – by alienation and false consciousness to use Marxist language.

The real issue, then, is not the public and the private: it is the contrasting articulations in the two general models of the relationship between social practices and economic activity, both of which generate subjectivities, and the reformulation of their relationship in such ways that will make possible more positive and sustainable lifestyle, relational and psychic possibilities that humanize rather than dehumanize their subjects. What is essentially different between the two models is the nature of the desired outcome, the quite different analysis of the mechanisms through which institutions achieve or violate this, and the distribution of benefits from those outcomes. In the neoliberal model, the outcome is presumably growth, absorbed via consumption by an increasingly large population, while profits accrue to relatively few and the distribution of the ability to consume is actually highly unequal. In the 'alternative' model, the outcome is almost invariably (and we will turn to examples shortly) some vision of human satisfaction and fulfilment independent of consumption and leading to high levels of social equality, cultural access, equity in the distribution of goods, and ecological responsibility and sustainability. The key, then, turns out to be the question of consumption and commoditization, and I will go on to suggest that it is this, not the question of communal labour characteristic of many alternative systems, that is the most important to address. This also suggests why people living under neoliberalism often express resistance to the dehumanizing and calculative aspects of capitalism via the subversion of consumption, and also poses what is perhaps the basic question at the root of economic anthropology as a whole: the relationship of people to objects and the reasons they want things in the first place, and indeed what they do with them when they have them. The problem for most alternative theorists, and a very practical question for those working in development, is how to have consumption without greed and unsustainable expansion of desires, and how to enhance consumption of things, services and activities that are not commodities. The education of desire lies at the basis of all attempts to define an alternative to the neoliberal growth model.

Objects do indeed embody and create patterns of social relations, as anthropologists have long known, although they did not always pursue the logic of this much beyond the theme of exchange into issues of production, use, disposal and embodied memory until the advent of Marxist-inspired economic anthropologies (Clammer 1978), the interest of, in particular, French social theorists in the 'system of objects' and the social meanings attaching to them (Baudrillard 1968; Barthes 1984), and the rather belated recognition by anthropologists of the significance of consumption and its relationship to the fundamental question of why people want goods (Douglas and Isherwood 1980). But the issue of people's relationship to objects is a crucial one for any alternative economics. For while, as Miller (1987) has pointed out, in a capitalist system that is increasingly abstract and remote from immediate social relationships people may turn to objects to attain a sense of identity and spatial and temporal continuity, this does not provide them with an alternative, but merely ameliorates their current alienated situation through the cultural resources immediately available, generated by that same capitalist/commodified system. As a form of resistance 'subversive' consumption or decreasing consumption is inevitably partial, compromised and ambiguous, and does not in itself generate any serious counter-theory.

But before we turn to more articulated alternatives in detail, we should consider several factors. The first of these is the need for a kind of 'ethnography of the future' – a serious discussion of what might be in terms of social, cultural, economic and political forms, on the basis of the huge accumulation of anthropological data now available. Up until now this has been rarely attempted – the ethnographic present or the past providing a safe environment for anthropologists to ply their priestly rather than prophetic functions – as keepers of the knowledge rather than as adventurous speculators of what might be done with that knowledge given the range of social, economic and environmental crises that we have ourselves induced. Second, the entire debate needs to be framed within the context not simply of capitalism but of its contemporary globalized expression and its many effects. This will help us to reveal both the kinds of linkages that exist between global subsystems (economy/ resources/environment/migration/debt/underdevelopment) and the scale on which these problems must now be approached (Augé 1999). Third, economics is to a great extent politics, not science, even as economics itself, especially in its 'virtual' form, has almost entirely colonized politics to the exclusion of almost any other issues. In discussing both alternatives and the staying power of the neoliberal model, the political dimension and the interests involved need to be incorporated, just as much as any concern with the relationship between the micro and the macro. Anthropology suggests that there is no need to succumb to the hegemony of the economists in defining the structuring of the social field. If socialists and utopians have hitherto been the main generators of alternatives, it is now time for anthropologists to see that they too are in possession of a vast body of data and accumulated wisdom on ways of doing and being. This knowledge now needs to be turned to socially and environmentally constructive uses. I will attempt to show how this might be done by showing how anthropological knowledge can inform and modify the arguments of thinkers who have specifically attempted to articulate alternative economic principles to that of the neoliberal model.

Post-capitalism and anthropology

Anthropological knowledge then needs to be related to the attempts of Boris Frankel's list of 'post-industrial utopians' (Frankel 1987). By these he means primarily the German anti-capitalist, anti-industrial Green thinker and writer Rudolf Bahro; author of works on post-industrial socialism André Gorz; the Australian mixed-economy theorist and politician Barry Jones; and the well-known futurologist Alvin Toffler. Frankel's review of this group of different but related post-industrial economy positions is worth briefly reviewing. Frankel starts from the observation that the exhaustion of the traditional left requires that attention be paid to some of the emerging alternatives, including small-is-beautiful, Green and the huge variety of localist, small-scale and craft-based or communalist models and experiments that are available. In the light of the crises emerging from the unfettered application of the neoliberal model, Frankel argues for some variety of 'eco-socialism' and for learning generally from the new social movements, even when they have failed to achieve all their objectives, while at the same time avoiding buying into a simple futurism, especially one consumption-led or one extolling uncritically the alleged virtues of technology (such as IT, GMO or cloning), as these just represent capitalism's utopia, not true alternatives. In contrast to some post-industrial theorists, Frankel sees the problems of the future being continuing scarcity rather than some predicted abundance, lack of work, deskilling, a continuing rolling back of social services, and persisting war and conflict. The key issue for the post-industrial utopians (the collective name for his four primary thinkers and a larger group of related ones such as Herbert Marcuse) is that of 'revolutionizing work patterns and dominant forms of consumption' (Frankel 1987: 16) and generally harmonizing human objectives with social reality.

But having identified this as the basic issue, Frankel then finds all his selected theorists wanting in some crucial respects. Bahro's model is based on ideas of radical and unilateral deindustrialization and the abandonment of high-technology and high-energy economic activities. Toffler, while a prophet of high-technology solutions to current ills, fails to show how it would work in practice to have a society based on localization and decentralizing utilizing such technology (the 'electronic cottage') and how his avowal of this localism fits with his equal enthusiasm for globalization. For Jones, the problem identified for his friendly faced mixed economy is that of providing and funding non-oppressive social welfare systems in a post-industrial society. For Gorz the problem is seen as explaining how non-alienating work can be generated in a post-industrial socialist society in which labour is still necessary (and not all of it necessarily pleasant). In short, Frankel sees the problems of articulating a serious alternative to capitalism *in toto*, or even of conceiving of some greatly modified and socially more responsible form, to be threefold. The first is the lack of serious alternative economic theory that can in any way rival mainstream and neoliberal versions in sophistication. The second is a range of unresolved or unaddressed problems for any alternative model, including women's issues and the overcoming of systematic discrimination in any future form of economic organization, military policy (to disarm or not?), North–South relations and explanations of underdevelopment after capitalism, ecological and energy issues, the provision of welfare services, a post-capitalist legal system, new forms of family relationships, the redefinition of the public/private spheres and their relationship, the continuing role (if any) of the state, the articulation of relationships between the local and the global, and the issues of political agency and structures and post-industrial political cultures and institutions. The third is the failure to spell out a politics of transition – of how to get from here to the desired future – and a lack of imagination in describing what actual concrete alternatives might look like as opposed to literary or science-fiction utopias in which basically anything is possible.

In practice these alternatives tend to fall into one of several rather predictable categories: decentralized, small-scale, non-market, craft-based village republics of a communitarian nature, low in resource use, low energy consumption and deindustrialized (Bahro). Or mixed economies in which the state will still have a major role and in which technology will be central (Jones and Toffler). Or, yet again, socialist with centralized planning, but decentralized production based on egalitarian communities employing low-energy but labour-saving technology (Gorz). While the first group are mostly opposed to globalization or higher levels of integration, the second group are globalizers – the globalization being understood to be shorn of the negative effects of the current system; the last group appear to vote for international connections with other societies while retaining local democratic and economic control, the connections being presumably for mutual trade and cultural exchanges. A politics of self-sufficiency, localism and some level of autarky tends to dominate the alternative models, especially the first and third varieties, the more radical of which are also seen as de-monetarized and are implicitly anti-urban and almost always strongly ecologically oriented. There are also splits within the alternative camp, Gorz for example seeing communal autarky as impoverishing and limiting, while Bahro sees it as providing the basis for human fulfilment. Frankel's own solution is to argue for what he calls 'semi-autarky' with the claim that 'small-scale social institutions have the best chance of thriving inside the boundaries of nation-states, themselves democratically organized along lines that aim at self-sufficiency' (Frankel 1987: 250).

Where and how does economic anthropology speak to these issues? I will suggest that the answer lies in several directions, which I will now sketch out schematically.

1. By demonstrating that the range of historical or actually existing economic systems is rather greater than that imagined by the post-industrial utopians, whose models are curiously myopic in their cultural range or actual possibilities. The ethnographic data reveals a huge amount of experience of economic arrangements, ecological adaptation, the management of scarcity and abundance, culturally defined notions of poverty and wealth, and social arrangements including kinship and political arrangements for managing a large range of environmental and economic conditions.

2. Although the anthropology of work is a rather underdeveloped field (see, however, Wallman 1979) the analyses currently available suggest many pointers for culturally differing attitudes to work, the merging or separation of work and leisure, devising non-alienated work, creating cooperative and communally based projects, resource sharing, efficiency and culturally conditioned notions of productivity, output, sharing, saving and egalitarian uses of the resources (game, fish, fruit, crops) generated by work.

3. Curiously none of the post-industrial utopians appears to have any underlying theory of the ideological unity that anthropological and sociological studies of communitarian movements have shown to be essential to the social sustainability and longevity of such experiments (Kanter 1973; Moore and Myerhoff 1975). Whether these ideologies be religious or secular, anthropology does suggest that a rich shared symbolic and ritual life is a basis for communal continuity, yet the post-industrial utopians, perhaps driven by a modernistic secularized frame of thinking, discount entirely this crucial aspect of social and cultural organization. In fact a common weakness of all the examples discussed by Frankel is that an analysis of culture and of cultural life after the transition to post-industrialism is absent. Oddly they too in this respect, like the neoliberal model that they explicitly oppose, credit primary explanatory power to the economy, assuming culture to be epiphenomenal. Although political economy tends to be concerned primarily with the relationships between the economic, the social and the political, the absence of the cultural dimension is a serious omission.

4. Although technology plays a significant role in all the post-industrial models (either pro- or anti-), it is neither theorized nor problematized in any of them. Anthropology, especially the anthropology of development, has accumulated a great deal of information on the impact of technology, the incorporation of

appropriate technology, indigenous building methods and architecture, and ecologically efficient technologies. Such knowledge of the actual socio-cultural effects of technology and technological innovation is of direct relevance to issues of technology planning in any future society.

5. Among the critical questions for any future economics are those of how to achieve satisfaction (psychic as well as material) given the resources to hand and without destructive overconsumption, and how to distribute resources equably in the new economy without exploitation and without introducing or perpetuating sources of social inequality. These are both issues widely addressed in practice by many societies known to ethnography.

6. Anthropology deals not only with the apparently static, but of necessity with processes of socio-cultural change. This has important theoretical implications for the anthropological analysis of the current industrial system and its associated patterns of consumption, and in which there is a relative move from the production of goods to the production of services and towards information and information-based economies (Lash and Urry 1994). In this context in 'advanced' economies material things and production become relatively less central and new subjectivities arise accordingly, and as they do so the meaning of the 'social' itself undergoes transformation as the configuration of the relationships between 'the family', 'the economy' and 'the state' have changed, which calls into question the continuity of the assumed relationship between these zones or fields of social life, along with others such as 'the political'.

Where the post-industrial utopian models tend to be weakest is not in the sincerity of their visions, but in their lack of rooting in any kind of ethnographic reality. This is important because whereas proponents of the neoliberal model (and paradoxically older forms of Marxism too) tend to characterize non-Marxist socialist (e.g.

Gandhian; see Rao 1970) and other alternative attempts at defining a different reality as negatively utopian, in fact anthropology might suggest that it is the neoliberal model itself, and perhaps the whole system of capitalism, that is absurd in comparative terms. This is because of its assumptions about need and satisfactions, and because of the extraordinary poverty of its social vision – restricted largely to the idea that satisfaction, happiness and fulfilment are defined as ever-expanding consumption to meet equally ever-expanding 'needs' generated by the system itself, and with little higher conception of what human life might involve or be like. Against this impoverished vision, anthropology by its very existence raises a huge variety of alternatives, many of which have been swept away not because of their non-viability, but because of the voracious expansion of the neoliberal model itself and its 'one dimensional man' understanding of the range of human possibilities.

Most utopian theorists operate at a level of abstraction that has little place for the ethnographic. Krishnan Kumar suggests rightly that utopianism is a form of social theory – 'all the more effective for looking at familiar problems from an unfamiliar angle and in a different light' (Kumar 1991: vii), while also recognizing that most utopian projects are weak on concrete descriptions of the economic arrangements that would sustain them. But Kumar, although a sociologist, stops short at the level of suggesting that the real power of utopias is in their critique of existing circumstances and institutions, rather than as constituting alternative models as such (e.g. Kumar 1991: 87–8). Yet Fred Polak, one of the most perceptive commentators on utopian thought, both argues that classical economics, which, like Carrier and Miller, he sees as having its origins in Bernard Mandeville, is the great enemy of the social utopia, and also – uniquely as far as I am aware among the major surveyors of utopian thinking – specifically relates such thought to anthropology (Polak 1973). In an important section of his book, titled 'Utopianism and Cultural Anthropology', Polak relates utopianism to comparative ideas in ideology, myth, politics, ethics and science, all of which he claims are best illustrated by the data of anthropology rather than treated as abstract categories by philosophy, although surprisingly he does not include economics in his list.

Yet, in every major attempt at sketching a utopia the economy is necessarily vital. Marcuse, for example, while not a utopian in a systematic way, but coming rather from a neo-Marxist perspective, argues that 'The theory of society is an economic, not a philo-sophical system. There are two basic elements linking materialism to correct social theory: concern with human happiness, and the conviction that it can be obtained only through a transformation of the material forms of existence' (Marcuse 1968: 135). While clearly drawing on Marx, Marcuse's position, however, agrees with the neoliberal model in one important respect: the very Western idea that the economy is basic to the definition of human subjectivity. Where he begins to suggest the outlines of an account transcend-ing this is in his theory of needs, the 'education of desire' and the replacement of false needs with true ones. For Marcuse the goal is human happiness, something primarily to be achieved by abolishing restrictive material conditions of existence through non-alienating labour and the abolition of scarcity. Scarcity, Marcuse suggests, is a historical condition, not a natural one, and so can be overcome, in part at least, by the liberating potentialities of technology and also by the containment of wants. Scarcity can be reduced, if not totally overcome, if sufficiency and not surplus is the principle. While there are unclarities in Marcuse's underlying theory of needs and of the ability to distinguish real from false need, he does pose the interesting anthropological problem of the ways in which this very issue is resolved, or at least constantly addressed, in a range of very different actual human societies. In recognizing that the power of capitalism is its ability to satisfy in large part the (false) needs that it itself has created, Marcuse not only succeeds in raising classical questions of false consciousness, but also puts his finger on another essential issue: not that of labour and its conditions, but of wants and the ways in which these are alternatively defined in a variety of cultures, and so might, drawing on this bank of human cultural experience, be redefined in an actual possible future society.

It is a weakness in addressing precisely this problem, and in failing to give it any cultural grounding, that besets one of the areas in which such issues are far from being only of theoretical interest – notably development studies. Much of the work characterized as 'alternative development', or even more radically as 'post-development' (e.g. Rahnema and Bawtree 2003), has as its basis a programme very similar to that of the post-industrial utopians, but using a different discourse. In his discussion of varieties of development theory, Jan Nederveen Pieterse suggests that although many of the specific critiques and recommendations of alternative development have been incorporated creatively into mainstream development thinking and practices (for example, the importance of grassroots participation, the significant role of NGOs, people-centred development, sustainability), such thinking has 'failed to develop a clear perspective on micro–macro relations, an alternative macro-approach, and a coherent theoretical position (Nederveen Pieterse 2001: 74), and, while being successful in introducing a language of participation, is weak in explaining agency – who will transform the dominant development paradigm 'from below', and how? But while Nederveen Pieterse, again like Carrier and Miller, sees a key to the main issues lying in the realm of the relationship between the micro and the macro, he also intuits that an equally major challenge for alternative development is not in that relationship per se but in the reconceptualization (or reimagining perhaps) of the macro itself, since post-development positions, while passionate in their critiques of the mainstream, are frequently very weak (unlike the post-industrial utopians, who at least offer a vision of an alternative future) at the constructive task of defining what that future might look like. It is also true that although anthropologists are increasingly involved in development activities, neither alternative nor post-development discourses make more than the most cursory use of anthropological data or insights.

This is an oversight, since what alternative development sees as being its critique of the general discourse of developmentalism is in fact essentially identical to post-industrial utopian critiques of the neoliberal model and its social consequences. While, rightly in my view, arguing for a redefinition of development as social transformation (the enhancement of human possibilities) rather than as growth, alternative development, like the post-industrial utopians, fails also to develop an adequate theory of globalization. Yet a thoroughgoing theory of globalization is vital, as it uncovers the essential characteristics of the neoliberal model in action as a practice, and, by identifying the social consequences of globalization, also reveals the crucial areas on which an alternative or post-development paradigm needs to concentrate. An adequate theory of globalization is in the contemporary context the necessary condition for a fuller theory of social transformation. Likewise, with rare exceptions, alternative approaches to development have not learnt much from the ideas of Pierre Bourdieu, who carries forward the expansion of the concept of capital from its purely economic usage to a much wider set of references including social capital, cultural capital and symbolic capital, and the connections of all of these to conceptions of social justice and inequality (Bourdieu 1999). For in suggesting that economics is not a science but politics in disguise, alternative development both begins to identify the seed from which a full-scale critique of the neoliberal model might grow, and suggests that the key concept of 'capital' cannot, even within that model, be consistently understood in purely economic terms. If, in post-development theories, the solutions to such pressing issues as poverty are seen to be found outside of market mechanisms, then they too will not only have to address the question of culture, a good starting point for which is obviously anthropology, with its considerable expertise in this area and experience of societies and economies outside of the market in its neoliberal sense.

Nederveen Pieterse concludes his book by suggesting that 'The challenge facing development is to retrieve hope from the collapse of progress' (Nederveen Pieterse 2001: 163) and that an approach capable of doing this must be a reflexive one, aware of complexity and the fact that in the North societies are moving from scarcity to risk, while in the South societies experience both scarcity and risk, and must be concerned with reconstruction emerging from the necessary, but purely preliminary, step of critique. Ernst Bloch wrote years ago about the task of the human sciences being that of 'reclaiming the future'. He was correct, I think, and it has been a major failure of social and cultural theory that it has largely relinquished this task to futurologists and science-fiction writers and has pushed alternative discourses to the margins of the social sciences. While we at first sight seem to live in an age of dystopias rather than utopias, in fact alternative thinking flourishes beyond, and often beyond the ken, of conventional social theory – in Christian liberation theologies, in Islamic economic thinking, in Engaged Buddhism, in some sectors of the New Age movement, in social movements, among artists, among communards and the creators of intentional communities, in community revival and self-help movements, in Gandhian and countless other experiments in the South, in organic farming, in co-operatives and feminism in the West and in Japan, in new religions and post-religious spiritualities, in the deep ecology movement, in post-socialist and post-New Left circles, in populist political movements, and in intellectual resistance, often allied with contemporary forms of the labour movement (e.g. Bourdieu 1999), in peasant and farmers' movements, and in any number of artistic, literary, theatrical and even architectural innovations (the literature is vast; for a good survey, see Hawken 2008).

Despite this luxuriant variety there are a number of common themes to most of these approaches, the sheer variety of which (and the far from complete or uniform penetration of globalization), reassures one that the hegemony of the neoliberal model is far from total. While these movements do not represent a united front, they do form the seedbed of a stronger opposition to the ecologically, socially and culturally destructive consequences of the unchecked expansion and psychic colonization of the neoliberal capitalist system, in part by defining the key issues to be addressed – the articulation of the micro and the macro; the problem of scarcity; the achievement of unalienated work, including the issue of domestic labour and child care; the 'education of desire' and its embodiment in forms other than consumption; the articulation of the relationship between oppositional struggles in the cultural sphere, now rightly seen by many as a major site of political struggle, and the economic sphere; and an analysis between local-level struggles and the global. So, while with Marx and Marcuse we might not want, or be able, to pre-empt history by stating in final terms what the alternative(s) would be like, not to do so at all is to fail to see the possible in concrete terms, represents a failure of oppositional imagination, and is to refuse to concretize the directions in which alternative theories logically lead. It is in fact to succumb to the hegemony of the present and of its currently existing structures and institutions, when history is in fact open and waiting to be made according to new patterns if we are willing to discover or invent and then to apply them. There are many steps that might be made in that direction, and here I am simply suggesting one simple methodological step – the bringing into dialogue with one another the largely separated discourses of anthropology (the true science of the possible), post-industrial utopian thinking, and the struggles of alternative and post-development theory against the anti-human and anti-nature ravages of 'progress'. This step, together with the imaginative but wholly possible operation of putting the social and the cultural back at the centre of debates about human identity, necessarily means challenging not economics as such, but its distorted and ideological varieties that stand that identity on its head. This is not only to avoid the colonization of the social and the cultural by the economic, but to rethink the nature of the economic itself, including re-examining the interfaces between the spheres of total social life, spheres separated by Western disciplinary discourse, but found bound together in quite different configurations than the limited and limiting model that neoliberal economics seeks to impose on us all.

Mapping the future

The current conjunction of environmental crisis, financial and eco-nomic chaos and the visible inequities of unrestrained globalization have triggered a significant upsurge of new literature confronting the issues that have been raised in this chapter. Some have drawn on slightly older investigations of the desire for a people (and nature) centred economics – works such as E.F. Schumacher's celebrated *Small is Beautiful* (1979) and his less well known *Good Work* (1982), or Erich Fromm's *To Have or To Be?* (1982). Others represent the thinking of social movements such as PROUT – the Progressive Utilization Theory movement of Indian origin, but now worldwide (Maheshvarananda 2003), while others have taken the form of either literary utopias directly addressing our multiple crisis, especially its environmental aspects and the forms that an ecologically sustain-able and socially equitable and non-alienating economy might take (Callenbach 2004), or of in-depth analyses of possible future and community-based economies, among the most significant of which is Bill McKibben's *Deep Economy* (2007). Others have systematically addressed what a post-capitalist economy might actually look like and how it might work (Theobald 1999; Korten 1999). Other such significant initiatives include the emergence of what is being called 'Solidarity Economics' or 'Social Economy' – economic activities that are sustainable ecologically, just in social and gender terms, support and create communities rather than undermine them, that are rooted in their local bio-regions; that create a culture of cooperation and sharing rather than of competition; and the outcomes of which are devoted to the creation of social solidarity and sharing rather than to profit (e.g. Fretel 2009). Yet another is the 'Transition' movement with its pursuit of a low-carbon, localized, sustainable and convivial economy (Hopkins 2008). In each case at least two moves are evident: a critique of the current forms of economic theory and activity that have led us into the systemic and mutually self-reinforcing multi-dimensional crisis in which we now find ourselves, and an attempt to define what economic activity, work, social policy, communities, politics and technology might look like, in Bill McKibben's words, 'after growth'. The thrust of this chapter has been quite simple: to suggest that there is already a vast body of data available on actually existing and historical 'alternative economies' that provide innumerable pointers to how possible sustainable futures might be shaped, this being the largely untapped resource of anthropology. But slowly the recognition has been dawning – initially in the development field (Gladwin 1994), but now with a much wider application to the issue of post-industrial futures and the creation of sustainable post-crisis societies in general – that anthropology, and in particular economic anthropology, provides a rich and still unexplored way of relating not only to economies and societies, but to the pressing question of creating a sustainable future for all inhabitants of the earth, both humans in the overdeveloped North and those in the still struggling South, and the rest of the biotic community upon which we are all ultimately dependent.

SIX

Culture and climate justice

Discussions of the biological, geographical and physical aspects of climate change, and of their probable economic consequences, are now part of a widespread public discourse. Less common, however, are discussions either of the probable social and cultural consequences of significant shifts in climatic patterns as a result of global warming on different human populations, including the immense social suffering likely to result, or of the cultural factors that have contributed to the ecological crisis in the first place, and how, in searching for possibilities of adaptation or mitigation, cultural and sociological factors are in fact paramount. This chapter will, at least in summary form, attempt to address these two related issues. What links them is the concept of climate justice, or, if you prefer, ecological justice, terms that I will shortly define in more detail.

Culture and climate

The first of these issues – the likely consequences for vulnerable populations of major climatic changes – has now attracted quite a substantial literature (e.g. Glantz and Ye 2010; Burroughs 2005; Adger et al. 2009). It is widely accepted that the negative consequences will fall first and with greater intensity on the poor, who cannot protect themselves by physical movement or installing air conditioning and other mechanical means to keep rising temperatures, rising sea levels and more chaotic and extreme weather conditions at bay; those who live in physically vulnerable locations such as sea coasts, on low-lying riverine environments and islands; on those whose agriculture (particularly rain-fed farming) depends on natural cycles such as predictable monsoons; and on those who rely on irrigation from natural river systems whose sources of flow (such as the Himalayan glaciers) are shrinking. While some farmers may benefit from enhanced growing seasons or more rain in previously dry areas, the uncertainties of weather and increasing unreliability of previously taken-for-granted natural climatic cycles are likely to have negative effects for a far greater number, most of whom are concentrated in the global South or occupy marginal land in either the North or the South. The North is certainly not exempt from these effects, as evidenced by severe and prolonged droughts in Australia, water shortages and massive forest fires in California, unusually powerful hurricanes in the Caribbean and Japan, and exceptionally severe winter weather in the American north-east and elsewhere. While these effects most obviously and immediately impact agriculture and are likely to trigger migration, dislocation and landlessness (so-called 'environmental refugees'), displacement of fisheries and inundation of coastal land, they also affect cities, many of which are vulnerable to flooding and the disruption of social structures and patterns of reciprocity ruptured by forced migration. While the social traumas of war and of major acute humanitarian disasters have been studied (Eade and Williams 1995), the slower and hence less immediately visible traumas of climate change – loss of home, livelihood, social networks and disruption of long-established patterns of culture – have as yet rarely been given much consideration. Yet all these issues as much raise questions of social, ecological and economic justice as do the more traditional issues of class, poverty, gender and marginalization that have hitherto preoccupied mainstream development studies.

The other dimension of the interaction between culture and climate is that of the cultural factors that have promoted the climate change in the first place. While we tend easily to blame corporations and the forms of industrialization that they have promoted since the Industrial Revolution, we have also to recognize that we are all complicit with this by way of our own patterns of consumption, greed and movement. The key factors can easily be listed: industry in both its polluting and its resource-extraction modes, consumption cultures with their unlimited 'needs' or rather wants, our addiction to travel (especially by air), the unnecessary long-range transportation of goods (often available locally) by ship, plane and truck, the car culture which now dominates our cities and countryside, our failure to recycle except in trivial amounts, our addiction to plastics, and the widespread failure to adopt even those environmentally friendly technologies that already exist such as rainwater harvesting and alternative energy generation (solar, wind, tidal and so on). What is frightening is our path-dependent relationship to these practices: despite the widespread and easily accessible knowledge of the severity of our environmental crisis, few politicians, business people or even individuals are doing anything to avert it. We rush on towards the abyss in the delusional belief that the future will just be like the present but hopefully a bit better, not only as individuals but from the perspective of governments too, as witnessed by the charade of the 2009 UN-led Copenhagen Climate Change Conference. Perhaps a paradigm case of this blindness and profit-driven short-sightedness was the launch in 2009 by Tata Heavy Industries of India of its so-called 'people's car', the Nano, a small and relatively inexpensive vehicle, but conventionally petrol-driven. This at a time when oil shortages can only but intensify, when Indian cities are clogged with barely moving traffic and intolerable vehicle-generated pollution, and without situating this profit-driven decision (even though hybrid and other environmentally sensitive technologies are widely available) in any kind of national transport or city-planning policy, which evidently does not exist. The idea of restricting private transport, greatly expanding and making more efficient public transport (buses and trains), discouraging long-distance goods transport, utilizing water transport on rivers and canals and in coastal regions, and greatly expanding non-oil-based alternative sources of energy does not seem to have occurred to Indian planners. No integrated policy, then, appears to exist, in this case in India, but just about everywhere else as well. While the idea of making private transport available to those on modest incomes seems to be a policy aimed at social equity, it makes no ecological sense at the present time, is unrelated to a broader transport policy, and is unrelated to the idea (found in Singapore for example) of making private car ownership so expensive, even for the rich, that it makes sense to use public means instead.

We can conclude from this that cultural practices, many of them deeply embedded in what the French sociologist Pierre Bourdieu called 'habitus' or our everyday sets of largely unexamined assumptions and daily patterns of life, are strongly implicated not only in the production of climate change, but also in the production of climate or environmental injustice. Let me briefly pause here to define these terms and their range of application. The more familiar notion of social justice implies equal or at least reasonable access to social and economic resources (jobs, income, education, political representation and so on); protection from illegal or extralegal punishments, detention, banishment or torture, and equal access to fair judicial procedures and outcomes should these be necessary; and the broad application of the provisions of the Universal Declaration of Human Rights, including the rights to free assembly and free movement. The notion of climate justice/environmental justice extends this definition to the right to free and reasonable access to an environmentally attractive and healthy environment to all people regardless of class, caste, ethnicity, religion or gender. It is significant that earlier attempts to formulate lists of human basic needs, while these always included basic subsistence and shelter needs, also listed aesthetic, recreational and health needs in their lists (Dube 1984). And rightly so, as the emergent field of eco-psychology consistently shows, deprivation of nature and natural beauty and lack of access to attractive environments are a major source of stress, illness and possibly even crime. In the past the notion of environmental justice has been closely tied to ideas of environmental racism/classism: the fact that the poor tend to get the worst living environments, often close to or even on toxic dumps, trash heaps, polluted canals, poor soils and devastated or traffic-ridden industrial parts of cities, while the wealthy can live in gated communities with gardens, trees, lakes, views, clean air and water, regular garbage disposal and 'security' – that is, the ability to keep out those threatening poor or minorities who inhabit the least desirable and most polluted parts of the city outside the walls of the rich.

The idea of environmental/climate justice extends this idea in a number of directions. At the macro-level it is to point out that the climatic stresses now being laid on the already poor and marginalized are for the most part not their fault, but that they are the victims of policies and practices that have made some people and some parts of the world rich while they have been sustained in poverty in many cases by those very processes and practices. At a more micro-level it raises the question of the visual and environmental quality of life spaces and the impact of these on life chances and life quality. The simple question is: why should only the rich enjoy beauty, attractive living environments and unpolluted spaces, and the health, lifestyle and longevity benefits that derive from these privileges? And at a legal level it raises the question of just compensation, both for the poorer countries and island states that now face crisis as a result of industrial and transport policies pursued for decades with impunity by the global North, and for individuals damaged by specific instances of such policies. One thinks, for example, of the Union Carbide incident in Bhopal (central India) where, more than a quarter of a century ago, a massive toxic gas leak killed and maimed a huge number of people and where, after a derisory initial compensation by the multinational company to the survivors the cases seeking proper benefits have only just been resolved in the Indian courts, while those responsible for the slipshod maintenance of the plant have long retired or have fled abroad. The idea of environmental justice, then, is multifaceted but is essentially an extension of the idea of human rights from political and social elements to environmental ones: that no one has the right to destroy the natural environment for personal or corporate gain, and that everyone regardless of social status has the right to dwell in a clean, attractive and unpolluted living situation with the aesthetic, cultural and health benefits that such a dwelling space confers.

If such justice does not in fact widely exist, we have to ask ourselves why. We can, of course, simply blame industrialists, but a slightly deeper analysis suggests the much broader cultural and social implication of all who have benefited from that process. It points indeed to the somewhat uncomfortable idea that it is our entire civilization that is to blame, our patterns of consumption and short-term goals in particular having given rise to the problems in the first place. If this is so, then the obvious implication is that it is our civilization that needs changing: that in its present configuration it is simply unsustainable and cannot continue on its present course. Without drastic changes, civilizational collapse, which has indeed occurred in the past to many other cultures (Diamond 2005), will be the terminal outcome for our culture, but with the additional fact that this time we have done so much irreversible damage to the total biosphere that simple recovery or mitigation may no longer be an option. And, as Diamond suggests, civilizations do not simply collapse: they in a sense choose to do so, knowing full well the outcome of the irresponsible and path-dependent course that they are following. The problem from a justice point of view is that this 'choice' is made by those who benefit most and will suffer least, and not by those who are without the power to choose except in minor ways and so become the victims of other's greed and hubris.

In his largely excellent book on the idea of a post-corporate world, David Korten suggests that 'To create a just, sustainable, and compassionate post-corporate world we must face up to the need to create a new core culture, a new political centre, and a new economic mainstream' (Korten 1999: 261). He is correct, although his book, in common with many 'alternative' writings, focuses only on the last two needs: the question of a post-capitalist culture is left untouched, except to suggest that what has basically led us amiss is our (false) 'Big Picture' – the familiar notion of the world dominated by a mechanistic, non-organic and managerial world-view that has outlived its usefulness and now badly needs to be replaced by a new Big Picture that will direct us to the interconnectedness of things, the analogies between biological and sustainable economic and social processes, and the affirmation of life rather than profit. Again he is right, and this can be verified by looking at many aspects of contemporary culture, from our social theories, which until very recently have argued for a radical separation between humans and nature, to the nature of education. I have personally counted MBA courses internationally running into many hundreds; at the same time I have been able to locate only a handful of development studies institutes, almost no serious 'futurology' ones actually considering the likely outcome of our present course and what its implications might be for our future culture and social organization, and very few alternative educational organizations offering their students the intellectual and spiritual tools to think through and creatively manage the coming transitions. On the whole, in fact, a kind of fatalistic cultural pessimism seems to reign, summed up in the title of a book by the Italian social forecaster Roberto Vacca, *The Coming Dark Age* (Vacca 1974), which predicts a future of resource wars, social conflict, the collapse of complex systems such as electricity supply and transport systems and the rise of a generalized barbarism. The cover of my paperback copy indeed announces 'This is your future and it's starting now.' It is clearly up to us to ensure that this is not our future. And, as I shall now go on to argue, culture plays a major role in ensuring that this bleak picture remains as it should be – a piece of dystopian science fiction.

Culture and core values

A number of cultural and value researchers, including David Korten, have identified what is being called a shift to 'a new integral culture that affirms life in all its dimensions' (Korten 1999: 214). Two of Korten's associates, Duane Elgin and Coleen LeDrew, define this as follows:

> An integral culture and consciousness involves a new way of looking at the world. It seeks to integrate all the parts of our lives: inner and outer, masculine and feminine, personal and global, intuitive and rational, and many more. The hallmark of the integral culture is an intention to integrate – to consciously bridge differences, connect people, celebrate diversity, harmonize efforts, and discover common higher ground. With its inclusive and reconciling nature, an integral culture takes a whole-systems approach and offers hope in a world facing deep ecological, social, and spiritual crises. (Elgin and LeDrew 1997: 19)

What this statement suggests, of course, is that we do not yet have such an integral culture, an idea that would be supported by figures as diverse as Gandhi, Ken Wilber among contemporary alternative cultural/spiritual writers (Wilber 2004), deep ecologists, and a few sociologists. Among the latter the problem is often phrased a little differently – as in fact the failure of modernism, the socio-technological-artistic movement that was supposed to deliver us from the shackles of the past into the emancipated and even utopian future envisaged by many nineteenth- and early-twentieth-century social and political figures. This project of modernity, the heir to the eighteenth-century 'Enlightenment project', has led in fact to the wholesale environmental destruction that we now see all around us, to violence on a scale never before seen in history, as witnessed by the First World War and its successors and the use of the atomic bomb in warfare for the first time. It has, as the sociologist Zygmunt Bauman argues, culminated in the Holocaust, an act or process of almost unbelievable violence perpetuated in and by the European country that prided itself on having the highest level of culture, and since then by a succession of cruelties and forced displacement of peoples from Rwanda to the Balkans (Bauman 1999, 2004). This certainly proves that the possession of culture as such does not insure against barbarism. Only a certain kind of culture can do that: the role of cultural analysis and cultural studies as a result becomes not only the description of cultures but, on the one hand, a critical and deconstructive approach to them revealing their hidden or concealed assumptions, biases, hierarchies and often classed or racialized nature, and, on the other, the constructive programme of conceptualizing and creating the integral culture that is the key to a sustainable future.

One of the major counter-cultural gurus of the 1960s, Herbert Marcuse, writing about the hegemony – and hence, in a sense, totalitarian nature – of late consumer capitalism, coined the phrase 'the education of desire'. That phrase seems to me to encapsulate the key issue in the creation of a culture that is both socially and environmentally just. For these are intimately linked. As the development ethicist Denis Goulet puts it:

> The ecological imperative is clear and cruel: nature must be
> saved or we humans will die. The single greatest threat to nature
> – menacing, irreversible destruction of its regenerative powers
> – comes from 'development'. This same 'development' is also the

major culprit in perpetuating the 'underdevelopment' of hundreds
of millions. The task of eliminating degrading underdevelopment
imposes itself with the same urgency as that of safeguarding nature.
These twin concerns have spawned two ethical streams of protest.
Yet almost always the streams flow in opposite directions: one
is concerned with protecting nature, the other with promoting
economic justice. This dissonance is tragic because it is the identical
pseudo-development which lies at the root of both problems. The
only antidote to pseudo-development is a working ethic of what
is generally called 'sustainable development', but which is better
termed 'integral authentic development'. Such an ethic joins the
two normative streams, linking the concerns for environmental
responsibility with the drive for universal economic justice.
There can be no sound development ethic without environmental
wisdom and, conversely, no environmental wisdom without a solid
development ethic. (Goulet 1995: 119)

Goulet goes on to argue that a major obstacle to the quest for new
and alternative development models is what he calls 'the worldwide
paralysis of creative imagination', a situation made worse by the fact
that, on the one hand, most of today's global institutions are relics
of a now past age, and, on the other, that alternative institutions,
although often talked about, do not yet for the most part exist. A
great deal of 'alternative' thinking and experimentation, however,
does (for a broad survey, see Hawken 2008). The problem methodologically and politically, however, is scaling up these many local
and sometimes international initiatives so that they can effectively
challenge the entrenched structural forms and institutions of the
dominant world order,

> and, in this specific context, to challenge the inherently
> environment-destructive industrialization, resource extraction,
> pollution and consumerism of the current hegemonic order which
> is, whatever 'green washing' it may go in for, inherently destructive
> of nature. (Kovel 2002)

As many have suggested, the key to this lies in education. Although
he is speaking here specifically of the universities, the comments of

the eco-theologian and cultural historian Thomas Berry here are very relevant to all educational institutions and programmes:

> Of the institutions that should be guiding us into a viable future, the university has a special place because it teaches all those professions that guide the human endeavor. In recent centuries the universities have supported the exploitation of the Earth by their teaching in the various professions, in the sciences, in engineering, law, education and economics. Only in literature, poetry, music, art, and occasionally in religion and the biological sciences, has the natural world received the care that it deserves. Our educational institutions need to see their purpose not as training personnel for exploiting the Earth but as guiding students towards an intimate relationship with the Earth. For it is the planet itself that brings us into being, sustains us in life and delights us with its wonders. In this context we might consider the intellectual, political and economic orientations that will enable us to fulfill the historical assignment before us – to establish a more viable way into the future. (Berry 1999: x)

The problem, however, is the inability of our educational institutions to respond to these pressing challenges in an effective way. As Berry laments,

> The pathos of these times, however, is precisely the impasse that we witness in our educational and religious programs. Both are living in a past fundamentalist tradition or venturing into New Age programs that are often trivial in their consequences, unable to support or guide the transformation that is needed in its proper order of magnitude. We must recognize that the only effective program available as our primary guide toward a viable human mode of being is the program offered by the Earth itself. (Berry 1999: 71)

The role of culture is hence crucial and is clearly the neglected dimension here, since culture encompasses education and the socialization processes that it embodies, meaning systems (religions), values and quotidian practices (de Certeau 1984), including those of consumption and spatial and temporal movement, and cultural and socially constructed notions of nature, of the body (obviously closely connected to the former), and of material needs and wants.

It also encompasses expectations – of dreams, hopes and desires of a non-material nature, which includes art, spiritualities of a non-institutionalized character, literature and the whole immense universe of fantasy, imagination and creativity – processes that lie at the very heart of culture. A new ecological and planetary consciousness may indeed be emerging – evidence of which is reflected in the works of writers as diverse as Sri Aurobindo, Rudolf Steiner, the major 'New Age' theorists such as Marilyn Ferguson and Joseph Chilton Pearce, process thinkers such as Fritjof Capra (e.g. Capra 1998, 2003) and deep ecologists and philosophers of nature such as Arne Naess, and many others. As the liberation theologian and social activist Leonard Boff rightly puts it, in arguing for transformative practice as well as transformative thinking that will bring together the needs of the environment and the desperate needs of the very poor,

> Having a new cosmology is not enough. How are we to spread it and bring people to internalize it, so as to inspire new behaviors, new dreams, and bolster a new kindness toward the Earth? That is certainly a pedagogical challenge. As the old paradigm that atomized human beings, isolated them, and set them against the universe and the community of living beings permeated through all our pores in our lives and created a collective subjectivity suited to its intuitions, so now the new paradigm must form new kinds of subjectivity and enter into all realms of life, society, the family, the media, and educational institutions in order to shape a new planetary man and woman, in cosmic solidarity and in tune with the overall direction of the evolutionary process. (Boff 1997: 119)

The first level of the achievement of climate justice is the reformation of the cultural institutions that prevent its full expression, including environmental law, laws governing corporations and their behaviour, industrial practices such as waste disposal, and the achievement of what Vandana Shiva has called 'Earth Democracy' (Shiva 2005). The second level, which is much more fundamental and long term, is the creation of new key culture values compatible with a future that is not only sustainable, but also equitable.

This is not the place to develop a whole theory of what a post-capitalist culture, sensitive to the demands of nature and our inter-connectedness with the total biosphere, might look like. This is, however, a vital project, as we have as yet few guidelines as to what form such a culture might take – and furthermore there is no *a priori* guarantee that a post-capitalist culture would necessarily be an ecologically oriented one. But we can, I believe, at least see the outlines of what a cultural configuration that is both environmentally and socially just would look like – not in the details of its cultural expressions, but in its structural form and in the means by which we might reach it. The first element is clearly that the human relationship to nature, rather than being simply one element among many in our total cultural universe, would be central – the point from which other forms of cultural production and creativity would emanate. In his book on transformative learning, the Canadian educationalist Edmund O'Sullivan spells out the educational consequences of this in terms of what he calls 'Quality of Life Education', implying a 'Transformative Ecozoic Vision'. This he sees as having a number of elements: the re-enchantment of nature, seeing education in a planetary context, nurturing the idea of an ecological self, the resiting of our culture in the context of what he calls, following Thomas Berry, the 'universe story' (the unfolding and evolutionary development of the total cosmological context in which our culture and institutions exist) and the revisioning of education as being for what he terms integral development – a holistic conception of the creative human person within the primal matrix of the earth itself (O'Sullivan 1999). Much of the methodology for such a cultural transformation, away from the purely human, from consumption and growth, from short-sighted short-term planning, from an ego-centred notion of the self, is spelt out in another book by fellow Canadian Brian Murphy, who roots his analysis in the belief that substantive change is indeed possible in individuals and in their wider society, especially if the psychosocial dimension of social and cultural change is given its due consideration and we can move beyond what he calls the 'psychology of inertia' that impedes so many social change initiatives. This involves many concrete steps, including the challenging of the 'established rationality' that posits as normal what is in fact the social, economic and eco-pathology of everyday life in the consumerist–corporatized world and a revolution in education towards transforming the perception of the young about their place in the wider universe and their creative role in shaping it rather than simply being shaped (Murphy 1999).

These transformative visions are hard to argue with, but we should also recognize that they are up against not only the psychological inertia of which Murphy speaks, but also a perhaps even deeper social inertia. In his influential and best-selling book *Collapse: How Societies Choose to Fail or Succeed*, the American geographer Jared Diamond (2005) explores in detail the ecological collapse of a range of civilizations and societies from ancient times up until the recent past and comes to some disturbing conclusions. Instances include the evidence that many societies have not responded to approaching ecological crisis, either by failing to anticipate the coming problems or by succumbing to what he terms 'creeping normalcy', the ignoring of small signs that something is wrong until they accumulate to the point where they tip into irreversible crisis; short-sighted profit-driven policies and lack of legal frameworks to enforce or encourage environmentally sensible industrial or resource extraction while there is still time; the pursuing of 'rational bad behavior' that leads, for example, to the 'tragedy of the commons', the idea that even if a resource is scarce and declining (a fish species for example) if I don't catch it someone else will, leading of course to the depletion of the resource for everybody including myself; and the clinging to disastrous values long after their functional utility is obviously spent. At a recent time meeting of the Convention on International Trade in Endangered Species (CITES) a ban on fishing for Atlantic and Mediterranean tuna (both severely endangered by overfishing) was proposed by the international conservation community to allow regeneration. This entirely rational move, however, was bitterly opposed by Japan, a society that consumes 10 per cent of the total world fish catch, on the grounds that tuna is a mainstay of the traditional Japanese dishes of sashimi and sushi and that these are cultural values that cannot possibly be given up. The same argument has been used in Japan in opposition to bans on commercial whaling, whale meat being also an element at one time in Japanese cuisine, and the skirting of such bans by the practice of 'scientific whaling' for 'research' purposes, despite the endangered status of the whales being thus harvested and of course consumed. Here we see a conjunction of disastrous values and rational bad behaviour, no long-term consideration being given to the renewal of the 'resource' or the inherent right to life of the species being hunted to extinction to satisfy human appetites, legitimized by the label of culture.

We are not, then, short of knowledge. The problem is the core values of our culture and the difficulty of changing them even when rationality points to the need, and indeed the necessity, for urgent and radical change. What is needed, as a number of the thinkers that we have cited have suggested, is a 'new story' – a new conception of the earth, its history, our place as one species among many in that story, and our vision of what we want our collective (human and non-human) future to be like. This is fundamentally not a question of politics, but of culture, the site of our core values, habitual practices, modes of expression and creativity and models of selfhood. It is not, then, just a matter of changing culture in more humane and ecologically just directions: culture is the *means* by which those changes take place. This, I would suggest, contains two essential elements, or perhaps just one seen from different perspectives. Michael Lerner suggests that ecological sanity requires spiritual transformation and argues specifically that 'the upsurge of Spirit is the only plausible way to stop the ecological destruction of our planet. Even people who have no interest in a communal solution to the distortions of our lives will have to face this ecological reality. Unless we transform our relationship with nature, we will destroy the preconditions for human life on this planet' – and this transformative process Lerner calls 'Emancipatory Spirituality' (Lerner 2000: 138). Indeed, although others, eschewing the word 'spirituality', have looked to other creative resources shared by all human societies, such as art, in the belief that the re-enchantment of art both signals and leads a re-enchantment of the universe that it visualizes, interprets and represents (Gablik 2002b). Still other resources exist in the field of anthropology – the study of actually existing or historically recent real societies, some of which have failed ecologically, but many others of which have worked out long-term highly sustainable and socially just relationships with their natural environments – yet anthropology, as the premier science of culture, is rarely invoked in discussions of contemporary human–nature relationships.

This is what Thom Hartmann in his classic study *The Last Hours of Ancient Sunlight* (2004), however, does when he invokes what he calls the 'Older Culture' (as opposed to our 'Young Culture') view of human–nature relationships, and where he cites the examples of the San and Kogi peoples as examples of cooperation with each other and with the environment, and the Kayapo people as an example of long-term sustainable agriculture. He invokes the idea of the study of tribal cultures as examples of egalitarianism, political independence, locally based economies (while acknowledging that others also engaged in conquest and had hierarchical social structures), and suggests that modern post-ecological crisis and post-capitalist intentional communities can be based on what we can learn from anthropology. And we can learn much, although the problem remains of how we scale up the solutions of low-population-density, usually rural, often hunting–gathering and low-technology-use peoples to our own urbanized, globalized and corporatized world.

Culture and justice

Cultures, however 'authentic' or integral and uncontaminated by the infiltrations of globalization and commoditization, if any such exist, are not in themselves necessarily just. Tribal cultures of the kind that Hartmann invokes have practised cannibalism, warfare, ecological destruction, female circumcision and scarification, and many have had anything but egalitarian social structures. It is as a consequence constantly necessary to interrogate cultures and not to be deflected from criticism and deconstruction of their ideologies by claims of 'tradition', essential identity and other such self-serving and often reactionary arguments. Although cultural analysts like to point out that cultures are dynamic and changeable, they do not always take up the practical implications of this quite correct claim and rarely undertake the actual cultural work necessary to bring about such cultural transformations. We may constantly now talk about 'transforming our relationship to nature', but not only has this to be done, but, as we have argued throughout this chapter, such a transformation must include an environmental and a social justice dimension. A future ecological consciousness and, indeed, many existing New Age ones, which simply make us feel 'closer' to nature, or somehow one with it, absorbed in it or enchanted by it, can easily lead right back to a new quietism, a mysticism of contemplation without the corresponding action. This is to be avoided at all costs otherwise our latter state will be little different from our former since the institutions and structures, including the economy and the attitudes that it has engendered, need to be transformed along with our consciousness. Popular notions of 'bio-happiness' or even of the notion of 'biophilia' propagated by the well-known entomologist and sociobiologist E.O. Wilson need to be expanded politically and culturally into the emergent idea of 'bio-civilization'. Social justice and environmental justice are but two sides of the same coin, and both together are not products of, but are rather generators of, bio-happiness, and to achieve this new forms of social and cultural imagination are required (Wielenga 1999).

To achieve this requires not only a transformation of our cultural stories and cultural myths – of unlimited growth, of the inevitability of technological 'fixes', of the historical triumph of capitalism and globalization – but also of our institutions, including some of the most sacred in a secular society such as the law. Law that primarily defends private and corporate property is now obsolete: the need today is for a legal system that respects not only human rights but also the rights of nature – the earth community context in which all human activity takes place and the biosphere on which we ultimately depend for our existence – and that is prepared to face the changes in governance structures, culture, education and the functioning of institutions that this entails (Cullinan 2011). Environmental justice requires for its full flourishing two equally important dimensions: an attitude of fairness and justice towards nature itself, including the rights of other species, animal and vegetal, to exist in their own right quite apart from their utility for us as humans; and equally the equitable access of all humans to clean, beautiful, and spiritually and psychologically satisfying experiences of the nature that is the final sustaining principle of all life and certainly the bedrock of human health and happiness. Without these dimensions and without active policy to express them in concrete forms, the sum of social suffering and of biotic suffering can only increase to a truly critical and unsustainable level.

PART III

Development, culture and human existence

SEVEN

Narratives of suffering:
human existence and medical models
in development

From many perspectives suffering is a paradigm of the human experience. This was certainly true for the Buddha, who saw suffering as
the foundational quality of human experience (and who, of course,
also offered a method for overcoming it), and is today true of most
medical sociology, which is predicated on the fact of suffering and
could hardly exist without it. As we will see in the subsequent
chapter, trauma (surely an extreme form of psychic and emotional
suffering) is a common by-product of war, revolution and criminal
violence. Hinted at there, but here to be considered in detail, is
the relationship between development and suffering. While underdevelopment and its manifold deprivations can certainly be described
as both a form of violence and a form of suffering (Scheper-Hughes
1992), a case can certainly also be made that so is development. The
erosion of cultures, displacement of peoples, forced landlessness and
urbanization, the economic and social impacts of globalization, all
force upon people experiences that they have not chosen and that
certainly do not necessarily better their lot. Yet despite the ubiquity
of suffering, it has attracted little attention from the social sciences
– remarkably and perhaps scandalously little. To speak of 'poverty'

is to name an abstract category, an economic status, but does little to reveal the experience of deprivation that the category label conceals; to speak of 'untouchability' is to name a social status in a hierarchical system of castes, but it does little to illuminate the daily humiliations of exclusion and denigration and its immense psychic effects that the status entails. Anthropology has been particularly remiss in this respect. For all its vaunted self-advertised expertise in ethnography, in practice concern for such disciplinary preoccupations as kinship, ritual, oral tradition or local-level political organization have led to a resounding silence on the question of the inequalities and everyday suffering that frequently pervade the societies that anthropologists mostly elect to study (for a notable exception, see Kleinman et al. 1997).

Earlier studies, if not of suffering per se, at least of the structures of inequality that frequently give rise to them, have been largely swept under the anthropological carpet. Significantly, studies of suffering in society show that it is frequently generated by the cultures of those very societies as much as by 'objective' forces of war, revolution or economic restructuring. Many of these studies have come primarily from theologians, especially those associated with liberation theology (Chopp 1986; Gutierrez 1983), while empirical research has come mainly from those who have followed the endemic violence of societies such as Guatemala, El Salvador and Argentina (for a range of examples, see Feitlowitz 1998; Grandin 2000), postcolonial theorists and students of the violence of modernity such as Enrique Dussel (1995) and Zygmunt Bauman in his later writing (e.g. Bauman 2004). Implicit in many of these studies, although rarely stated as such, is the question of the violence of development. Certainly colonialism, the process of modernity and their latest manifestation as globalization are all of them complicit in containing or advancing by another name the concept and practice of 'development' (Sachs 1995). The links between modernity, violence (especially structural violence) and development are clear. The question then becomes how to place the suffering that they generate and/or that is generated by the existential qualities of being human centre-stage in social analysis, so that its causes can be more fully understood with a view to its alleviation, and by what methodology such suffering might be grasped and understood.

Development theory has a tendency not to engage in dialogue with other sectors of social theory, and yet in empirical development studies issues of health are one of the central concerns. Medical sociology and medical anthropology, while focused on cultural constructions of illness, patterns of medical care and the cultural management of illness through ritual and other mechanisms, in fact have at their centres the problem of human suffering even if they do not explicitly identify it as such. The interesting methodological possibility then arises of linking the discourses of development sociology and the sociology of medicine by way of the analysis of the causes and management of suffering. The question then is, can medical models illuminate the problem of suffering in development contexts? The answer is certainly a qualified yes, and what follows is an exploration of this potentially creative interface and its implications for development discourse and practice.

Suffering and development

The problem of suffering has always been central to humanity and its cultures. A great deal of what passes for religion is in fact a wrestling with the problem of suffering, whether expressed in the idiom of Buddhism (suffering as arising from attachment and desire), or, as in the Judeo-Christian tradition, defined primarily as the problem of evil. Although perhaps posed primarily as a theological or metaphysical question, in practice it is the cultural negotiation of suffering that preoccupies most people – cultural explanations of suffering (as with Azande witchcraft), the diminution of such suffering by way of magic, ritual, healing techniques and medicines, the identification of specialists in the relief of suffering (doctors, shamans, witchdoctors, mediums), and techniques of prevention and protection. Such an approach applies particularly, although not exclusively, to illness, but may in some cases also be applied to more 'structural' forms of suffering such as war; natural disasters; the social, cultural and economic displacements of modernization and development (forced migration because of dam construction, loss of traditional livelihoods as a result of the expansion of agribusiness and plantation agriculture, loss of land for airport or road construction); or through the violence of colonialism and the new economic activities (slavery, mining, plantation labour) that it enforces on subject peoples (for a classic instance, see Taussig 1980). It is also the case that cultures themselves are a major source of suffering for their own members by way of patterns of social exclusion, torture and other methods of punishment, warfare, socially sanctioned forms of violence, neglect, and educational, psychological and other performative stresses and expectations. Social theory is itself often complicit in this. Its recent preoccupation with the 'Other' and with the politics of difference extended not only to humans but to nature as well, rather than with seeking a philosophy of interrelationship and mutual dependency, has if anything intensified the tendency to see cultures as separating rather than as including, even as critical theory and postmodern deconstructionism have proved very efficient at critique, but very weak indeed at any positive form of reconstruction. The interplay of structural violence and individual suffering then becomes a key interface. Exploring this interplay in the context of development then becomes our objective.

Suffering, as the Buddha clearly saw, is part of the human condition, and not just a peripheral part at that for much of our species. As David Morris suggests, 'Unlike robots or rabbits, humans possess a tendency towards repeated and often protracted illnesses that seem finally less a flaw in our design than a mysterious signature' (Morris

1998: 1). And even as the search for perfect health is a universal and ancient impulse, so too is the search for the perfect society, as evidenced by the perennial attraction of utopias throughout history. If the perfect society cannot be found, at least we seek the good society – the best that the imperfections and limitations of human thinking and conduct can conjure. Whatever the criticisms that have been made (often quite rightly) of the concept of 'development', what can certainly be said in its favour is that it does (or should) represent the impulse towards the alleviation of unnecessary suffering and the achievement of higher and potentially reachable levels of social justice. But just as illness has been attacked by the mechanical and science-based intervention of biomedical medicine (with its many victories, but with the corresponding marginalization of traditional medical systems and their accumulated wisdom), so the problems of underdevelopment have been attacked with all the resources of a 'scientific' economics and all the managerial paraphernalia of policy science, planning and forecasting. Both depend on a mechanistic model and the assumption that there are objective 'problems' to be 'solved' by the application of scientific reasoning. Neither has taken seriously the necessary convergence between, on the one hand, biology and culture and, on the other, between culture and development. The result has been not only the very incomplete treatment of illness by biomedicine and even the generation of what Ivan Illich has called 'iatrogenesis', medically induced diseases, the existence of which led him to the conclusion that 'The medical establishment has become a major threat to health' (Illich 1990: 11). Its more radical critics would say that the same thing is true of development. Both certainly operate in an environment of very incomplete knowledge, strongly political agendas often driving their allegedly scientific objectives, little awareness of the long-term outcomes of their well-intentioned interventions, and little insight into the deep subjectivity of the subjects of their activities – patients or those being 'developed'.

Yet, for all their limitations, hidden often behind their hubris, and lack of acknowledgement of the very failures from which as much can be learnt as from the successes, is a common concern with human suffering, whether expressed in illness or in the deprivations and exclusions of poverty. And they are in any case connected: poverty, with its attendant chronic or acute malnutrition, is the basis of many if not most of the sicknesses experienced in the 'Third World'. While culture shapes and provides (however imperfect) models for suffering, the afflictions that provide so much of the 'signature' of being human are common to all of us. While politics is the cause of much suffering, suffering itself lies beyond politics – it is a universal language and as such the basis for a new form of philosophical anthropology – not the seeking for an 'essence' of human nature, but a critique of the nature and sources of that suffering, a critique that points to such remedies as are within our power. This modesty is necessary as a clear lesson to be derived from the limitations of both biomedicine and development: while each has very honourable intentions, each may be working with the wrong model that still controls thinking, education and practice in the respective fields – a biomedical one in the case of medicine and a still (despite disclaimers) largely economistic one in that of development. While both have shown remarkable successes in addressing certain (especially acute) crises, neither provides a clear model of health or of the good society. Both tend to operate with the false philosophical view that there are discrete, concrete 'problems' to be 'solved' rather than with a view of the embeddedness of their particular fields in the complex and indeterminate context of culture and in relation to deep change – the slow and fundamental shifts rather than the easily discernible and measurable 'social trends' – in which global society is now and has always been situated. Much as we desire one, there is no 'cure', no ultimate 'fix': rather, there must be a new model of understanding suffering as a key interface between the existential condition of being human – our species-being, to use Marx's term – and the cultural negotiation of that suffering. While the issue certainly and ultimately touches upon theological questions, here it will be understood as a matter of sociology, but of a deep sociology that goes beyond the empiricist and mechanistic premises of so much conventional sociology (Clammer 2008).

Any adequate (especially culturally adequate) conception of development must accordingly encompass the economic, political and natural conditions that define its parameters, and also the experience of those faced with the actual life-conditions of underdevelopment and the often wrenching transformations that accompany change, perhaps to a better state, or perhaps just to a different one. This, as we have seen in Chapter 4, is a somewhat different notion from the recent anthropological rediscovery of 'indigenous knowledge' (e.g. Sillitoe 1998; Sillitoe et al. 2002). In that approach the ethnoscience of developing societies is seen as being functionally recoverable and applicable to the development process, in particular in such areas as agriculture and healing. It says little or nothing, however, about the experience of development or of the destruction, transformation or renegotiation of that traditional knowledge under the impact of development or its larger frameworks such as globalization or colonialism. Again an analogy with medicine greatly helps to clarify this. David Morris discusses the case of the critic Anatole Broyard, who, prior to his death from prostate cancer in 1990, kept a diary reflecting on his own illness and his relationship to the medical system that was attempting to treat him. In that diary Broyard emphasizes the power of narratives to make sense of experience, including in his case a not statistically uncommon, but personally devastating, experience. As Morris summarizes it:

> He emphasizes that narrative contains or releases therapeutic powers. A sick person, he contends, can make a story out of illness as a way of trying to 'detoxify it'. In seeking to detoxify his own illness, Broyard experiments with inventing 'mininarratives' and exploring the resources of metaphor: 'I saw my illness as a visit to a

disturbed country ... I imagined it as a love affair with a demented woman who demanded things I had never done before. (Morris 1998: 45)

Such narratives, of course, do not need to be written: the oral history of development and maldevelopment is undoubtedly richer than the sparse written record. What is significant about them is that they allow the 'victims' of even apparently intolerable situations to find, if not meaning, certainly humour, a sense of self-worth and a meeting with reality (change, struggle, deprivation) on their own terms rather than being the victim of determinism. As Morris summarizes the case, 'The patient', he insists, 'has to start by treating his own illness not as a disaster, an occasion for depression or panic, but as a narrative, a story. Stories are anti-bodies against illness and pain.' The storyteller – according to Arthur W. Frank (another cancer patient who turned his experience into narrative) – 'is the new figure of the postmodern patient: no longer a victim of disease, not the object of medicine, but a person struggling to recover and to reshape the voice that illness so often takes from us' (Morris 1998: 48).

Narrative, development, empowerment

Narrative, then, is a form of empowerment, available alike to the very poor and to the very rich. And its necessity may be increasing as, with the advent of the 'risk society' with its unknown, diffused, untraceable dangers and problems, the sense of lack of control over the environment by the average individual increases. The disempowering consequences of development as much as of medicine, then, need to be confronted. And again we can see the parallels between development and mechanistic biomedicine:

Postmodern illness, because of its complicated links to the culturally constructed environment, ultimately demands that we rethink the sources of medical knowledge. Laboratory tests and scientific studies cannot reveal everything that doctors need to know.

The social, cultural and personal dimensions of illness must be understood through other means, and one neglected but useful source is narrative. Narrative, we might say, constitutes a mode of understanding appropriate for situations too variable and too untidy for laboratory analysis. Further, storytellers thrive at the margins of power, casting a skeptical eye on contemporary culture, and their somewhat independent status permits them to offer impassioned critiques, visionary alternatives, and an outsider's objectivity. Narrative may also require readers to confront self-consciously the ways in which their culture has taught them to think about illness, to imagine ways in which they might experience a healthier relation to the earth. The United Nations reports that fourteen million children die annually from causes related to environmental degradation. For the children, if not for ourselves, we need to hear from voices silenced or overwhelmed by the prevailing biomedical discourse of science, policy analysis, and cost containment. We need a knowledge that comes with narrative. (Morris 1998: 89)

As with medicine, so with development. Morris here, however, seems to be speaking mainly of the writer, the outsider. Here, though I prefer to speak, as with the case of Anatole Broyard, of the voice of the individual: the average and actual person caught up in the process of forced change and of the personal opportunities, energies and restructuring of subjectivities that it so often entails.

An obvious parallel between development and medicine is that both involve a sense of violence being done to the self – medically through illness and the sense that one's body has been 'invaded'; development through forced, unchosen and uncontrollable changes that come not primarily from the natural world (although with the human manipulation and modification of the environment, even that is becoming increasingly part of 'culture'), but from 'artificial', that is to say humanly engineered, interventions – dams, agribusinesses, urbanization, industrialization, new economic forms – that are the source of migration, land loss, famine, new illnesses, cultural loss. Furthermore, decades of 'development' have not had an appreciable linear effect on disease eradication. Not only have 'new' diseases (AIDS, SARS, avian flu, for example) emerged, but older diseases such as malaria, asthma and rabies have made startling comebacks, in the case of malaria almost certainly as a result of climate change as well as resistance to the overuse of pesticides. Development has proved to be like one of those games in which no sooner is one peg knocked into its hole than another one pops up. In fact a general law of all policy science would seem to be that the application of any given policy will have unforeseen consequences not anticipated in the original plan, which will give rise to the need for yet further policies. Much development, then, like much biomedicine, is devoted to the eradication of symptoms, and not necessarily of the underlying disease or its ultimate causal factors, which reside as much in the complex relationships between illness/development and culture as they do in the biological or socio-economic environments.

> The main point is that, although life expectancy has increased, a high-tech, energy dependent, consumer lifestyle has not brought the developed world a period of unprecedented health. Historian Roy Porter rightly warns against the facile and long standing prejudice that equates civilization with the spread of disease [Porter 1993]. The serious question is not about the health value of civilization but about what kind of civilized society we want. Along with their benefits, unfortunately, affluence, technological development, and biomedical progress in Western nations have accompanied the rise of new or intensified illnesses. By-products of development have in fact left industrial nations vulnerable to a growing list of maladies that bodes ill for future generations. (Morris 1998: 104)

There are additionally two major consequences of this pattern of development – its immense negative impact on the environment (which in turn has disease generating implications) and its unequal impact on the so-called developing or underdeveloped nations which may well be the victims of global processes (global warming being just the most obvious) of which they are in no way the authors.

This has some important ramifications: the aforementioned principle that all policies contain unexpected outcomes; the recognition of the principles of ignorance (we are doing our best, but in an environment of very incomplete and constantly evolving knowledge) and of caution (when we are not sure, as is usually the case, of the outcome of our actions/policies, proceed with great slowness and care); that there are no 'solutions' but only temporary fixes that will dissolve in the ever dynamic environment in which cultures exist and shifts of perception. This last point is important: even as the construction of a meaningful narrative of suffering confers meaning on illness to a patient and may indeed, and often does, lead to healing, even paradoxically in terminal cases (Levine 1987), so too the experience of the violence of development can and does lead to the transformation of that experience through parallel means.

An equally important consequence is the recognition of imperfection, of what Ian Craib has called 'the importance of disappointment' (Craib 1994). Even as we have learnt that perfectionist utopias all too readily lead to totalitarianism despite their imaginative possibilities and stimulation (Jacoby 2005), so too in development the grasp of the fact that there are no final solutions and that development is in fact an art rather than a science becomes apparent (Kaplan 2002). The objective problems exist, but they can be managed, if only to an imperfect degree, both by the techniques of development and by the subjective relationships to the processes of development expressed through articulated or unarticulated narrative forms. There are no conclusions, only temporary closures. But the process of development itself, as experienced in particular by those being 'developed', requires listening as much as prescribing, as much as it does in the context of biomedicine. It also requires attention to that profoundly neglected dimension of culture, the emotions. Loss, grief, excitement, powerlessness, empowerment, fear, apprehension – a whole geography of the emotions shaped by the particular culture and its specific vocabulary of feelings – attend the experience of change and the reshaping of society around oneself (e.g. Clammer 2000). The external processes of so-called social change and the inner processes of the reshaping of subjectivities go hand in hand and are in fact interpenetrating and dialectical experiences. As the old 'basic needs' approach to development insisted two decades ago, it is the *quality* of experience that makes any development process a success, not its delivery of material goods, which are only a means to enhancing that quality of life, not in themselves the goal.

Medical models and development

Development requires a critical holism: a perception of the (often hidden) linkages of things and events and an awareness that the artificially separated dimensions of development – economics, gender, sociology, environment and so forth – in fact constitute a single interactive system often obscured by ideology, bad methodology or the arbitrary nature of academic disciplinary boundaries; and a constant vision of what 'development' is ultimately for – presumably the alleviation of human suffering and the establishment of the conditions for the best possible quality of life for the greatest number, that quality of life including the enhancement of sustainable relationships with the larger biosphere on which all life depends. Within that understanding of development, growth is secondary to other considerations and pre-eminently to social justice – a term encompassing not only equitable distribution of resources and rewards, gender and age equality, political access and representation, the meeting of basic human (including psychic and emotional) needs and freedom from torture, trafficking, forced labour and similar unsought impositions, but also a sense of fairness, autonomy and creativity. While the former factors can to a large extent be measured, the latter are, while equally important, more subjective and are expressed, among other means, in the narratives and autobiographical accounts of life experiences that peoples of all cultures constantly generate and tell or perform.

Medical sociology has begun to recognize something very similar: that illness is not just an objective condition, but also a relationship to the world that must be made sense of in some way by the patient, and also by the medical practitioner whose therapeutic interventions are likely to be much less successful if the 'story' in which the patient's experience is embedded is not acknowledged and to some extent empathized with. Anthropologists working with traditional health systems which do centrally acknowledge those stories, and modern biomedical systems which mostly do not, yet which are rapidly encroaching on and eroding the traditional modes, have clearly identified the critical role that the narrative of suffering and the supposed causes of that suffering play, both in the ontological environment of the indigenes and in the success of biomedical or alternative therapies (Samson 2004). Development theorists, however, have not drawn on the vocabulary of medical sociology, and medical sociologists have not for the most part related their work to the development context. So clearly a potentially very valuable interface exists here waiting to be explored. Probably the only point of contact has been with the elaboration of the notion of 'social suffering' explored by Arthur Kleinman, Veena Das and Margaret Lock and their collaborators (Kleinman et al. 1997) in which a number of in-stances of collective suffering are explored, including the Holocaust, political widowhood in South Africa, torture, the Chinese Cultural Revolution, and the relationships between religions and suffering. It is significant that two of the three editors of the collection are medical anthropologists, and Kleinman has devoted an entire book (Kleinman 1988) to the analysis of illness narratives, a study to which we will shortly return.

In the introduction to their collection, Kleinman and his co-editors define social suffering as that 'assemblage of human problems that have their origins and consequences in the devastating injuries that social forces can inflict on human experience' (1997: ix) and point out that this suffering is a shared and therefore social experience, and that while this can occur anywhere in practice it falls disproportionately on the poor and powerless. The issues that they list, including political violence, social breakdown, uprooting and forced migration, infectious diseases and mental health problems, have their roots in the political economy of globalization and underdevelopment, and sometimes in the bureaucratic or well-intentioned policies designed to alleviate the suffering that they in the end intensify. The representation and experience of suffering all too often become 'professional' problems to be dealt with bureaucratically by 'experts' or 'agencies' and, in a phrase resonant for students of development studies, 'Existential processes of pain, death, and mourning are metamorphosed by these historically shaped rationalities and technologies, which, again all too regularly, are inattentive to how the transformations they induce contribute to the suffering they seek to remedy'. Whether the result of violent or of routine suppression, 'social suffering ruins the collective and intersubjective connections of experience and gravely damages subjectivity' (x).

The outcome is that a fresh methodology is required to address these issues of suffering:

> The authors discuss why a language of dismay, disappointment, bereavement, and alarm that sounds not at all like the usual terminology of policy and programs may offer a more valid means for describing what is at stake in human experiences of political catastrophe and social structural violence, for professionals as much as for victims/perpetrators, and may also make better sense of how the clash among globalizing discourses and localized social realities so often ends up prolonging personal and collective tragedy. (Kleinman et al. 1997: xi)

This is important for the exploration of the linkages between culture and development, as not only are cultural representations of suffering involved, but experiences of suffering are often used for current political purposes – to fuel hatred, for example, as we have seen so graphically in the Balkans, giving rise to yet another cycle of suffering.

It is also important to overcome the impoverishment of theory that stems from its failure to acknowledge suffering and the fact that much of this suffering is a societal and cultural failure and is indeed caused by certain forms of culture. It is also often the case that theory itself divorces the humanistic analysis of meanings, feelings and subjectivities from the 'hard' world of social policy, yet the whole thrust of the argument here (and that of Kleinman and collaborators) is that this is an entirely unwarranted separation and is itself the cause of further suffering. Poverty lies at the base of a huge amount of social suffering; and, as Oscar Lewis demonstrated decades ago (leaving to one side his controversial 'culture of poverty' thesis), poverty is also an experience, one demanding endless survival strategies, adaptations and daily confrontation with the starkness of an existence without safety nets or fallback positions. To confront both the structural and the existential dimensions of poverty it is necessary to grasp the full dimensions of the problem and of the experience. And to do so is to render easier the expansion of the moral community, which in a globalized environment is to move a little closer to the ideal of a genuinely global or cosmopolitan sense of citizenship and solidarity (in the context of conflict situations, see the deeply sensitive analysis in Lederach 2005). And since the ultimate end of both academic research and social policy should be the relief of suffering through understanding and action, a holistic grasp of its fullest dimensions is a prerequisite for its alleviation and response at the deepest human level. Integral development requires holism: the relating to one another or the synthesis of the various disparate levels at which social science and policy discourse operate. The key to this is culture: the mechanisms through which subjectivities are formed and expressed and the narratives which give shape to life experiences, including, perhaps especially, extreme ones, those that exist within the realm of suffering.

It is for this reason that Kleinman's attention to the interpretation of the illness *experience* is particularly significant (Kleinman 1988).

I will discuss his insights here with a view to relating them to the broader question of social suffering, the very problem that 'development' is charged with resolving. This is important, I think, because it suggests a whole new model of approaching development, a truly humanistic one rooted in culture and with a convivial, equitable and sustainable culture as its final outcome. At the beginning of the book Kleinman relates how, through two experiences with quite different patients of greatly differing ages, he came upon the central theme of his study: that it is possible (for the doctor, usually fixated on the disease) to hear from the patient about the actual experience of illness, and that listening and witnessing can help to order that experience in ways that can have great therapeutic value (Kleinman 1988: xii). This, he realized, pointed to a holistic model that connects body, self and society. This complex set of relationships is inevitably mediated by culture even as it points to universal qualities of the human condition:

> The study of the process by which meaning is created in illness brings us into the everyday reality of individuals like ourselves, who must deal with the exigent life circumstances created by suffering, disability, difficult loss, and the threat of death ... Illness narratives edify us about how life problems are created, controlled, made meaningful. They also tell us about the way cultural values and social relationships shape how we perceive and monitor our bodies, label and categorize bodily symptoms, interpret complaints in the particular context of our life situation. (Kleinman 1988: xii)

We can at once see the resonances of this statement with development, as it is the narratives of the subjects of development that take centre stage and as the development practitioner is recast in the role of interpreter rather than as the agent of intervention in the lives of others that s/he may not and probably does not fully or even partially understand. But, on the other hand, contact with development realities and the experience of real social suffering can shock the practitioner and the planner out of their own culturally mediated and common-sense view of the world into a deeper grasp of the extent and structure of the problems that stand revealed to them – not as statistics, but experientially, as truly human life as it is lived by a scandalous majority of the world's population.

Furthermore, chronic illness, like trauma, displacement and the manifold dislocations of development, 'becomes embodied in a particular life trajectory, environed in a concrete life world' (Kleinman 1988: 31), to be endowed with both personal and interpersonal meanings, particularly when the ties that bind the individual (emotional and affective as much as purely social ones) are severed or damaged. Sociologists who have belatedly discovered both the body and the emotions as key elements of culture and social behaviour will recognize that the affective relationship to events, personal and collective, is a vital aspect of the relationship to, and management of, change. The parallels, again, between the medical field and development are close, and for the development practitioner as for the doctor:

> The role of the health professional is not so much to ferret out the innermost secrets … as it is to assist the chronically ill and those around them to come to terms with – that is, accept, master or change – those personal significances that can be shown to be operating in their lives and in their care. I take this to constitute the essence of what is now called empowering patients. (Kleinman 1988: 43)

Here we see a powerful corrective to the domination of the objective, structural or technical aspects of development. The process of change, especially when it involves displacement, cultural loss and the cutting of emotional bonds to places, kin, work and familiar nature, deeply involves the emotions and subjectivities of those affected, their self concepts and their sense of personal worth and competency. These are questions that involve the ethics of development every bit as much as the technologies of development.

But to stress only the violence of development would be a mistake. Also involved, and indeed stimulated by change rather than by the stasis and immobility of a traditional and conservative lifestyle, is the possibility of human transformation and of positive social and cultural changes that lead to greater empowerment and freedom. Knowledge of the forces that are creating change can dramatically increase the strategic possibilities of the relatively powerless by understanding, and thus to some extent controlling, the mechanisms of exploitation that abound in most societies. To borrow from Habermas, this is the point at which the lifeworlds of the developee/patient intersect with the social system and a negotiation of meaning and strategic possibilities begins in which, as far as possible, the subject seeks the possibility of the decolonization of the personal lifeworld by the forces that have made unacceptable incursions into it, whether this is done by personal resistance or by political or cultural means, including recourse to myth, religion, fantasy and the freedoms of the imagination (Clammer 2009b), all mechanisms against demoralization. The practical need, then, for the most part is not to 'represent' those undergoing development, but to give them voice and to hear those voices when they speak. As a patient of Kleinman's so appositely puts it, 'We have powerful techniques but no wisdom. When the techniques fail, we are left shipwrecked' (Kleinman 1988: 142).

Healers and 'developers', then, have much in common: both are concerned with listening as well as doing, encouragers of the recounting of narratives of suffering and displacement to emerge, empowerers rather than simply technicians, and operating in a deeply and inevitably cultural context, one in which culture is not merely an added extra to the technical interventions of the developmentalist, but is the very medium in which the whole discourse is embedded and expressed. As with the chronically ill, in development there may be no 'cures'; rather, in order to address what are often intractable and permanent conditions, a new methodology is required: 'The essence of that methodology is captured by the words *empathetic listening, translation,* and *interpretation*, which I take to be the craft of the clinician who treats illness, not just disease' (Kleinman 1988: 228). The necessity of ethnography, in clinical practice and in development, is thus paramount. Rather than the practice in many development agencies of having a token anthropologist to perhaps review the 'cultural impact' of technical, infrastructure or economic policies that are going to be implemented anyway, the deep understanding and appreciation of culture becomes a prerequisite for any satisfactory development intervention, on the one hand, and the maintaining and advancing of the integrity of the culture in question should be an absolutely central part of any development policy, on the other. The necessity of discovering the models that the developee/patient is employing is vital if the developer/physician is to know what they *want* from the situation. Such knowledge is necessary to help efffect the empowerment of the subjects of the development process, or what Kleinman calls the 'remoralization' of – the instilling or rekindling of hope in – those subject to wrenching changes that force them to redefine their own place in the world of meanings and social networks on which they have previously relied as their primary maps.

Seen from this perspective, development itself becomes a meaning-centred activity in which the central methodological elements are care rather than control, and empowerment rather than management (a perspective that has major implications for development education and the teaching of development studies). None of this is intended to exclude the political and structural dimensions of development, but rather to infuse them with the spirit of cultural sensitivity and compassion that is sadly lacking in so many mainstream development models and has rightly led to attacks on the very concept of development itself by Wolfgang Sachs and others. In fact such an approach to development requires a grasp not only of those political and structural factors but also of the cultural and moral ones – which the field of 'development ethics' has emerged to fill (Goulet 1995) – and of history. As the philosopher Alastair MacIntyre has wisely observed, 'In successfully identifying and understanding what someone else is doing we always move towards placing a particular episode in the context of a set of narrative histories, histories both of the individuals concerned and of the settings in which they act and suffer' (MacIntyre 1981: 197). By so often cutting itself off not only from the study of culture, but also from history, postcolonial studies and theories of modernity and postmodernity, development studies has done itself a grave disservice, one not only of intellectual concern, but even more so because of its damaging effects on practice and policy in the real world.

Suffering and methodology in development studies

One of the main thrusts of this book has been that the existential issues that engage people on an everyday basis are actually what 'development' is all about, and that culture, often treated as an abstract category with little real or concrete content or as an essentialized notion of some kind of collective identity, is in fact a shorthand for the strategic means by which people attempt to manage the tensions and problems (including illness). This has some fundamental methodological implications. In the words of Kleinman and Kleinman:

> Humanizing the level at which interventions are organized means focusing planning and evaluation on the interpersonal space of suffering, the local, ethnographic context of action. This requires not only engagement with what is at stake for participants in those local worlds, but bringing those local participants (not merely national experts) into the process of developing and assessing programs. Such policy-making from the ground up can only succeed, however, if these local worlds are more effectively projected into national and international discourses on human problems. (This may represent the necessary complement to the globalization of local images. Perhaps it should be called the global representation of local contexts.) To do so requires a reformulation of the indexes and instruments of policy. Those analytic tools need

to authorize deeper depictions of the local (including how the global
– e.g., displacement, markets, technology – enters into the local).
And those methodologies of policy must engage the existential side
of social life. How to reframe the language of policies and programs
so that large-scale social forces are made to relate to biography and
local history will require interdisciplinary engagements that bring
alternative perspectives from the humanities, the social sciences,
and the health sciences to bear on human problems. The goal is
to reconstruct the object of inquiry and the purpose of practice.
(Kleinman and Kleinman 1997: 18–19)

That is indeed the goal. But to reach it requires a new blend of
the detailed and ethnographic analysis of culture and its existential
dimensions, a grasp of the structural qualities of globalization, and
an awareness of the social justice aspects of social change.

In illustrating this necessary triangulation the Kleinmans' analysis of the methodological characteristics of a humane approach to
contemporary world problems continues as follows:

Ultimately, we will have to engage the more ominous aspects
of globalization, such as the commercialization of suffering, the
commodification of experiences of atrocity and abuse, and the
pornographic uses of degradation. Violence in the media, and its
relation to violence in the streets and in homes, is already a subject
that has attracted serious attention from communities and from
scholars. Regarding the even more fundamental cultural question of
how social experience is being transformed in untoward ways, the
first issue would seem to be to develop historical, ethnographic, and
narrative studies that provide a more powerful understanding of the
cultural processes through which the global regime of disordered
capitalism alters the connections between collective experience and
subjectivity, so that moral sensibility, for example, diminishes or
becomes something frighteningly different: promiscuous, gratuitous,
unhinged from responsibility and action. There is a terrible legacy
here that needs to be contemplated. The transformation of epochs
is as much about changes in social experiences as shifts in social
structures and cultural representations; indeed, the three sites of
social transformation are inseparable. Out of their triangulation,
subjectivity too transmutes. (Kleinman and Kleinman 1997: 19)

This viewpoint relates not only to the understanding of past and present development contexts, but also to potential future ones, especially where suffering is likely to be involved and which can be anticipated:

> Well-intentioned intervention after the fact is no substitute for strong action to prevent atrocities from arising ... Perhaps it is time to admit that atrocity in the past does not discourage but in fact *invites* atrocity in the future. From the scandalous carnage of World War I to the innumerable murders of the Leninist and Stalinist regimes, the countless victims of the Holocaust (condensed into a single abstract figure, six million) to the bloody outrages in Bosnia and Rwanda, our age of atrocity slips into and out of consciousness with the casual appeal of a transient news item. We fail to decipher the clues that would rouse us to an alarmed vision. (Langer 1997: 54, 59)

Widening the moral community

Suffering, while individually felt in the pain of each discrete individual, is also, then, a social phenomenon – it has its roots all too often in the unnecessary infliction of that pain by social, cultural, economic and political mechanisms that could well be otherwise. Mourning can be for individual loss, but also for collective trauma – 'ethnic cleansing' in the Balkans, the 'disappearances' of the years of military dictatorship in Argentina, intercommunal atrocities in Rwanda, vicious civil war in Sierra Leone, the deep violence of colonialism in the Belgian Congo, the experience of hunger in the Ethiopian famine, or the post-cyclone devastation in Burma, made immeasurably worse by the incompetence and intransigence of the desperately corrupt military regime there.

The recognition of this collective dimension has fundamental moral, political and methodological implications. The key to these is the recognition that we are all complicit in one way or another – by our silences and our ignoring or turning away from these glaring problems and the obscene poverty of a vast mass of the human family; by allowing the activities of our 'democratically' elected governments and their actual secrecies, corruption and quiet violations of human rights in far-off places in the interests of business or 'national security'; through our consumption habits, which allow us to benefit, perhaps unconsciously, in the objectively negative and destructive dimensions of globalization and neo-imperialism; through the ways in which the media romanticize poverty and commodify other people's experience of starvation, abuse or atrocity. Methodologically we have to grasp the extent to which our 'scientific' and managerial approaches to development diminish the full dimensions of the experience of suffering, and to allow back into analysis a significantly cultural (including religious) dimension. As Vera Schwartz puts it, 'The Jewish view of suffering insists that pain can teach us something in proportion to our willingness to question the limits of human knowledge itself. Simply put, suffering both humbles us and clarifies our minds' (Schwartz 1997: 127). Suffering is perhaps the primary challenge to human knowledge, yet an epistemology of pain hardly exists (and, interestingly, the sketches for such a project that do exist are mainly in the realms of literature and art, not in the analyses of the social sciences – e.g. Sebold 2003).

The rather recently discovered field of the sociology of the body, for example, has yet to assimilate fully the fact that suffering is, often quite literally, inscribed on the body – through torture, illness, malnutrition, disfigurements caused by constant hard labour – and that such disfigurement is itself a cause of social stigma, loss of confidence and withdrawal. Anthropology, too, is complicit here: despite the critiquing of the moral and other consequences of cultural relativism, especially from the view point of the formerly colonized, 'this rethinking has not yet eroded a tendency, registered in many of the social sciences but perhaps particularly in anthropology, to confuse structural violence with cultural difference. Many are the ethnographies in which poverty and inequality are conflated with "otherness'" (Farmer 1997: 277). The notion of culture, then, is very loaded. Arguments for 'multiculturalism' or the rights and dignities of particular communities, 'tribes' or 'races', or even, as Amartya Sen has pointed out, of religions (Sen 2007), can easily become arguments for exclusion, stigmatization or persecution, of special privileges for some and the denial of those same resources or rights to others. 'Multiculturalism' is not a neutral term and is embedded in one dimension in the particular lifeworlds and experiences of specific communities, their historical experiences, local ecologies and social arrangements, and in another in the larger politics of an unevenly globalized world. This includes its cultural politics, which contains inevitably ideas and prejudices about ethnicity, gender, religion, class and the other classical dimensions of social inequality together with the agency of actors – individuals, on the one hand, negotiating their identities in a shifting socio-economic environment, and states and multinational actors (including, very centrally, business) with their own agendas of power and profit, on the other. The problem of suffering focuses these issues like perhaps no other, and for this reason must be located at the core of debates about globalization and about the nature (and responsibilities) of culture.

So, too, does the problem of suffering raise questions about 'professional' involvement in development. In much the same way that Ivan Illich has argued that the medical profession has become a major threat to health, so it might be argued that a culturally ill-informed development practice is a threat not only to health, but also to lifestyles, memories, rootedness and a strong sense of the self. Speaking of medically induced diseases Illich proposes that 'My argument is that the layman and not the physician has the potential perspective and effective power to stop the current iatrogenic epidemic' (Illich 1990: 12) and to reverse the counterproductivity of so much 'development' when measured against the ideals of human happiness (see McKibben 2007). He continues:

A professional and physician-based health-care system that has grown beyond critical bounds is sickening for three reasons: it must produce clinical damage that outweighs its potential benefits; it cannot but enhance even as it obscures the political conditions that render society unhealthy; and it tends to mystify and to expropriate the power of the individual to heal himself and to shape his or her environment. The medical and paramedical monopoly over hygienic methodology and technology is a glaring example of the political use of scientific achievement to strengthen industrial rather that personal growth. (Illich 1990: 16)

Even as the proportion of doctors, clinical tools and hospital beds has not significantly affected the emergence of disease patterns – morbidity is redefined but not reduced – so too the vast development and aid budgets at the disposal of development 'experts' have not significantly reduced the incidence of poverty or produced notable progress in the achievement of the laudable UN Millennium Goals. Large systems and their staffing with 'experts' in fact can and do easily produce what Illich terms 'social iatrogenesis':

I will speak of 'social iatrogenesis', a term designating all impairments to health that are precisely due to those socio-economic transformations which have been made attractive, possible, or necessary by the institutional shape health care has taken. Social iatrogenesis designates a category of aetiology that encompasses many forms. It obtains when medical bureaucracy creates ill health by generating increasing stress, by multiplying disabling dependence, by generating new painful needs, by lowering the levels of tolerance for discomfort or pain, by reducing the leeway that people are wont to concede to an individual when he suffers, and by abolishing even the right to self-care. Social iatrogenesis is at work when health care is turned into a standardized item, a staple; when all suffering is 'hospitalized' and when homes become inhospitable to birth, sickness and death; when the language in which people could experience their bodies is turned into a bureaucratic gobbledegook; or when suffering, mourning, and healing outside the patient role are labelled a form of deviance. (Illich 1990: 49)

As with medicine, so also with development that is not rooted in culture and genuine human needs.

As Illich rightly notes, many of the factors that influence human life and satisfaction are beyond the intervention of experts anyway. Supplementary to his notion of social iatrogenesis, he also proposes the concept of 'cultural iatrogenesis':

> It sets in when the medical enterprise saps the will of people to suffer their reality. It is a symptom of such iatrogenesis that the term 'suffering' has become almost useless for designating a realistic human response because it evokes superstition, sado-masochism, or the rich man's condescension to the lot of the poor. Professionally organized medicine has come to function as a domineering moral enterprise that advertises industrial expansion as a war against all suffering. It has thereby undermined the ability of individuals to face their reality, to express their own values, and to accept inevitable and often irremediable pain and impairment, decline and death. (Illich 1990: 133)

This is not to paint a gloomy picture of human life as nasty, brutish and short: it is to indicate that the barriers against it being nice, humane and long are often generated not by factors beyond human and social control, but by the very interventions that those same humans and societies, often in the name of progress, development, growth or science, impose on each other.

It is what Illich calls the 'specific counterproductivity' of too much or inappropriate institutional intervention that in his view brings about these effects and results not in the alleviation of poverty, but rather in its modernization.

> The persons most hurt by counterproductive institutionalization are usually not the poorest in monetary terms. The typical victims of the depersonalization of values are the powerless in a milieu made for the industrially enriched. Among the powerless may be people who are relatively affluent within their society or who are inmates of benevolent total institutions. Disabling dependence reduces them to modernized poverty. Policies meant to remedy the new sense of privation will not only be futile but will aggravate the damage. By promising more staples rather than protecting autonomy, they will intensify disabling dependence. (Illich 1990: 220–21)

Illich, unlike Kleinman and his collaborators, specifically includes development agencies, welfare, aid and international relief efforts among these counterproductive institutions. While this may be a difficult position to defend in contexts of humanitarian emergency, in broader structural terms we see here a convergence between the arguments against overinstitutionalized medicine and overinstitutionalized top-down development. The recovery of health and the recovery of ecological sanity and just development are parallel and interlinked processes. Given that a huge amount of suffering is man-made, the tools to counter this are at hand, but they do not reside by any means exclusively in technical and managerial methods, but in culture, values, spirituality, resistance, imagination and the ability to draw on experience in order to design a more desirable, rational, attractive and ecologically supportable future. If many of our current problems are the side effects of strategies that were designed to alleviate these very problems, then it is to this dysfunctionality of our planning processes that critical attention must be directed. And of course, as we have suggested, culture is implicated in this too – not only as a source of solutions, but often as the source of the pain. But if it is our civilization that has brought us to this impasse, then it is our civilization that must change. This is where the role of the cultural critic takes a central place and not a subservient role to that of the economist. If what lies after 'development' is the good life, then that life must be defined in cultural terms, but in full awareness of the fact that culture is not necessarily neutral in the generation of human suffering. The goal then becomes to nurture a culture that is genuinely humane, enriching and ecological and that builds and sustains the human relationships and economic patterns that contribute to the creation of the communities in which the best flowering of the human spirit can flourish without injustice and in full realization of our position as but one species in an intricate and marvellous total biosphere.

EIGHT

Towards a sociology of trauma: remembering, forgetting and the negotiation of memories of social violence

The notion of 'social suffering', then, has belatedly entered the vocabulary of the mainstream social sciences, especially in sociology and anthropology (Bourdieu et al. 1999; Kleinman et al. 1997), building on work that addressed the existence of violence as a central part of the fabric of everyday life in many developing societies (Scheper-Hughes 1992). Although this dimension of social analysis has not been extended as much as it should be, its very existence suggests a new mode of critical theory. This is especially so when it is triangulated with the concern for memory that has emerged in the social sciences at the same time (e.g. Connerton 1995; Freeman 1993; Rubin 1996; Tonkin 1992), and with the pervasive social violence of the contemporary world – war, development, crime, risk, domestic, caste and many other forms. This new form of critical theory transcends or at least complements the older Marxist and Frankfurt School varieties by substantially deepening the addressing of the actual existential issues that lie at the core of human social and personal life. Many forms of social inequality and social injustice are subtle and diffused through everyday life structures and experiences, and carry with them the hidden injuries that bruise and scar so many lives (O'Brian and Howard 1998). Suffering is the point at which the subjective and objective aspects of society so poignantly meet, and becomes the medium in which the *experience* of war, migration, 'development', colonization, state violence, crime and dispossession, both physical and psychic, is rendered.

This chapter is an attempt to sketch out some of the major outlines of a sociology of trauma as an integral part of development sociology, concentrating on experiences of development, war, colonization and other forms of social violence, and to demonstrate how memory and narratives of suffering are utilized as existential necessities in the face of such displacements, but also manipulated, mythologized and restructured to serve larger political and nationalist ends. Methodologically I will also continue to suggest that the centrality of narratives in accounts of social suffering imply a model of analysis and interpretation closer to that of medical anthropology than to conventional sociologies of development or of social change with their generally neutral stance and their exclusion of the subjectivities of the actors and victims (see, however, Clammer 2010b).

It is surprising and revealing that here we have stumbled on one of the great silences of the social sciences. For while there are developed sociologies of crime, elaborate sociologies of development, and many attempts at providing sociologies of social change, there is little effort to address the issue of systematic violence built in to these processes. In so far as this has occurred at all, it has been largely left to historians, who have not, however, for the most part drawn any significant theoretical conclusions from their narratives. Here I will suggest that of particular significance sociologically are the relationships between memory, forgetting, mythologizing and negotiating social violence (as distinct, that is, from natural disasters and personal domestic conflicts experienced by individuals) as a social process; that is to say, the ways in which societies memorialize or suppress and inevitably edit collective memories of their own violence or the suffering of the violence of others.

The memorialization of violence

Most societies have recognized forms for the memorialization of war or other extreme situations of experienced social violence. Many of these take the form of physical memorials – monuments, statues, cenotaphs, specially constructed sites of memory such the Vietnam Memorial Wall in Washington DC, or the architecturally very similar Heiwa no Ishiji in Okinawa commemorating the enormous casualties, many of them civilian, in the fighting on those islands during the last big land campaign of the Second World War. Others are preserved sites of catastrophe or horror – the A Bomb Dome in Hiroshima, the Buchenwald concentration camp near Weimar in Germany and its counterparts elsewhere in Germany and Poland, or the massive monuments and acres of graveyards that mark the carnage sites of the First World War in northern France. Many of these sites are linked to nearby museums, as in Hiroshima and Okinawa, or to special days of ritual memorialization. But does any museum yet exist for the victims of maldevelopment, or of the displacements and violence that have followed from 'development', as in the oil delta of Nigeria or the plantations and goldfields of Amazonia? In fact many of the remaining public rituals of modern life are related to the memorialization of events of social violence, but a closer examination of them suggests that they are rarely concerned with the causes of the events that they recall, but are rather subtle forms of nationalism, self-glorification of the victors, or opportunities to assert the victim status of the losers.

Memorialization, then, can take many forms, especially, on the one hand, by those who perceive of themselves as victors or civilizers, and, on the other, by those who perceive themselves not so much as losers but as victims, and whose memories are consequently reconstructed rather differently (for a comparative study of Germany and Japan in this respect, see Buruma 1994). Often lost in between these positions are the memories of those who participated and suffered – destruction of home, death of family members, rape, exile, displacement, experience of concentration camps, and the loss of possessions, hopes and futures that would have accompanied a normal existence untraumatized by conflict and violence. While public memorials send one message, the voices of the injured masses are often lost, or more likely turned to other and more politicized ends by the managers of national myths.

Many varieties of this co-option of memory take place. As Kali Tal asks in her study of the literatures of trauma,

> What happens when a survivor's story is retold (and revised) by a writer who is not a survivor? How are survivors' stories adapted to fit and then contained within the dominant structure of cultural and political discourse? (Tal 1996: 3)

Her own answer is that traumatic events

> are written and rewritten until they become codified and narrative form gradually replaces content as the focus of attention. For example the Holocaust has become a metonym, *not* for the actual series of events that occurred in Germany and the occupied territories before and during World War II, but for the set of symbols that reflect the formal codification of that experience. There is a recognizable set of literary and filmic conventions that comprise the 'Holocaust' text. These conventions are so well defined that they may be reproduced in endless recombination to provide us with a steady stream of additions to the genre. (Tal 1996: 6)

A key sociological issue, then, becomes that of analysing and deconstructing the politicization of memory even as the victims themselves attempt to resist the pressure to revise their own stories or give up control over the representation of their experiences to powerful forces: commodification, romanticization, current political goals, or the desire of the wider community to forget or to resist the perpetual reminders that the survivors represent. Refugees, or even long 'assimilated' minorities originally displaced by conflict, globalization, colonialism or other forces, will be well aware of the discrimination and exclusion to which they are so often subject, despite their own innocence in the conditions that led to their displacement in the first place. Thus although memory is a key category here, so also are forgetting and the active erasure of history.

Of course the current political and cultural situation of the community of survivors is of major significance here. While Jews in the United States, comprising now a powerful and wealthy lobby with above-average educational levels, can keep the memory of the Holocaust very much alive, this is less the case for descendants of the survivors of the Turkish holocaust of Armenians, denied in the country in which it was perpetuated and only known to many people through recent films or novels such as Louis de Bernières's massive *Birds without Wings* (de Bernières 2005), or the victims of the great Bengal famine of the 1940s which killed millions despite the availability of food in India as a whole. The individual trauma and existential experiences of suffering on the part of the individual and the corresponding attempts to give some sense of meaning or continuity to life, while felt at some level that is beyond sociological understanding or explanation, are nevertheless culturally coded and are expressed or suppressed in political and sociological contexts that fundamentally influence their modes of presentation. Tal indeed goes so far as to argue that survivor texts (testimonies, narratives, memoirs) pass invariably through a sequence that starts with 'sacred' survivor texts, through what she calls 'contextualized' texts to terminate in 'appropriated' texts (Tal 1996: 59). While I think that her general typology is correct, she overlooks the dialectical nature of the process and the fact that there are multiple feedback loops, such that the appropriation of memory characteristically triggers new forms of testimony concerned with recapturing in its 'purity' the original event and its representation. In the development context this can and does take the form of the 'developees' discovering what the developers are saying about them (anthropological texts or development plans for example) and responding in their own terms to the perceived misrepresentations contained in those texts.

An event, especially a traumatic one, is a floating signifier. 'Vietnam', '9/11', the genocide of Pol Pot, ethnic 'cleansing' in Bosnia or Rwanda, or the displacements caused by the flooding of vast areas of farmland by the Kabini dam in south India are not all simple objective events that can be recovered in their entirety by historical or sociological analysis. They are, rather, constantly subject to revision and reinterpretation, a fact that keeps university scholars in business for generations. As Philip Beidler suggests in his study of the literature generated by the war in Vietnam, the collective mythology or cultural myths (in this case in and of the United States) predetermined to a great extent the understanding of what were at the time current events, a process that also works retroactively as the past is reinterpreted as new cultural myths emerge and have a profound if subterranean influence on future decisions and readings (Beidler 1982).

When we speak in the abstract of 'memory' it is often assumed to be some sort of mental category, when we should know in fact from the literature on the anthropology of memory that it is profoundly social. But an anthropological conclusion is not always drawn from this, notably that those who are the possessors of memories (in this context traumatic ones) find themselves occupying a strange and ambiguous social location. Eric Leed, in his study of the complex identity issues faced by surviving veterans of the First World War trench warfare and building on the rites of passage theory of the anthropologist Arnold Van Gennap, suggests that, unlike normal ritual participants (such as in a wedding or graduation ceremony), who pass from one status to another via a brief liminal state during which one has shed one's old status but is not yet fully incorporated into the new one, veterans forever continue to occupy a liminal state. In Leed's words, 'He derives all of his features from the fact that he has crossed the boundaries of distinctive social worlds, from peace to war, and back. He has been reshaped by his voyage along the margins of civilization, a voyage in which he has been presented with wonders, curiosities and monsters – things that can only be guessed at by those who remain at home' (Leed 1979: 193–4). Identity is transformed not only for the survivor of extreme violence, but also for those with whom s/he must thereafter associate, since the psychic and experiential relationship between the two parties has forever changed. The survivor, far from being necessarily or permanently a hero, is suddenly a disturber of the peace: 'He is a runner of the blockade men erect against knowledge of "unspeakable" things. About these he aims to speak, and in so doing he undermines, without intending to, the validity of existing norms' (Des Pres 1976: 42).

Strategies of containment

The public memorialization or appropriation of memories of violence is not the only strategy available. Among the most important attempts to come to terms with the traumas of social violence have been the Truth and Reconciliation Commissions that have been established in post-apartheid South Africa and elsewhere, and the Winter Soldier movement among Vietnam War veterans. The essential difference between them lies in the fact that in the latter ex-soldiers who had participated in or witnessed atrocities confess to their peers, but not to the victims, who are far away in Vietnam, whereas in the former there is not only public confession, but also personal confrontation between the victims and the perpetrators (Paris 2000). In the one case there does often occur genuine reconciliation and restitution, while in the other, while providing catharsis to the perpetrators or witnesses, little is done to build bridges between them and their victims.

The sheer number of societies emerging from conflict in the contemporary world (Cambodia, Afghanistan, Iraq, Sudan, Sudan, Northern Ireland, Bosnia, Kosovo, Columbia, among others) has given rise to a whole body of analysis and scholarship addressing the issues of post-conflict reconstruction, reconciliation, peace-building and the prevention of future conflict, security, physical reconstruction, reparations, restoration of property, and restoration of trust applicable in these all too common situations (Newman and Schnabel 2002; Lederach 2005). This literature dovetails in significant respects with the growing sociological literature on risk and uncertainty, much of it stimulated by Ulrich Beck's seminal book on the subject, *Risk Society* (Beck 1992), and with the analysis of the social effects of natural disasters and the growing recognition of the critical and truly global nature of ecological damage, pollution and humanly induced climate change. But there is little in the development studies literature that addresses the similar problems that arise from many 'development' initiatives – civil wars, oil spills, blood diamonds, forced migration and displacement, plantation agriculture and ecological devastation and even civilizational collapse (see, however, Diamond 2005 on the latter; and Hecht and Cockburn 1990 on environmental destruction). The links between conflict studies, natural disaster analysis and development studies, however, are potentially very strong and fruitful, and out of a dialogue between them might emerge a new vocabulary not only of crisis *management*, but also of crisis *understanding*, not only in terms of causes but also, and most significantly, reflecting the perspectives of the victims.

Much of the literature that does exist is technical in nature and compartmentalized within specific approaches or disciplines. But, as John Paul Lederach points out in his sensitive and experience-based study of mechanisms of reconciliation and peace-building, technical solutions are only part of the picture: behind them lie the narratives of suffering that are the soil out of which existential as well as physical reconstruction must grow, and without engagement with and listening to these needs no future lasting peace (or development) is possible. We need, then, to work at three nested levels: the grasping of the place of violence in its manifold forms in the constitution of contemporary life; an analysis of the dialectical relationship between war, development and suffering; and an understanding of the narrative strategies that survivors of social violence may deploy in giving shape to their experiences and defending them from appropriation.

Reflections on violence

In approaching social violence it is necessary to incorporate an interpretative dimension that retains the centrality of subjectivities, intersubjectivity and reflexivity, in which cognition and emotion, body, selfhood and issues of identity formation and maintenance are all encapsulated. In her study of a mixed Jewish–Palestinian village in Israel that has become an internationally known centre for peace education and dialogue, Grace Feuerverger notes that typical encounters at the 'School for Peace' workshops in the village would go through three phases: what she calls 'narratives of vulnerability' in which participants who saw themselves as the oppressed (the Palestinians) would have to encounter those they saw at the oppressors (the Jewish Israelis), followed by a longing for legitimacy in which claims for identity on both sides were staked out, and finally a deconstruction of the discourse of victimhood that not only had the Palestinian participants brought to the encounter, but surprisingly many of the Jews as well (Feuerverger 2001: ch. 4). The perceptions of social violence experienced by the minority group – the 'victims' – were substantially modified when brought into reciprocal contact with the perceptions of the 'oppressors' (see also Barenboim and Said 2002, where the same issues with the same national-religious groups were approached through cultural, and specifically musical, contact).

In 1970 Hannah Arendt wrote her now classic essay *On Violence* in which she argued that public life was being progressively colonized by violent practices and ideologies (Arendt 1970). In his extended commentary on Arendt's essay, Fred Dallmayr suggests that while this was written at the height of the Vietnam War, the history of the world since then has vindicated this view, and that we have witnessed the progressive erosion of the rule of law both domestically and internationally, and, despite all the talk of civil society, actually possess a weakened public sphere that can little influence the outcome or nature of political, business or development decisions (Dallmayr 2004: ch. 6). Tracing the lineage of ideas about the 'purity' or regenerative power of violence from Georges Sorel through Frantz Fanon to Jean-Paul Sartre, even in 1970 Arendt saw social violence as increasingly underwritten by emerging ideas in sociobiology and biological anthropology, in which violence and aggression are seen as being integral parts of human nature and as necessary to evolution, and by ideas in social theory, especially the preoccupation with power and with the idea that war pertains to the essence of states. Even Derrida put his prominence as a post-structuralist behind this effort, arguing for the primacy of transgression such that even justice involves what he calls 'irruptive violence' and indeed requires it, something that places violence beyond theoretical rationality and hence beyond the reach of any real intelligibility or human understanding, as an un-deconstructed form of 'madness' (Derrida 1992).

The thrust of Arendt's position, however, was not only to describe or document the existence and spread of social violence a quarter of a century after the last great global conflagration, but equally to argue for a more civilized conception of politics, on the one hand, and, on the other, to draw attention to the forgotten factor in all this academic theorizing of violence: the victims. These are what her commentator Bat-Ami Bar On calls the 'subjects' – those who actually experience the 'shattered worlds and shocked understandings' of their worlds and whose lives are shaped by the 'work of mourning', as was Arendt's own life as refugee, Jew and exile (Bar On 2002). The understanding of violence involves several interacting levels: a grasp of its progenitors (social systems of oppression, imperialism, resource competition, development, clashing ideologies and religious antagonisms, and so forth); the specific mechanisms of the sparking of actual violence from these underlying factors and the dynamics of conflict once it emerges, including its course and resolution or termination; and, very significantly, the experience of those involved, both perpetrators and victims, even if their respective claims may not be morally comparable.

In many cases, furthermore, the violence may not be acute as in war, but chronic as in situations of maldevelopment, such as in the Brazilian *favelas* studied by Nancy Scheper-Hughes in which the brutality of everyday life is the consequence not only of crime, drugs, the easy availability of weapons and police violence, but also of poor or non-existent health facilities, lack of sanitation, severely substandard housing, lack of access to education, male machismo, poverty, extensive unemployment and distorted patterns of urban development. Social violence certainly need not be equated with war, but often, as in Foucault's conception of power, is pervasive, uncentred, yet acts on all around it. Or, as Susan Buck-Morss puts it, 'The metaphysical problem of evil in the modern world is not only that of intentionally inflicted pain, but of the cultural dismissal of this pain; not only the fact of Auschwitz, but of the everydayness of its horror' (Buck-Morss 2000: 259).

The anthropology of memory and the anthropology of suffering

In a revealing and in many ways chilling essay, Mart Bax analyses how, behind the noisy rhetoric and ideological and religious posturing that much of the Western media took to be the truth about the vicious conflict in the former Yugoslavia, there were in fact 'micro-foundations' or factors in local social organization that led both to the outbreak of large-scale violence and to its perpetuation in smaller but longer-term ways. When Bax insisted that one of his local informants take him to see a monument raised to commemorate Cetnik (Serbian) victims of World War II pogroms by Ustasi or Croats operating independently or under the authority of local warlords near the village of Surmanci, he discovered the monument to have been blown up by Croat partisans. When the anthropologist commented on this, the informant replied: 'We killed the dead because they kept them alive.... To us here, Surmanci is dead ... we want to forget' (Bax 2004: 180). As Bax pointedly states, this is the ultimate form of ethnic cleansing.

Bax's study goes on to show how a long history of violence and enmity between even closely neighbouring communities, and held in abeyance by the stronger hand of the state during the communist period, even if inflamed after the death of Tito by ethno-nationalist extremists, never ceased and was in fact preserved and perpetuated by collective rituals, especially those focused on war monuments, which in this context are also often mass graves. In the area studied by Bax, animosity dates back at least to the mid-sixteenth century, when under Ottoman domination certain small towns, in this case the large village of Zitom, were largely Muslim in population and controlled the surrounding areas through the collection of tribute, and exacting tolls on traffic between the interior and the coast and between the market towns and the villages and hamlets. With the beginning of the collapse of the Ottoman Empire in the late nineteenth century, Serbs from Montenegro captured Zitom, killing or exiling its Muslim population and provoking vigilante and resistance groups among the local Croats. The bitter animosities created at that time were kept alive by memory and further fuelled by World War II atrocities, including the mass slaughter of most of the population of Zitom, and subsequent local policies under the Tito regime, including that, until the late 1960s, all Croat families with any links to the Ustasa movement (meaning in practice all of them), had to pay off so-called 'war debts'. Humiliation continued even beyond that; for example, with Croats being forced to work on the monument to the Cetniks at Surmanci.

These memories lived on, even after the collapse of formal Serb control in 1992 and the economic boom brought about by the

Marian apparitions at the village of Medjugorje. Bax suggests that conventional theories of ethnicity fail to account for these kind of phenomena: 'It will be clear that this is only one of many possible models for conceptualizing and experiencing cultural differences and similarities, for different people have different notions and ideas about what determines who they are and to what category of people they belong' (Bax 2004: 185). What is needed is, rather, a dynamic theory of identity which includes mechanisms of inclusion and exclusion and competition between groups. In a peasant society people may construct notions of identity in line with their own experiences, rather than with the official state forms of categorization, which is essentially what has happened in the former Yugoslavia with its deep historical, ethnic, religious and cultural divides, animated by a long record of violence and intolerance between competing rather than cooperating social groups, a situation equally familiar in many development situations. Ritual sites become naturally the locations at which dramas of dependency and domination play out, in this case on the part of the Serb dominators and the Croats, which is also why with the crumbling of Serb power all of the ritual sites of memory/ power that Bax could locate (sixteen in all) had been destroyed by Croat militants eager to kill even the dead of their former oppressors. Forgetting is as of much importance as remembering when either the individual or the society are confronted with traumatic and tragic events that cannot be assimilated into the normal frameworks of everyday life. This can be as true of the disruptions of development as it is of war and civil conflict, and the nexus between war and development is one that has still to be systematically explored historically and in the contemporary world.

War, development, suffering

Actual experiences of suffering, while certainly culturally coded and memorialized, differ little in their existential qualities from place to place or time to time, but it is still instructive to ask to what extent the context of the violence that has occasioned the suffering has shifted, and with it differing interpretations of that suffering. War has been a part of human experience for probably most of human history. Development in a systematic sense has been part of that experience for a much shorter time. Mass-technologically mediated destruction, however, is relatively new, as is massively aid-funded development with all its attendant and now well-documented problems. In low-intensity warfare and localized development, the possibility of some human contact between perpetrator and victim remains – something that deeply affects post-conflict reconstruction – while in high-technology killing there is no such mediation. In this respect it shares many characteristics with terrorism, for in both the victims are largely random and anonymous and are simply ciphers for the society that is being attacked.

The great historical shifts of the past two centuries – industrialization and its corresponding rural displacements and urbanization, colonialism and its confusions, civil wars and international conflicts, accelerating ecological destruction and massive population displacements and the generation of huge numbers of refugees among the most significant ones – have likewise brought huge suffering in their wake, suffering concealed behind the claim that the benefits have far outweighed the disadvantages of development and modernization. Development itself, despite its progressive aura, has proved in many cases to be violent. This violence includes the social displacements that it has entailed; cultural and language destruction; vast environmental damage and loss of biodiversity; the corruption, militarization, racism, gender inequality and caste-ism that have accompanied so many development projects; and the indebtedness and corresponding tax burdens and 'belt-tightenings' of the citizens of countries whose governments have indulged in irresponsible borrowing from the multilateral lending institutions (Roy 2002). As Bax has shown, many modern civil wars are not primarily about ethnicity, but have much more deep-rooted sources in historical memories and experiences, exacerbated by subsequent political cultures and structures and by the maldistribution of development, and are worse in their intensity and propensity to atrocity precisely because the combatants or local civilians *do* actually know each other, a fact tragically underlined not only in the Balkans, but equally in such examples as Northern Ireland and, perhaps the most extreme case, Rwanda.

Given these facts, we are faced with a complex mapping of the possible narratives of suffering and the routes through these to recovery. These can be illustrated by looking briefly at three case studies of the experience of social violence: the only recently concluded (at least formally) civil war in Sri Lanka; caste riots in Bihar (India); and the atomic bombing of Hiroshima, as each illuminates a different but related facet of the ways in which violence, memory and recovery are related, sometimes in paradoxical ways.

In her study of the militant Tamil movement in Sri Lanka, Chitra Sivakumar shows how 'what is missing in this concern for social suffering is the possibility of a reversed situation, where violence itself can be an expression of unfathomable pain and anguish' (Sivakumar 2001: 304–5) in a situation where the perception of an intolerable predicament led many members of a minority group to accept violence and armed struggle as the only way left to establish a degree of autonomy, security and identity compatible with their cultural and political concepts of selfhood. Sivakumar attempts to show this through the personal narratives of some of the leaders of the major Sri Lankan Tamil militant organizations, arguing that these narratives embody a theory of violence and social transformation that arises out of anguish, anxiety and frustration, and is as such, the product of a certain graspable logic. The discriminatory policies of the Sri Lankan government in education, language and land ownership provide the political basis for such narratives, rather than there being hostility to individual Sinhalese as such. As one of her informants graphically put it,

If blood needs to be shed, we will shed it. Most crucially, it is a question of being alive, and then to be able to live in self-respect and dignity as Tamils. Instead of getting killed by Sinhalese, we would rather fight and die. If we don't like to engage in violence, what is the option? We subject ourselves to being killed by the Sinhalese and let the whole Tamil race be erased from the soil of Sri Lanka. (Sivakumar 2001: 315–16)

Sivakumar's other informants provide variations of the same story: violence as the only option left when faced with an intolerable and very dangerous (and for many Tamils murderous) situation in which non-violent struggles, which had continued for the previous three decades, had proved fruitless. What she and they do not directly point out is that this was a crisis of development and misapplied development policies as well as of ethnic and political discrimination. The deprivation of the fruits of development had bred the very conditions under which violent attempts to seek both dignity and resources would seem to be the only remaining option.

The traditional social imagery of the Tamils was conservative, security-conscious, religious and oriented to education. The vicious anti-Tamil riots of 1983 radically changed this posture. That event was the collective trauma that precipitated a violent response, a counter-violence as an act of balancing that was designed to redress the shattering effect of the initial violence on its peaceful victims and to restore the self-image of the survivors. In his moving study of the Tamil victims of violence, Valentine Daniel shows how even long after the experience of torture or atrocity, the pain is still seen as being quite literally inscribed on the body. When all photographs of the disappeared have been destroyed, even parents begin to find it hard to recall the features of their lost loved ones; totally unrealistic expectations that dead or disappeared family members would one day appear took root; when the experience could not be spoken of at all, the surviving victims retreated into silence (Daniel 1997). Trauma is not a passing event, but leaves lasting traces on the cognitive, affective and ontological dimensions of the victims (Young 1997), who, even years later having married, established careers and to all external purposes 'recovered', still carry un-erasable scars that surface in dreams, suicides decades after the original trauma has passed, or in guilt for having survived when so many others perished. This is very true of Holocaust survivors, for example, as Lawrence Langer has so eloquently documented in his studies (Langer 1997). One often overlooked consequence is lack of fundamental trust, in individuals, governments or the ways of the world in general. In the Sri Lankan case, Sivakumar suggests that 'Violence and death became metaphors for Tamil recovery' (Sivakumar 2001: 334). But to live with this extreme existential condition, she suggests, requires in her terms a 'transformative hermeneutics of death' in which cognitively or at least publicly fear of death is denied and martyrdom becomes a route to achieving (posthumous) heroic stature. In the formerly Tamil-controlled zones of northeastern Sri Lanka the ritualization of this existential extremity differed little from that in Bosnia: memorials, war graves as semi-sacred sites, songs of heroism and martyrdom, and the annual celebration of *Mavirarnal* or 'Great Heroes and Martyrs Day'. Death for the Sri Lankan Tamil militants 'became a polysemic emblem, signifying not merely the recovery of dignity, honour, self-respect, nationhood and freedom, but also an instrument for the recovery of the Tamil ontic self in its "hiddenness" – the sense of authentic being destroyed by the originating trauma' (Sivakumar 2001: 336–7).

This hermeneutic, however, has an ensnaring quality, for the violence it engenders is not only directed against the military and police of the perceived oppressor, but is also turned inwards. Violent internecine struggles took place among the rival Tamil liberation organizations, resulting in killings, assassinations, elimination of members who attempted to leave or defect to a rival group, and the torture of members seen as having infringed some rule of the camp or organization. Likewise it was directed outwards at innocent non-Tamil civilians, whose only 'crime' was being Sinhalese and whose age or sex was immaterial, atrocities being committed against small children or the aged for example simply because of their ethnicity. In often less expected sociological outcomes, it fuelled a culture of pornography and promiscuity on the principle of make merry today as tomorrow we may well die; the generation of a large number of orphans and widows; the understandable unwillingness of young women to marry a militant; changes in the nature of play and child-hood experiences among children growing up in militant-controlled zones or buffer and contested zones of great insecurity and instabil-ity; huge physical destruction of once familiar neighbourhoods; and daily insecurity leading to the almost total cessation of cultural life. Violence as the new social imaginary of the Tamil militants soon began to consume its own children, the attempted reconstruction of the self through violence leading inexorably to the denial of other, far more significant, aspects of personhood.

Another facet of the prism is provided by Badri Narayan Tewari in his study of caste riots in central Bihar between 1970 and 1990 (Tewari 2001) in which inter-caste violence broke out over perform-ances of dramas featuring Chuharmal, a folk hero of the lower castes of the region, who represents the victory of the downtrodden over the upper, wealthier and landowning castes. While the low castes are eager to keep the legend alive and to see it performed, the 'feudal castes' (to use Tewari's terminology) are just as eager to suppress it, by violence if necessary. This latter strategy is indeed one to which they have resorted, in one notorious incident by shooting the actor playing the role of Chuharmal while he was performing on stage during a dance-drama in the village of Ekauni in June 1978. In this case a folk 'memory' has become a badge of caste identity, and despite its mythical origins has become the line of division and source of violence between upper and lower castes, both of which retain the 'memory', but for entirely opposite reasons. Its framing role in the generation of caste identities makes it a genuine instance of social or collective memory, and to keep it alive as a social force it is not simply sufficient to recollect the original memory, but to reinforce it through repetition and its inscription in a number of cultural sites and activities, including monuments, religious rituals, plays, folk tales and family lore. While the forces of social resistance (the deprived castes) want actively to preserve these memories and performances, the local power elite equally wishes to erase them. Memory – or its surrogate, cultural myth – becomes the site and instigator of struggle for recognition and social justice (Tewari 2001: 355).

For the lower castes these 'memories' are now strongly reinforced by upper-caste acts of violence, including the public murder of the actor depicting Chuharmal, and at least four other murders since then. Tewari suggests that the structure of memories in central Bihar is largely determined by the social location of the actors. In a society deeply divided by caste, class, religion and a highly unequal distribution of social, economic and political power, and of the fruits of development including levels of village electrification, access to land and irrigation water, market access and availability of rural credit, there is no master narrative of identity, but rather fragmentation and polarization. Most of the land is owned by upper-class people, while most of the lower class are landless labourers, artisans or marginal subsistence farmers on the least productive land. Yet demographically the 'Backward Castes' together with the members of the Scheduled Castes (Dalits or so-called 'untouchables') and Tribals (the term still officially used in India) comprise over 50 per cent of the total population. In central Bihar we see a classic instance of concentration of wealth in the hands of a small group of landlords and large farmers coexisting with extensive poverty, deprivation and exclusion for more than half of the population. As Tewari phrases it, 'Their long history of subjugation and discrimination and their growing aspirations, restlessness and assertiveness in the face of upper caste groups unwillingness to relinquish their power and privilege, explain, to some extent, the growth of violence in

Bihar' (Tewari 2001: 359). In a society where literacy is low and oral culture predominates among the lower castes, myth and folk memories become the tools of identity and a means of protest, fed in Bihar by the existence of many travelling theatre groups often with radical political ideologies, and by the ritual performing of the myth that keeps the folk memory alive.

In very diverse places and contexts we see remarkably similar mechanisms at work for negotiating the interface between social violence and social memory, whether these situations be ones of war, civil conflict or maldevelopment. We most certainly see the conflict of interests between those whose agenda is to keep alive memories of social violence, injustice and social suffering, and those who wish to suppress or 'tame' those memories. These conflicts are animated and informed by differing hermeneutics: the radically differing Serb and Croat versions of Yugoslav history; not only differing Sinhalese and Tamil versions of the sources of conflict in Sri Lanka, but also competing versions among the rival Tamil militant groups; the different texts of the Chaharmal legend circulating in Bihar and 'owned' by different caste groups; the landlords and peasants of James Scott's celebrated study of rural resistance in a Malaysia undergoing rapid modernization and, for some, development (Scott 1985).

In her study of the memorialization of the Hiroshima atomic bombing, Lisa Yoneyama illustrates how the memory of war, or in this case one overwhelmingly traumatic event in the context of a war, has resulted in a complex and contested politics and hermeneutics of history (Yoneyama 1999). The multiple formulating and reformulating of the bombing of 6 August 1945 include debates over the nature and orientation of the Peace Memorial Park that now occupies the former downtown commercial district that was the epicentre of the bombing and of the various monuments that it contains; the spatial politics of the 'taming of the memoryscape' through the rebuilding of the city and its self-conscious repositioning of itself not as a city with memories of militarism (the reason it was selected as a possible target), but as an international city of peace; the shifting nature of the narratives, or what Yoneyama calls 'testimonial practices', of the survivors; the nature and contents of the museum that stands at one end of the Peace Park next to an international conference centre; and the very contentious issue of the (currently marginal) location of a memorial to the Korean forced labourers who were also victims of the bombing. The result is that Hiroshima – in common with other highly charged memory sites such as Auschwitz (Webber 1992) – attracts what Yoneyama calls an 'excess of memory', highly politicized memories of great social density or weight. Structurally the issues in these various cases of civil war, international war and underdevelopment are similar. If Hiroshima and the Nazi death camps are now seen as universal symbols of social suffering, and the folk rituals of a Bihar village as very localized ones, they share very similar formal characteristics, including resistance to the erasure of memory and its intense politicization.

War/development, memory/narrative

In studies of Latin America and Africa, in particular, a number of scholars, including Kay Warren (2003) and Patricia Marchak (1999), have pointed to what Warren calls 'heterogeneous formations of violence on a global scale', notably convergence of forms of violence across cultures and the social and political dimensions and consequences, including counter-insurgency states in Latin America and South Asia and the violence perpetrated by both insurgents and the state in such contexts, colonial and neocolonial regimes, the globalization formed and fed by predatory capitalism, the chronic violence that accompanies weak or failed states, and the unstable nature of border zones. These large-scale forms are reflected in their sociological and cultural consequences: the blurring of the line between the military and civilians, lost of trust within one's group and towards surrounding groups, opportunism and cycles of uncertainty and insecurity, and the fact that endemic violence unmakes both morality and community. Mixed in with these are complex patterns of colonial history, population displacement, land issues, neoliberal forms of globalization, identity and gender politics, ethnicity and the uncertain effects of peacekeeping operations, humanitarian interventions, and post-conflict reconciliation and reconstruction. State terrorism – terrorism by the state against its own people, often in Latin America with the complicity of elements within the powerful Catholic Church – further intensifies the chronic insecurity of everyday life, when denouncements, disappearances, and torture are the background against which everyday life is lived, where there is no clear boundary between personal opinion and political heresy and where there is no real civil society separate from the state. All of these characteristics are typical of the developmental state and of its more extreme manifestations in the mixtures of capitalist-led development, state violence, corruption and cronyism and tolerated crime that have marked some developing societies in Central America, Latin America, Africa and parts of Southeast Asia.

Studies such as those by Leed and Beidler, cited earlier, focused on wars and the postwar experiences of veterans. But in the development context, as well as in the war situation, attention must necessarily shift to the civilians, those who suffer despite being non-combatants or bystanders in a process of development or displacement, or who even suffer brutally at the hands of their own 'protectors', as was the case in Okinawa, where so painful are these memories that elderly survivors are deeply reluctant to talk about them, yet are constantly reminded of militarism by the huge US bases on the islands (Ishihara 2001). This has a number of anthropological implications. The first is the linking of social violence to its social context. Past forms have been largely associated with conventional wars and with the internal terrorism of many forms of state socialism (Fulbrook 2000). But newer forms are increasingly associated with developmentalism in some form or another: globalization, resource competition, the failure of postcolonial states, corruption, militarization, cronyism and ethnic conflict, factors that have seen once-rich countries such as Zimbabwe, Burma or the Philippines sink towards the bottom of all conventional development indicators lists.

The second implication is the increasing salience of the language of human rights in assessing development progress, aid and the combating of social violence. While many activists now draw on this language, as it stands at present the Universal Declaration of Human Rights (UDHR) is not fully comprehensive, especially when applied to abuses arising from non-democratically conceived and applied development policies. For, as Anthony Woodiwiss points out,

> although Article 4 declares that 'everyone has the right to life, liberty and the security of person', many of the subsequent articles make it clear that the state may deprive anyone of these rights, provided only that this is not done arbitrarily or with the use of directly inflicted pain. In other words, the UDHR in no way reduces the inequality of power between the state and the citizen but instead, in the name of the limited form of reciprocity summarized by the term human dignity, imposes some limits on the possible consequences of such inequality by insisting that the state as well as the citizenry should be subject to the rule of law. (Woodiwiss 2005: 6)

The UDHR sees the problem of social violence in legal rather than sociological terms, and the creation of the International Court at the Hague has extended this principle by now acknowledging that individuals, including heads of state, who carry out acts of war and violence even within their own 'sovereign' boundaries are no longer immune from international law, and recognizing that crimes against humanity no longer have any geographical boundaries. In situations of war or extreme internal suppression such as genocide or ethnocide this makes good sense. But what of the slower violence of so many development policies and projects – of the displacements caused by dams, the destruction of human and natural habitats through deforestation and industrial pollution, the massive consequences of climate change in the Third World caused by industrialization, overconsumption and vehicle use in the First World, and the destruction of agriculture and the generation of huge number of environmental refugees by these activities? Against these there are no laws.

The third is that, while the anthropological analysis of memorialization and ritualization of memory is a valid approach, in itself it does little to explain or prevent the social violence and suffering. What anthropology should point to is a more comprehensive theory of violence, and some steps towards this are indeed made by Michael Jackson in his work on African societies. Jackson suggests, on the basis of detailed case studies of social violence in Africa, that

> Unless one has been caught up in a war and experienced the terror that comes from knowing that hundreds of heavily-armed individuals are bent on one's annihilation, it is hard to realize that most violence is not motivated by evil, greed, lust, ideology or aggression. Strange as it may seem, most violence is defensive. (Jackson 2005: 57)

Building on William James, Jackson suggests that the primary motivation of violence is fear – that if one does not kill, one will be killed, by the enemy or even by one's own organization (as we saw in the Sri Lankan case). Constant anxiety and the fear and vulnerability that come with it are what, in this model, provoke the torching, shootings, taunting and abusing: violent activity that conceals the fear and impotence beneath it, and represents the cry for recognition and voice denied the perpetrator in the real world.

This is an interesting theory, but it has its weaknesses. It suppresses the injustices, powerlessness, deprivation (relative and absolute) and sense of victimhood that come from exclusion, displacement, loss of dignity and the ability to act meaningfully in the world that come from so many experiences of unsought social change. It also overlooks the extent to which, while fear is undoubtedly a major component in initiating participation in violence against a perceived enemy, in many cases sadism exists that, whatever its ultimate psychological causes, is indeed evil and has profound implications for the understanding of self and of others. This Klaus Theweleit has shown in his study of the pre-war German *Freikorps*, the vicious militia formed in the closing months of the First World War to fight the perceived Bolshevik threat on Germany's eastern border and later the internal left in general during the ensuing Weimar Republic, many of whose members later formed the core membership of the violent elements in the Nazi Party in its rise to power during and after the 1930s (Theweleit 1987, 1989; Clammer 2010b). The weakness of a purely 'ritual' theory of war, as Jackson recognizes, is that,

> although war and peace are both products of the same forcefield, and may be construed as variations on the theme of renewal, war rapidly becomes entropic – transforming social distinction into radical otherness, taking life rather than creating it, and losing the ludic power that gives myth and ritual their regenerative power. To invoke the Bambara metaphor, fire gives birth not to fire but to ashes – which is to say that the social ceases to reproduce itself and produces the antisocial. (Jackson 2005: 72).

Fear produces fear: the reciprocal form of the fear of the perpetrators of violence is fear in those upon whom it has been visited. An important element in Jackson's account of violence is what he terms 'the prose of suffering' – the ways in which the people in his field situation (Sierra Leone in the wake of a long civil war that had torn apart the country for a decade and generated thousands of refugees) had negotiated and come to understand that violence. As he points out, a favourite anthropological theme has long been that of initiation; and initiation, often accompanied by the infliction of pain or deprivation, is a way in which the neophytes acquire the virtues of fortitude and imperturbability (Jackson 2005: 143). In much of the African world-view, pain is seen as an unavoidable part of life, but the problem with the erratic and incomprehensible fluctuations of civil war and its outcome for many as ending up as refugees in a camp in a neighbouring country, is the sense of being useless and powerless, of having no hope, of empty waiting, of the feeling that one's life is hostage to unknown and uncontrollable forces, of degrading passivity and dependence on the fickle ministrations of unapproachable aid agencies and humanitarian relief organizations.

But is recounting and recording the stories and memories of the victims of social suffering enough? In reviewing the possible approaches that genuinely concerned intellectuals and activists might take to the reality of human suffering, such as identifying empathetically with the victims, throwing oneself into administrative and bureaucratic activity so that the suffering becomes simply a 'technical problem' seeking 'solutions', speaking truth to power, or the placing of oneself in the position of the sufferer that Hannah Arendt calls 'training one's imagination to go visiting', Jackson acknowledges that all of these approaches to revealing, recording or representing the suffering of others are fraught with problems and moral issues. But one of his own solutions, not pursued in any detail, is perhaps methodologically potentially the most fruitful one. Referring to the work of the medical anthropologist and scholar of social suffering Arthur Kleinman, Jackson summarizes the former's position by stating that 'Kleinman argues that by subjecting the experience of human suffering to anthropological theorization we violate that experience in much the same way as medicalization delegitimates the existential reality of illness' (Jackson 2005: 153). Certainly this is a real danger, although the danger of silence on these same issues is arguably even greater. But Jackson overlooks the fact that elsewhere in his extensive work, as we have seen, Kleinman has devoted considerable effort to recovering the illness narratives of the sick and with great sensitivity has tried to understand and explore anthropologically the ways in which patients construct such narratives in order to make sense of their own physical suffering. In doing so he suggests that interpreting the illness experience is a tragically neglected art in the modern world of highly technological biomedicine and that the recovery of the social and personal dimensions of illness are fundamental to the humane treatment of disease, itself not simply a physical manifestation but a complexly culturally constructed category for the individual sufferer. In this approach, what Kleinman calls the 'life world as meaning' becomes central and as such creates the bridge of understanding, witnessing and helping (often mutual) between patient and physician (Kleinman 1988).

Here I would suggest that a variation of this model, much more fully developed in Chapter 7, brings us the closest to a morally acceptable and dialogic means of understanding the relationship between social suffering, social violence and the working out of and communicating those experiences in such a way that they become meaningful and perhaps even tolerable. This is as true of the experience of development and the associated social and psychological transformations that accompany radical change as it is of war. So far the *experience* of development is a tragically neglected area of development studies, although an overwhelming number of analyses have shown, as have studies of the social impact of globalization, that the effects, while benefiting some, are highly negative for others. Trevor Parfitt (2002) has argued that the 'post-development' position of thinkers like Wolfgang Sachs, who campaigned vigorously for the view that 'The idea of development stands like a ruin in the intellectual landscape' (Sachs 1992: 1), were mistaken and that an ethical form of development can indeed be conceived that is complementary to the emancipatory projects of the new social movements. But at the same time Parfitt implicitly agrees with the post-development position that development is an inherently violent process, when he argues for what he terms 'a development of least violence'. That statement alone raises a fundamental question: why in the process of seeking human freedom, happiness and fulfilment are violence and suffering assumed? Are there not other models through which we might pursue social justice, harmony with nature and the expansion of creativity? This would seem finally to be the really key question, and the pursuit of the answer the main objective of social, economic and political theory and analysis (Pim 2010).

NINE

The aesthetics of development

The subject of the ethics of development is, if not yet mainstream in development studies, at least an accepted part of the field (Goulet 1995). The same cannot, however, be said of what should perhaps be its partner in the humanizing of development theory, policy and practice – notably development aesthetics. In fact the subject as yet hardly exists and such attempts that have been made to introduce the idea seem largely to equate aesthetics with the cultivation of the self (Quarles van Ufford and Giri 2003: 23). Here I will propose, however, that aesthetic considerations are central to development issues and that the introduction of this perspective, with aesthetics being understood in a broader sense, can have a profound impact on the whole way in which 'development' is conceived.

The visual plays an essential but understated role in cultural identities, and indeed many of the controversies in critical cultural and cross-cultural studies are precisely about the issue of representation (Said 1985, 1993). Significantly, in the older 'basic needs' approach to development popularized in the 1980s by such thinkers as Johan Galtung and Carlos Mallmann (Dube 1984) the issue of beauty inevitably appeared in the guise of the necessity of at least a relatively attractive environment and of a satisfactory relationship to nature, the latter now re-emphasized in the emergent field of eco-psychology. In fact any cultural approach to development should quickly realize that an adequate model of human being-in-the-world necessarily involves aesthetics – its connections with emotions and the erotics of culture, the identification of spaces of identity and intimacy, the importance of memory and nostalgia, and the stories that people constantly tell about their environment, sense of belonging, loneliness, exile, suffering, fantasy and their utopian visions. All of these factors illustrate the primacy of the *imagination* in human culture and also suggest that beauty is as much a category of development as are concepts such as 'efficiency' or 'productivity'. Visual violence is as much violence as its more obvious physical counterpart and has equally deleterious effects. Michel Maffesoli has argued that ethics and aesthetics are intimately connected (Maffesoli 1990), and we will argue here that both are fundamentally linked to any adequate idea of a holistic or integral sense of development.

Development studies, as it has emerged as an academic field of study as well as a kind of policy science, is highly textual and pays little attention to the visual, sensory, sensual or erotic aspects of the specific aspects of life-in-the-world that it purports to analyse and understand. In fact the existential fullness of life as much involves these elements as it does the economic. Development studies exists in an almost wholly unexplored relationship with the visual and the sensory. In this chapter I will explore some of the interfaces between them and demonstrate how a deeper appreciation of these linkages transforms the concept of development itself, in ways that I will argue are more humane, ecologically responsible, poetic, spiritual and holistic than what has hitherto passed as the subject matter of development studies and development theory.

Development, having long been the imposition of the techniques and world-views of the powerful on the relatively powerless, has always been concerned, albeit at an unconscious level, with the construction and representation of the 'Other' – the subjects of development. And as it has undertaken this transformation of economic, political, technological and institutional fields, so it has also transformed the visual, musical and sensory fields, and by doing so has modified subjectivities in ways that are still hardly understood. While the subject of representation has bulked large in Western social science at least since Edward Said's classic *Orientalism* (Said 1985), very little research exists regarding the effects of this on its subjects. While in the field of religious studies substantial attention has been paid to conversion and its profound effects on the culture, social networks and psyches of the converts (e.g. Viswanathan 1998; Clammer 2009b), little parallel work has been carried out on the aesthetic transformations that accompany development, which are, I would argue, equally profound. While in visual anthropology film and photography have been used to record cultures, the same techniques have been little applied to the documentation of social change. While some socially conscious photographers such as Tina Modotti have used photography to record poverty, war, famine and underdevelopment, little of this material has been assimilated into development studies. And while whole art forms exist depicting the encounter with development and modernity on the part of indigenous cultures (e.g. Sabapathy 1996), this whole zone of culture is left to art historians and rarely, if ever, in my experience, employed as actual material in the study of development.

Yet the visual (to take just one form of artistic expression) looms large in socio-cultural and economic change. For example, as consumption culture spreads, everyday aesthetics becomes increasingly tied in with the objects of consumption and is expressed too in architecture and design. One has only to compare the visual and architectural qualities – the buildings, shops, streets, malls and markets – of the capitalist city with those of cities in the developing world and one can see clearly that as an 'underdeveloped' city evolves and grows richer it takes on (often an ersatz version of) the architecture and consumption spaces of its developed counterparts (Bangalore, for example, or Shanghai, with its plethora of skyscrapers decorated with every possible architectural excess of turrets, spires, Greek columns, marble porticos and flashing lights). Development and aesthetics are consequently connected in at least two major ways: one, the empirical links between modernization and aesthetic transformation, usually in the direction of commodity aesthetics; two, at a conceptual level in which the whole notion of the good life is intimately tied up with an increase in and access to beauty. The aggressive ugliness of most cities in the developing world (and many in the developed) well illustrates the former: the yearning for a higher quality of cultural life, including the visual, signals the profound need for beauty for psychic health, and for an actual increase in the quality of the visual and sensory environment in which humans are forced to live out their lives.

Vision and justice/visual justice; or, why should beauty be the province of only the rich?

The concept of environmental justice has drawn attention to the fact that it is usually minorities that get stuck with the worst environments and are forced to live in unhealthy conditions, adjacent to or even literally on top of trash dumps, while the rich can move to leafy suburbs, protect themselves with technology (air conditioning, water filters, safe food) and move if necessary to safer environments. Here I would like to introduce the idea of visual justice, a parallel concept that indicates that it is minorities that are most likely to be forced to live in ugly, tiring and aesthetically fragmented neighbourhoods, while the rich can buy beauty in their external environments and also buy art to beautify their interior ones. A number of individual artists and art movements have recognized this unacceptable dichotomy and have attempted to remedy it by a number of means – Mexican muralists such as Diego Rivera through the production of public art, and movements such as that of the German Bauhaus through overcoming the distinction between arts and crafts and attempting to produce high-quality and aesthetically pleasing housing and everyday artefacts accessible to the proletariat of that time. The whole contemporary notion of public art in fact carries into the present the same inspiration (Miles 2000).

This points beyond a concept of development as simply economic, or even social, to a broader project of the evolution of a *social aesthetics* – a critical aesthetics concerned as much with the aesthetic critique of society and culture as it has traditionally been with simply works of art themselves. This is a project very different from what are sometimes termed 'social theories of art' – that is to say, sociological attempts to *explain* art in terms of the conventional sociological categories of class, race, gender, occupational background, and so on. Here we are concerned with the much more global project of not simply (difficult as it is in actual practice) situating particular works of art, or particular artists, in their social milieu, but of an aesthetic critique of society itself. Such a critique has a number of components: a concern with visual justice (the right for all to have access to and to inhabit aesthetically pleasing environments, housing, work and leisure spaces regardless of social status, ethnicity, gender or religion); the notion of development not only as freedom or external emancipation, but as internal also, the possibility of psychic, emotional and spiritual growth and transformation along autonomous lines; the broad enhancement of life and its quality; the acquiring of the mechanisms for the transformation of oppressive structures, institutions, environments and patterns of dependency by non-political or extra-political means; and the enhancing of the role of the imagination in social transformation, as the imagination is perhaps the most significant human faculty since where reason is limited, imagination is essentially unbounded.

Such an approach opens new conceptual and imaginative spaces. One is that social research itself becomes more creative and allows the social scientist legitimate access to areas of human life, emotion and culture that have hitherto been primarily the province of the artist, the poet or possibly the psychiatrist. Another is that it points us beyond an understandable but conceptually limited preoccupation with politics and power (Clammer 2005) and suggests the possibility of 'revolution by enlightenment' by way of refreshing and non-economic forms of human liberation and fulfilment which also have the potential to relink humans with the natural environments from which civilization so-called has become dangerously and self-destructively estranged. Indeed if, as many have suggested, the form of our industrial, environment-destroying, consumerist civilization is itself our central problem, then the question must arise of how we can conceive of different and less dysfunctional forms. The category of the aesthetic, then, re-emerges as far from a luxury item at the very edges of serious socio-political engagement, but rather as the primary means of recolonizing our lifeworlds, of restoring, revitalizing and reinventing culture, and of discovering new forms of expression, empowerment and autonomy: of redefining, in short, the good life.

Part of the problem here is a theoretical one: the lack of communication between development studies and cultural studies. The marginalization of the visual and the sensory in development studies has paradoxically occurred at the very moment when the visual has become important in cultural studies. But such limitations (at least on the part of development studies) are largely self-imposed. There are many potential new avenues of enquiry, possible fresh reworkings of conventional methodologies and new uses to which the valuable insights of parallel fields can be put, but which have not yet been explored or exploited. The key question in the context of this chapter is how to incorporate the aesthetic dimension in an authentic and integral way into the concerns of development studies and to demonstrate adequately the centrality of the aesthetic to the cultural dimensions of development and to the cultural critique which should be an important dimension of development seen as a holistic discipline. For the aesthetic is not only that which immediately presents itself to the senses, but equally that which invokes and enshrines memory and the recognition of sites of happiness and suffering, embodies emotions, nostalgia and modes of representation of the past and their projection into the present and the future. The recovery of some sense of the 'fullness' of the aesthetic dimension of human life and our life in nature is an important part of the attempt to reconstruct an appropriate philosophical anthropology for our time, and equally to recover a sense of the fullness of culture, not as a denuded and abstract concept, but as the cradle and expression of human being-in-the-world.

We can illustrate this by building on some remarks of Raimon Panikkar to the effect that rationality does not exhaust being. Panikkar's point had been that reason is not the only instrument for the human investigation of reality as demonstrated by the power of art, myths, mysticism and the role of play in human cultures, reflecting among other things, in Panikkar's words, that 'Man is not the whole of reality', a deeply ecological view that refuses to reduce the human to the socio-political (Panikkar 1993). In a world saturated with information and also what passes as 'knowledge', wisdom is often lost, whereas what really needs to be explored is the relationship between art and knowledge – alternative ways of knowing, one of which is embodied in poetry. Art in this view both creates and changes the world; it has a formative as well as a reflective aspect. In some Indian traditions the 'Fifth Veda' (the Vedas, themselves deeply poetic documents, are acknowledged as the essential scriptures of Hinduism), notably art, was created for those not permitted to learn the four orthodox Vedas by virtue of their gender or caste status. An important implication of this is the suggestion that, despite its technological prowess, our civilization is in fact in the process of shrinking – in terms of language diversity, biodiversity, ethnic diversity, as well as in terms of our conception of knowledge, which now excludes the insights expressed in the medium of poetry. Whereas songs and poetry are now read mainly as 'texts', they are in fact the distillation of wisdom and of forms of perception that often or usually fall outside the boundaries of conventional 'knowledge'.

This perspective on the arts opens up a number of avenues for exploration largely closed off by aesthetics itself, sociology and development studies, while providing the basis for an alternative form of critical theory rooted in a new mode of cultural criticism. In such a model art proves to be the boundary-crossing mechanism between the usually separated spheres of the 'spiritual' and the 'material' and does so in a way that goes well beyond the Marxist formulation of base and superstructure or its Weberian reversal, both of which assume and posit a particular causal epistemology. The critical dimension comes not only from revealing the violence in a great deal of contemporary visual culture and its own complicity in the system of capitalist commodification and the marketization of art; it also comes from revealing the extent to which the poor in particular are not only denied access to real beauty, but are doubly denied by only having access to ersatz versions – Bollywood, Hollywood and the virtual 'reality' of the video game. This in turn points to a very significant and little-discussed question – that of culture after capitalism, or, if you prefer, culture after development.

The education of desire

It is an endlessly repeated mantra that if the currently developing world (including the two giants, India and China) were to attain a standard of living comparable to the contemporary USA or Japan, we would require at least two and a half earth-sized and earth-endowed planets to sustain the vehicles, pollution, urbanization and resource depletion resulting from this 'development'. But even such a potential scenario is not sustainable given the current dominant model of development, since in a relatively short time even those one and a half extra earths would be reduced to the same state of ecological disaster, endemic violence, corruption and level of social inequalities as the present one, which is in fact of course the only one we have. The consequences of this are very hard indeed for many people to think through or to contemplate. Barring the very real possibility of environmental catastrophe bringing an end to the present world-system, the only possible outcomes are a drastic scaling down of living standards in the already 'developed' world and a corresponding and very painful realization on the part of the developing world that attainment of the industrial civilization and its living standards currently found in a small number of 'advanced' economies is impossible within the ecological constraints of the planet. The violence, resource competition (fuelling the next genera-tion of wars over access to oil, water, food and living space) and social upheavals consequent upon this awareness can only be realistically avoided by one alternative scenario – notably, development without greed, or what, building on a term used by Herbert Marcuse, we might term the education of desire.

Consumerism itself is, of course, socially sanctioned desire, conferring status and security on those able to access it. And it is consumerism that supports and extends the industrial resource-depleting economic system that is the main threat to the environ-mental integrity of the planet (Kovel 2002.). To move away from such a system implies an alternative set of desires focused on a very different relationship to the world than that primarily mediated by the possession or manipulation of things. As Gloria Orenstein puts it succinctly in her essay on 'Artists as Healers', 'It is imperative that we go about the task of creating an alternative society that is interconnected with nature *now*' (Orenstein 1990: 287). Underlying this objective are, I think, a number of important ideas, including that throughout human history new creative capacities not previously known before have emerged over and over again. These are in prac-tice associated with the great religious innovators (Abraham, Buddha,

Jesus, Zarathustra and company), major philosophical thinkers (Lao Tze, Confucius, Socrates et al.) and artists of various stripes (Homer, the unknown architects and craftsmen of the great Gothic cathedrals), down through the roll call of luminaries and the illuminated who have fundamentally changed human modes of perception and modes of engaging the world. In a sense all of these have pointed to ways of making the ecosystem and people's lives fuller, more enriched, responsible and meaningful, towards spiritual richness rather than material abundance, and realizing the infinite possibilities hidden in our everyday lives. This is deeply important as culture is the site on which our identities are formed and contested: the content and quality of culture are consequently crucial to the overall quality of human life. Yet it is often this culture itself which proves to be inhumane, imposing arbitrary or cruel modes of conduct, dress or livelihood and status on women, children, outsiders, members of religious minorities, the ethnically different or even its own privileged members. For many, their culture is an ordeal to be endured, rather than a source of liberation and fulfilment.

It is for this reason that the question of *representation* is so central to contemporary cultural studies. Edward Said has, of course, classically pointed out and analysed the ways in which representations of the Orient in literature and art, in particular, were fundamentally formative of Western and colonial attitudes to the Others that they encountered in their voyaging and colonial expansion, including the exoticizing, eroticizing and infantalizing of the inhabitants of the Middle East, North Africa and beyond, a tradition of scholarship that now has many followers (e.g. Thomas 1994). This issue remains central to any critical social aesthetics. As the art and culture critic Craig Owens suggests, the critique of representation is vital because representation so often means, in fact, subjugation; and the recognition of this points not just to the politically motivated goal of 'consciousness raising' but also to the mobilization of the spectator who needs to recognize that there is no one narrative of culture, but a plurality of aesthetics. The role of comparative aesthetics is to reveal the existence of a whole set of possible or alternative aesthetic systems (a recognition that, as Owens notes, can activate the realization of the intrinsic value of 'outsider' art and indigenous artistic forms and traditions. Representational systems are apparatuses of power, and the role of a critical aesthetics is to reveal the structure of these systems and so to deconstruct them, while also revealing the existence of alternative systems of representation/aesthetics that signal quite different ontological assumptions (Clammer et al. 2004). Art for Owens is not an *alternative* to reality (the Freudian model), but a *recognition* of reality, a mode of apprehending and representing it, of revealing, creating awareness, of defamiliarization. This, furthermore, is not simply a project projected onto the Other, but applies equally to the observer: 'Perhaps it is this project of learning how to represent *ourselves* – how to speak *to*, rather than for or about, others – that the possibility of a "global" culture resides' (Owens 1994: 326). This resonates very well with the observation of John Berger that art need not only represent the nostalgia of a class in decline (the aristocracy or bourgeoisie). Rather,

> If the new language of images was used differently, it would, through its use, confer a new kind of power. Within it we could begin to define our experiences more precisely in areas where words are inadequate. ... Not only personal experience, but also the essential historical experience of our relation to the past: that is to say the experience of seeking to give meaning to our lives, of trying to understand the history of which we can become the active agents. (Berger 1972: 33)

The cultivation of aesthetic appreciation is in principle one means of not simply practising self-cultivation, but of seeing the world such that its own depth and beauty (and the necessity of enhancing and protecting those qualities) become central to the individual's project of being-in-the-world. Awareness (and an awareness of the fragility of the environment) rather than the possession of things then becomes the dominant mode of cultural practice. This relates to but is rather different from debates within critical art studies that attempt to relate art less to 'self expression' and more to its potential political, social and environmental context, and to take it out of museums and galleries into everyday practice. In conversations with a range of contemporary artists, aestheticians and social activists, the art critic Suzi Gablik discovered that what struck a common chord was the shifting of aesthetic experience out of galleries into the broader world, that art should not be defined as a professional-ized or specialized category of objects or activities, 'but is a living process centered around daily life and vital human concerns' (Gablik 2000a: 32) and that it is modern aesthetics that is the anomaly. Art itself, in this view, is a natural and universal cultural practice and the human propensity for aesthetic expression has been distorted both by systems of education and specialization which relegate it to a largely fringe activity in daily life, and by wider societal trends which have allowed the economic, the managerial and the technical to fill the field of vital human endeavours. As a consequence art, like religion, has been driven to the edges of significant everyday practice and even regarded as a retreat from the 'real' world, when both should in fact be at the centre. Given that, to a great extent, we live by images, the corruption and trivialization of so many of those images in the mass media is a major factor in civilizational decline. Beauty is fundamental to life, and certainly to the good life, and is not the province simply of the 'arts', but is central to cultural well-being and to human appreciation of nature. Discussing her interview with the psychologist James Hillman, Suzi Gablik summarizes his (and her) basic philosophy as follows:

> Beauty in its sensate presence is, for Hillman, absolutely
> fundamental to life; it is not a cultural accessory, or some thing that
> belongs to the exclusive province of the arts. Beauty is the inherent
> radiance of the world, and its repression, he feels, is the most
> significant factor in our culture, because its loss is what keeps us

from caring for nature. 'Nature today is on dialysis', he says, 'slowly expiring, kept alive only by advanced technology'. When all is said and done, it is only love for the world, and a desire for rich, sensory contact with the beauty of its sounds and smells and textures that will save us. A truly aesthetic response, in Hillman's view, could affect issues of civilization that most concern us today which have remained largely intractable to psychological resolution. Like Satish Kumar, Hillman feels that beauty has been sequestered into the ghetto of beautiful objects by museums, by the ministry of culture, and by a professional cadre of artists. Indeed, he claims, we must cleave beauty altogether away from art, art history, art objects, art appreciation, because they posit beauty into an instance of it, when in fact, beauty is the manifest *anima mundi*, the very sensibility of the cosmos. (Gablik 2000a: 179–80)

This, then, is a different perspective from the idea of art being in the service of something (social issues in particular). It is a much broader claim that art itself is simply a particular cultural practice that applies certain culturally accepted techniques to produce certain types of artefact (such as paintings or sculptures) to be exhibited or appreciated in particular kinds of settings. Such art may be self-expressive or socially concerned, but in both cases it applies to a particular mode of cultural production. The point, however, is that the category of the beautiful far exceeds the limitations of art, so defined. It in fact refers to what used to be called in development discourse a 'basic need', an aesthetic orientation to the world more often violated than respected in development practice, urban planning and growth-oriented strategies. Changing desires in sustainable directions is hardly possible if this fundamental quality of human being-in-the-world is not granted pride of place.

Imagination and the erotics of development

If the subject of the aesthetics of development is rarely admitted into the dominant discourse, the issue of the *erotics* of development is even less so. Yet art is largely about the sensuous – depicting it, rendering it into a form that stimulates the imagination, and a great deal of that imagination is, in the broadest sense, erotic. Most images of the good life are not only concerned with the fullest play of the senses (all of them, not only the visual), but also recognize that spirituality need not be ethereal, but can be rooted, earthy, bodily. Even when 'human needs' are discussed as part of development discourse, such sensuous capacities are never mentioned or prioritized, but, if they exist at all, are assimilated into broad abstract categories such as the need for leisure or exposure to nature. In fact 'development' itself is a highly impoverished concept if it is only concerned with the exterior political and economic aspects of life, as it usually is. Yet in fact any sense of a life of fullness and satisfaction must include the expression of emotional needs, of bodily freedom and the ranging of the imagination. Sexuality is a major component of this wider sense of freedom. On the one hand art itself is closely connected to sexuality in many of its manifestations, while on the other sexuality does not exhaust the category of the erotic, which can encompass a far wider range of expressions of the primary contact between the body and nature (including other animals) – the source of some of the deepest feelings of well-being and health available to human beings.

The shallowness of much development thinking and practice derives not from its materialism per se, but from the shallowness of that materialism itself. A truly material existence involves intimate connections with the environment in all its manifestations – air, light, fragrance, and the means by which we experience it and participate in it – touch, taste, smell, vision. Contemporary society too often tells us what these sensations should be, which are legitimate and which are not, and encourages us by numerous mechanisms to give up our sensuous autonomy for the codified, even in cultures that still claim a close connection to the natural (Clammer 2000). But, as Susan Griffin puts it, 'If sexual desire, sensitivity to touch, taste, smell, love of color, movement, passionate emotion, all that which is the estate of those on earth, is consigned to others, it is also relinquished. What is lost is nothing else than the eros at the heart of existence' (Griffin 1995: 51–2). In the process of 'development', how much of the eros of indigenous cultures has been lost for ever, what range of feelings and sensitivities to the earth extinguished? In the overly cognitive models of Western anthropology indigenous *knowledge* has been given pride of place, without the recognition that in fact such 'knowledge' is not merely technique, but in actuality encompasses modes of feeling, of relating, of alternative modes of being in the world. Globalization not only reduces the economic and cultural diversity of the world (and biodiversity too), but also its emotional and erotic diversity, signalled by language loss, which is one of its causes, leading to a psychic deprivation of the highest order. The recovery or recolonization of this realm presents itself as a primary task for what might be called the poetics of development.

It is in radical environmentalism as well as in art that this truth has been recognized, in particular in the former's critique of the technological domination of humanity and nature that has been one of the major outcomes of 'development': 'Technology totalizes existence along one axis, the axis of utility, and all the other rich, poetic, wild ways in which a human being is able to encounter the world are excluded' (Manes 1990: 226). It also excludes or channels in particular ways (the computer game for instance) the full range of the human imagination. As the great Sufi poet Rumi rightly said, 'The world of phantasy is broader than the world of concepts. For all concepts are born in phantasy. The world of phantasy likewise is narrow in relation to the world out of which phantasy comes into being' (Arberry 1994: 202). The imagination, then, is perhaps the primary human faculty (not reason, as is so commonly supposed); it is through imagination that desire is formed and educated, and it is through it that the fullest life is achieved. As Henry James aptly put it, 'I call that man rich who can satisfy the requirements of his imagination.' Art in its various forms is one of the main ways in which this opening to/of the imagination takes place, and the deprivation of the aesthetic dimension is as much a form of poverty as material want. As the writer Pico Iyer has put it, 'It is not easy to explain that poverty can take many forms, and that poverty of horizon can seem as paralysing as the other kinds' (Iyer 2004: 189). Aesthetic deprivation, ignored as a factor or imposed actively by the ugliness of much development practice, is as much a violation of human rights as the deprivation of physical liberty, and conversely the presence of aesthetic qualities in the environment is a source of fundamental satisfactions. As the novelist and dramatist Albert Camus expressed it, reflecting on his own humble North African origins, 'Originally brought up surrounded by beauty which was my only wealth, I had begun in plenty' (Camus 1979: 18).

This view is indeed the consensus of the majority of practising artists and poets and sympathetic commentators on their works. Susan Murphy draws a parallel between religious insight and art: 'To understand this better, consider how great paintings rearrange us. You don't so much look at a great painting and figure it out as stand before it and, with a sense of the self dropping away, let it reorganize you from the centre of your being ... It is learning to be present with the whole body rather than just the pinpoint of the intellect and the customary buzz of thought' (Murphy 2004: 70, 205). The Columbian poet Eduardo Carrenza: 'If poetry does not make my blood run faster, open sudden windows for me into the mysterious, help me discover the world, accompany this desolate heart in solitude and in love, in joy and in enmity, what good is poetry to me?' (Marquez 2004: 252). Elias Canetti: 'Only an image can please you *totally*, never a human being. The origins of angels ... The inklings of poets are the forgotten adventures of God' (Canetti 1986: 2, 4). Even the philosophers agree: for the political philosopher John Finnis the universal categories of all human cultures are life, knowledge, play, aesthetic experience, friendship, practical reasonableness and religion (Finnis 1980). The aesthetic, then, not only stands at the heart of human culture; its performance leads to a relationship with the world unique in its inherent and undeconstructable authenticity.

The art of sustainability

The architectural historian James Wines has cogently noted that 'Without art, the whole idea of sustainability fails' (Wines 2008). This comment succinctly summarizes the core of the argument presented here: that without art, development fails. It becomes in fact all of the things that its critics have charged it with – ecologically irresponsible, resource-depleting, the principal generator of ugly, boring and unhealthy environments, and ultimately unsatisfying to the human spirit and its aesthetic, erotic, cosmological and utopian needs. The eclipse of utopia parallels the rise of growth-oriented developmentalism, its toxic modernist architecture and its assault on nature (Jacoby 1999; Kovel 2002). Without a fertile, organic and earth-rooted imagination the world becomes technocratic and sterile, and, as Suzi Gablik has rightly argued, the re-enchantment of art and the re-enchantment of the world go hand in hand (Gablik 2002b). Likewise art, as Michael Chanan has argued, is one of the principal fields of cultural experimentation, and its drive towards increasing rather than restricting our responses to the world is one of the main means of preventing the stagnation of our species, even when the experimentation seems outlandish and pointless, criticisms frequently directed at new art movements which later become assimilated into mainstream or establishment art – Impressionism, Expressionism and Cubism being exemplary instances (Chanan 1972: 146). The artist and poet, then, far from being marginal to true civilization, are its essence. They are the ones, as much as the scientist, who produce exploratory languages, whether of words or images, that point to new significations and meanings. Or, as Shakespeare puts it in *A Midsummer Night's Dream*, 'as imagination bodies forth / The forms of things unknown, the poet's pen / Turns them into shapes, and gives to airy nothing / A local habitation and a name.'

Obviously there will continue to be argument over the definition of art, even as there is argument over the definition of development. The critic Julian Spalding, however, is right to note that the increasing narcissism and failure to produce images of any real social consequence that characterize so much contemporary art are driving many people who would otherwise like to be open and appreciative of art to decide essentially that much of what they are asked to see is rubbish (Spalding 2003). Art that resonates with people's imagination and their primal experiences is powerful inasmuch as it gives access to alternative cultural resources rather than those purveyed by the dominant matrix: aesthetics can form the basis for a critique of instrumental reason; while it can be so easily co-opted by those forces, imagination, fantasy, desire and the urge to produce images can be directed to ends other than simply enhancing consumption. Art in fact has the potential for revolutionizing the image world and overcoming the atrophy of experience that is characteristic of the anomie of the industrialized world. It is not only through politics that utopia can be approached – indeed it is politics that has constantly been the betrayer of alternative futures. As the artist Joseph Beuys puts it,

> As our ageing old order muddles its way towards death, it is only by radically widening our conceptual understanding to embrace art, that we will be able to receive the powerful inspiration of art. And it is only such inspiration of creative art that can serve as evolutionary midwife to aid the birth of a new society. Such a society, celebrating liberty, equality and fraternity, would itself be a great work of art, and every person in it a deeply fulfilled artist. (Beuys 1977)

The realizing of such a vision places great responsibility on art; it becomes incumbent on actual artistic production to fulfil this mandate. It is also a statement that comes from a highly secularized social location. With the rise of new forms of spirituality in the contemporary world and the alliance of some of these with art, and many with an expanding ecological consciousness, any number of fresh syntheses and advances will undoubtedly propose themselves and point to alternative conceptions of society, culture and community.

The aesthetics of imperfection

Discussion of art in relation to development may for many have an idealistic ring about it. While that is understandable, especially given the social irrelevance of much contemporary art, the whole thrust of this book has been to show that in fact the aesthetic dimension of life is to be counted among the most basic of 'human needs', and that any fulfilling 'post-development' culture would be one in which creative faculties were given the fullest rein. The aridity of much current development practice derives from its ignoring of this crucial dimension of human existence. One could argue, too, that its lack of serious concern with the environment is equally derived from this diminution of any sense of beauty as an essential component of a rounded lifestyle.

But to say this is not to argue for some kind of perfectionism. In practice the world is a complex and messy place, always in the process of change and transformation and never in full equilibrium. Commenting on a line by the poet Wallace Stevens that 'The imperfect is our paradise' (Stevens 1954: 194), David Morris suggests that

> Suppose that the earth – what Dante emerging from hell called the 'shining world' (*chiaro mondo*) – is the only paradise we will know. Suppose that paradise is here and now, not in some future or perfect state: the world and all its people with their glaring deficiencies. We might then be called upon to begin working towards an aesthetics and an ethics of imperfection. The aim would be to base our values not in the quest for perfection but in an appreciation of the imperfect. (Morris 1998: 162)

In the light of suffering, itself a universal characteristic of life in the world, the need to give voice to this suffering falls as much on the arts as on religion, pastoral care or science. The objective is not, then, the attainment of utopia with all its attendant problems and the dystopias that the pursuit of perfection has so frequently engendered, but rather that

> We might then come to recognize in our inevitable imperfections
> – signs of the only paradise on earth that we will ever know – both
> the evidence of a shared humanity that makes an ongoing ethical
> claim upon us and the occasion for seeking to create a culture in
> which human life could be, as Karl Popper put it in his postwar
> critique of utopian thinking, thinking inseparable from Nazi
> fantasies of eugenics, 'a little less terrible and a little less unjust'.
> (Morris 1998: 163)

The embodied life carries with it the existential realities of illness, ageing, accident and death, the very existential dimensions of existence rarely if ever touched upon in conventional development thinking. As the sociologist Ian Craib has noted, disappointment – the non-realization in everyday life of desires and ambitions – is an essential not a contingent part of the tragi-comedy of everyday human life (Craib 1994). Nowhere is this more the case than in 'development' – in the pursuit of material goals that recede as they are approached, or which prove to generate even more and unexpected problems than they solve. It is precisely in this context that the capacities of the imagination are most needed, not as escapism (although that is a very undervalued and all too frequently maligned genuine need), but as a way of conceiving of alternatives and conferring meaning on existing suffering and disappointment.

In his literary biography of the great Greek writer Nikos Kazantzakis, Peter Bien sums up his subject's life project as follows:

> Both art and religion, far from being escapes from life, bring us
> into a more meaningful contact with reality than we achieve via
> quotidian experience. This is especially true of tragic art, which

teaches us to understand suffering and death; but it is also true of comedy, which celebrates human foolishness. To the degree to which art, whether tragic or comic, escapes subservience to everyday reality, to that same degree will it succeed in returning us more meaningfully to that same reality, because it will have concerned itself *with the meaning of being rather than of things*. Far from avoiding a confrontation with the problem of value, it will have placed itself in a position where value can be truly discovered and formulated. In other words, it will have refuted nihilism. The very 'playing with the world' commonly scorned as irresponsible aestheticism is precisely what strengthens our capacity to act in the world instead of merely making a picture or spectacle of it, because it teaches us to live in the truth. (Bien 1989: 231)

In speaking of the issues involved in the construction, experience and representation of pain, Veena Das supports this view by noting that

Some realities need to be fictionalized before they can be apprehended. This is apparent in the weight of the distinction between the three registers of the real, the symbolic, and the imaginary in the work of Lacan, and in Castoriadis's formulation of the necessity of working on the register of the imaginary for the conceptualization of society itself [Castoriadis 1987]. I shall allow myself three scenes, or phantasms, that provide a theoretical scaffolding to the issues that I address. In these three scenes I call upon the words of the philosopher Wittgenstein, the poet–novelist– essayist Tagore, and the short story writer Sadat Hasan Manto, as persons who responded to the call of the world in the register of the imaginary. (Das 1997: 69)

Enough said perhaps. The aesthetic is not merely a mode of representation, but also a mode of knowledge and of action. As Pablo Picasso well expressed his view of the social commitment of the artist during his politically active period after the painting of *Guernica*:

What do you think an artist is? An imbecile who has only his eyes if he is a painter, or ears if he is a musician, or a lyre at every level of his heart if he's a poet, or even if he is a boxer, just his muscles? On the contrary, he's at the same time a political being, constantly alive to heartrending, fiery or happy events, to which he responds in every way. How would it be possible to feel no interest in other people and by virtue of an irony of indifference to detach yourself from the life which they so copiously bring to you? No, painting is not done to decorate apartments. It is an instrument of war for attack and defence against the enemy. (Picasso 1945, quoted in Read 1997: 160)

Remembering, too, that art movements are also social movements, we can give the last word to Picasso's contemporary, the poet, writer and leader of the Surrealist movement André Breton. In the 1924 *Manifesto of Surrealism* Breton states in a comment that resonates well with contemporary conceptions of 'development as freedom':

Only the word freedom still exalts me. Among the many disgraces we inherit, we should do well to recognize that the *greatest freedom* of spirit is left to us. We ought not to misuse it. To reduce the imagination to slavery, even when it might lead to what one crudely calls happiness, is to evade whatever one finds, in the depths of the self, of supreme justice. Imagination alone tells me *what can be*, and this is enough to lift for a little the terrible interdict – enough also to allow me to abandon myself to this freedom without fear of self-deception.

TEN

Emotions of culture, social movements and social transformation

The entire thrust of this book has been that essentially any integral concept of 'development' has to be fundamentally concerned with the existential issues that form the basis of human life on this planet. These include embeddedness in culture, including its artistic dimensions, the religious dimension of human life, and, inevitably, suffering. Any concept of development concerned only with the external aspects of life – growth, accumulation, consumption, material resources and even politics narrowly defined – is profoundly impoverished. This text has attempted to show ways beyond that limited paradigm into a much expanded concept of human development and its place in the wider biosphere. Movements in other areas of the social sciences – such as the sudden concern with selfhood and personal identity, the discovery of the body as a subject of sociological and cultural enquiry, and the much belated insight that the emotions are a highly significant part of socio-cultural being – signal this move away from the purely abstract, instrumental, pragmatic, quantitative methodologies that have dominated so much social science, including development studies, towards a much more phenomenological, subject-centred and cultural approach. This is a good thing, but the problem has been that so much of the cultural studies approach to social reality has been narcissistic and has failed, like the postmodernism that gave birth to much of it, to address the larger questions of human life, including the highly uncomfortable ones of poverty, corruption, violence and environmental degradation. Additionally, at its core is a weak and inadequate philosophical anthropology – a failure to grasp the fullness of human being and as a consequence to develop the tools for a deeper understanding of processes of change and transformation. The result has been a philosophically shallow sociology rather than a deep one (Clammer 2009a).

When cultural studies confines itself to the field of culture, narrowly defined, it has proved to be quite an exciting and insightful enterprise, bringing into the field of sociology areas previously deemed frivolous or marginal – fashion, food cultures, sport, regimes of diet and fitness, for example, or, in its earlier incarnations associated with the Birmingham Centre for Cultural Studies, key issues of gender, ethnicity and class. Yet in its subsequent development, it has been in these latter fields that cultural studies and phenomenological and postmodernist varieties of sociology have proved weakest in their theoretical development. While a great deal of literature exists on these subjects (and indeed in many cases appears to have driven out of cultural studies the study of culture itself; see e.g Jordon and Weedon 1995), relatively little deepening of its grasp of fundamental issues in social change and transformation is at all evident, and there are very few attempts to relate the cultural studies approach systematically to the issues named by the concept of 'development'. Yet at the same time those concerned primarily with social change, and especially social movements theorists, make little reference to a cultural studies approach. Probably the point at which the two fields come closest is in the area of alternative or 'post-development' thinking where some very interesting attempts have been made to link culture and development in innovative ways (e.g. Carmen

1996; Rahmena and Bawtree 2003). In this closing chapter we will attempt to provide something of a new synthesis by sketching ways in which cultural studies and the study of social movements and social transformation can be better related, in ways that not only increase our understanding but also provide tools for action.

Culture, emotions and social movements

In *The Art of Moral Protest* social movements scholar James Jasper makes a systematic attempt to relate culture, emotions, values and the biographies of protesters and movement participants to an in-depth understanding of the genesis and development of social movements, particularly those concerned with the environment, the construction of nuclear power stations and animal rights (Jasper 1997). In this important respect his work is distinguished both from those whose primary concern has been with resources and mobilization techniques in social movements (a dominant motif in much 'classical' sociological social movements theory) and those who do include culture, but as a kind of afterthought, placed literally at the end of their book on the subject, even though the world 'culture' appears in the title (e.g. Buechler 2000). Jasper quite rightly argues that culture should never be contrasted with structural or 'objective' factors, because it is intimately involved in the genesis and operation of those very structures. Operating in any sociological context are not only these structural factors and culture (understood as collectively derived cognitive beliefs, emotions and moral evaluations), but equally biography, strategy and resources. A tendency of social movements theory has been largely to ignore the element of moral visions, which, as Jasper shows in his various case studies, play a very major role in mobilizing and sustaining protests of various kinds and the more systematic movements and organizations that often grow out of them. Commenting on five posters affixed to a lamp post outside his apartment announcing a range of upcoming meetings and protests about women's liberation, war, abortion, AIDS and military recruitment, Jasper suggests that

> The five posters touched on basic issues of human existence – war and peace, men and women, life and death – about which all of us hold passionate feelings and opinions. They are questions that touch our innermost sense of who we are and why we are, as well as our moral visions about how we should act in the world. Most of our institutions are silent about existential issues like these; protest is one of the few arenas where they are raised and examined. (Jasper 1997: 2)

And another is undoubtedly development, where, despite their exclusion from mainstream development thinking, values are now recognized by many as central to the task of, or even as defining, 'development' (e.g. Goulet 1995; Clammer 1996). Development is inevitably about change, yet few if any major textbooks on development look to social movements studies for insight as to how change occurs when stimulated by conscious action and not by impersonal factors such as the workings of globalized capitalism. Intentional change, however, is the key to being able to steer social processes in desirable directions, desirable in the sense of more equal, more just and more environmentally responsible.

As we have suggested a number of times in this book, aesthetics, values and emotions are primary constituents of the human experience and hence of the ends desired from 'development', a development which, because of its frequent violence, its materialism and its ignoring of fundamental existential issues, has not only failed to deliver the goods but also, as we now so clearly see, frequently made conditions (including ecological ones) considerably worse. What people care about and what development processes deliver are not necessarily the same things at all, and culture inevitably shapes the responses of people to opportunities, emerging possibilities, threats or risks. But realizing that there is a danger in the theoretical over-extension of concepts (making them carry too heavy a theoretical load), Jasper nevertheless argues that,

At the risk of the same kind of overextension, I'll argue that culture is not only an independent dimension alongside resources, biography, and strategies. It can be this, as when it is defined as cognitive grids that encourage or discourage solidarity, or as repertories of strategic know-how. But because all action involves intention and thought, culture also involves the construction of the other categories: what counts as a resource under what circumstances, what works as a strategy and why, what an individual absorbs through socialization. Neither resources nor strategies are 'objective' realities that can be identified outside of their social context, independent of the mental world of their users. Even physical resources such as bullhorns or fax machines require familiarity, habits, and messages for effective use. Sometimes culture is a simple causal factor that can be contrasted with other causal factors; at other times (or in other ways) it helps define these other factors too. At some times it is more explicit, at others more implicit, buried in action and the social construction of the other categories. There may be a tension between these two aspects, but I hope it's a creative one. The limitation of game theorists, mobilizationists, and process theorists is not that they are wrong, but that they don't look behind the curtain at the origins of the factors they take as independent 'givens'. This role of culture is the reason, I think, that a cultural perspective is good for helping us see the autonomy of all four dimensions [resources, strategies, culture, and biography] from each other. And by carefully demarcating the different roles of culture, I hope to avoid the conceptual overextension that has plagued most paradigms. (Jasper 1997: 41–2)

Likewise here: in placing the role of culture as central, it is necessary to place culture itself in the context of its dynamic interaction (causative, reactive, resultant) with other factors of the human existential situation – hope, fear, love and emotions in general, the situatedness of people in/as their bodies, suffering, future visions, the transcendent realm and embeddedness in nature. Sociology has tended to overemphasize cognition at the expense of feelings and embodiment. But any concept of integral development needs by definition to be holistic and hence involves all these aspects, together with the ethical (values) and the aesthetic.

It is significant, however, that while in recent social movement theory, and especially in European 'new social movement' scholarship, attention has been paid in great detail to the forms of social movements that began to emerge particularly in the 1960s – peace movements, feminism, ecology, anti-nuclear and attempts to create alternative lifestyles (Touraine 1981b, 1988; Sicinski and Wemegah 1983), no sociologist to my knowledge has considered art movements (for example, Expressionism, Cubism, Surrealism, the Bauhaus) to be social movements. This is despite their profound connections to the social changes of their day, which in many cases they (culturally) led rather than simply reflected, and few art historians have interpreted them as culturally transformative movements, but rather simply as stylistic and conceptual developments within art itself (e.g. Lucie-Smith 1995). This is remarkable, since not only are art movements among the leading sources of cultural innovation, but, as Alberto Melucci rightly suggests, the new social movements are utopian, representing and embodying 'a certain number of moral and totalizing expectations for happiness, justice and truth' and, even in their 'latent' or post-mobilization phases, involve the 'daily production of alternative frameworks of meaning, on which the networks themselves are founded and live from day to day ... Latency does not mean inactivity. Rather, the potential for resistance or opposition is sewn into the very fabric of daily life' (Melucci 1989: 82, 70–71). This leads to two important insights: not only is art a source of knowledge (not simply of symbols), but social movements themselves are among the major generators of 'alternative' knowledge – knowledge, that is, that contests the mainstream hegemony of what is thought to be either knowable or meaningful. This points to the significance of social movements not only as agents of social change, but equally and relatedly as generators of culture and, through that production of new cultural knowledge and new cultural subjects, as challenges to the underlying epistemology and ontologies of the dominant social structure. As Jasper phrases it, 'Culture not only bounds rationality but defines it. It provides the context and criteria for recognizing and judging rationality, which cannot exist in a pure form outside of social contexts' (Jasper 1997: 83).

Shared visions, the basis for action in and on the world, then, are necessarily collective and hence cultural, but that culture is highly dynamic and fluid, being a point in a feedback loop rather than a fixed point in itself. Culture shapes perceptions, but individual biography, personal motivations and objective structures shape responses to culture and bring about changes in it, as artistic movements so clearly indicate. Emotions, values and beliefs constantly intersect and interact in complex and ever-changing constellations. Emotions in particular are what Randall Collins calls 'the "glue" of solidarity – and what mobilizes conflict' (Collins 1990: 28). Cultural change lies at the basis of a great deal of social change, and often leads it, not only by creating new cultural forms (again as in art movements), but by articulating or demonstrating the real possibility of alternatives, often outside of the conventionally political. Society learns not only through innovations in technology, marketing (in capitalist societies) and institutional and legal reform, but equally through protest, philosophical, religious and artistic reflection and through new perceptions or awareness arising from the soil of existing culture. To this must be added incremental change and occasionally radical paradigm shifts (as with the advent of a new religion) in a culture – an ever-advancing and evolving matrix and complex of feedback loops that define the meaning patterns and appropriate behavioural responses of a human population at a given point in time.

Social movements, development and new knowledge

Anyone concerned with development will have noted that the vocabulary of alternatives has changed constantly over the past two or three decades – basic needs, participatory development, dependency, human rights and, more recently, indigenous knowledge. But underlying all of these is a single basic concern: the mechanisms through which social change occurs and the means by which such change might be fruitfully directed. It is exactly these issues that social movement theory addresses, and it is remarkable that it has not been brought into systematic dialogue with development studies. In almost no major textbook of development sociology or anthropology, for example is any discussion of social movements to be found. In fact social movement theory in its various and now extensive guises addresses a number of key questions for development studies. These include not only mechanisms of social change and mobilization, but also participation, the relationships between social movements and NGOs and ideas of civil society and citizenship, identity politics, responses to globalization, and the raising of new 'subjects' for consideration (peasants, women, sexual minorities, the disabled, child workers or child soldiers, for example, as social categories; or ecology, animal rights, abortion or nuclear power generation as issues) in development discourses. And, as I have argued elsewhere (Clammer 2004), social movements are of profound significance as generators of new forms of knowledge. While this is particularly true of all social movements that seek socio-cultural transformation rather than simply resisting or reacting to change, it is especially true of those kinds of movements most commonly omitted by mainstream social movement theory – art movements and new religions.

For, in discussing social change and social movements, the question is rarely raised as to where transformative ideas come from in society, who generates them and what kinds of social experiments are giving rise to these new ideas. For ideas rarely arise in a vacuum – they occur in the context of response, conflict, conquest, change or the necessity, often for unchosen reasons, to reinterpret a formerly taken-for-granted social reality in new and unexpected ways. Indeed if a new moral community is being established or proposed, an element of originality is almost inevitable (even among movements whose objective is a return to some kind of past model or putative golden age). Consequently, imagination flourishes in the new social movements in particular, but in concrete forms, since these are necessarily social and cultural experiments extruded into the culture at large.

Methodologically this kind of view of social movements takes us a long way from the perspective that sees them as primarily the expression of class interests in the context of capitalism, important as that larger context certainly was in the nineteenth century, seen by some scholars as essentially defining what kinds of movements are possible at all. As Arrighi, Hopkins and Wallerstein put it very clearly,

> In the course of the twentieth century, indeed defining it, a massive sea-change has been occurring in the social relations of accumulation. In a sentence, the relational networks forming the trunk lines of the circuits of capital have been so structurally transformed that the very workings of the accumulation process appear to be historically altered. It is this ongoing transformation that has continually remade the relational conditions both of the organizing agencies of accumulation (by definition) and those in the fundamental struggle with them, the antisystemic movements; and so have continually remade as well the relational character of the struggle itself and hence the nature of the movements defined by it. (Arrighi et al. 1989: 41).

Indeed, logically this is true: movements are always defined in part by that which they are moving against, and all movements exist obviously in a larger historical, economic and political context. But where this argument is weakest is in relation to religious movements, not discussed at all by Arrighi et al. For they do not seem to be able to understand movements that transcend the state, although they do grasp that the operative context is now not so much individual states, but rather the *system* of states (the term 'globalization' does not appear anywhere in their analysis). This leads them to argue that

> There is ... a set of consequential historical contradictions being formed through this recreation of all varieties of social relations

into networks within either inter- or intrastate frameworks. Many kinds of community – in the sense of communities of believers/ practitioners – form in a way 'worlds' of their own in relation to, in distinction from, and often in conflict with all others; that is, those who are not of their community, who are nonbelievers or nonpractitioners, hence nonmembers. These are often large, encompassing worlds: the Islamic world; the scientific world; the African world ...; the women's world; the workers' or proletarian world; and so forth. It is far from evident that such communities of consciousness can even persist, much less grow, within the structurally developing inter- and intrastate framework. (Arrighi et al. 1989: 45–6)

Apart from the shocking essentialism of this argument and its historical crudity, on a par with Huntington's 'clash of civilizations' thesis, it is evidently false. Not only do such 'communities of consciousness' flourish in the interstices of the state/interstate system, they in many cases transcend and will no doubt outlive it, having persisted in some cases for millennia.

This draws our attention to two factors: the weakness of much social science in explaining what it takes as its own subject matter (a shallow as opposed to a deep sociology), and the inadequacy of purely materialist methodologies. It is noteworthy that much of the most innovative thinking about deep change and fundamental socio-cultural structures has come from outside sociology and by thinkers largely or totally ignored by mainstream social sciences. Instances of such entirely neglected thinkers (who are, however, often prominent in 'communities of consciousness' of their own) might include Rudolf Steiner (e.g. 1985), C.G. Jung (Odajnyk 1976), Ernst Bloch, Albion Small (Becker 1971), and contemporary thinkers such as Michael Lerner (1996), Ken Wilbur (2004) and Fritjof Capra (2003), or Roy Bhaskar (2002), as well as people entirely outside the ambit of Western social thought such as Gandhi, Sri Aurobindo, P.R. Sarkar (the originator of the Progressive Utilization Theory) and Pandurang Shastri Athavale, the founder of the large Indian social movement known as Swadhyaya (Srivastava 1998), to name a few prominent examples from my own list of favourites.

Speaking of the role of culture in social movements and in the women's movements in particular, Steven Buechler points out, rightly, that culture is a key factor in many of the new social movements based around ecology, peace, nuclear power, and gay and lesbian themes:

> Such movements have a mixed record of instrumental practices and predictable tensions between cultural commitments and political aspirations. They nevertheless signify a major trend in contemporary social activism by reframing the Leninist question of organization from a strategic challenge in an instrumental conflict to a symbolic challenge in a cultural struggle. (Buechler 2000: 207)

This is indeed so, and, to reiterate an earlier point, such movements not only discover new subjects of knowledge, but themselves represent knowledge generation as praxis.

They do so, however, not simply as cognitive movements, but as expressive ones: those concerned as much with performance and the creation of what Kevin Hetherington calls 'emotional communities' (Hetherington 1998) in which celebration, liminality, play, choice, style, 'tribalism', theatre, art and new forms of spirituality take a central place. As such they challenge fundamentally the anti-humanism, textualism and determinism of both structuralist conceptions of identity associated with figures such as Lacan, Althusser and Lévi-Strauss and Foucault's notion that subjectivity is constituted in discourse, in subject positions within a space of power–knowledge in which, to use Hetherington's formulation, 'All we can do ... is use the subject positions in which we are located to write, not life-scripts, but little stories, poems, language games, in which we can rearrange our identities and our identification with others in partial and contingent ways' (Hetherington 1998: 24). A new form of agency, voluntarism and vitalism consequently enters the social and sociological scene. As postmodernists would argue, there may be no master-script, but then, while this constitutes a vast area of freedom, in postmodern thought it also leads to a politics of difference and a world-view characterized by fragmentation, uncertainty, contingency, multiplicity and ambivalence. While the postmodern critique of essentialism and realist views of identity proved to be a valuable move, by abandoning any conception of human nature, or even of 'nature' having any specific non-socially constructed qualities, it becomes problematic to talk about identity at all, except as a shifting field of relational positions, of 'Others'. Yet in fact most counter-cultural movements, far from expressing this free-floating, contingent and apolitical form, are actually utopian, meaning-generating and opposed to the instrumental and secular features of contemporary societies. As Cohen, Ben-Yehuda and Aviad express it,

> 'Post-modern' individuals ... seek to 'recentralize' their world
> through adherence to one of the symbolic-moral universes
> enveloping a host of competing 'elective centres' such as those
> proposed by the new cults and religions, new life styles and
> communal movements, as well as by radical movements. Each of
> these typically embodies a vision of some ultimate salvational goal
> and proposes a 'salvation path'. (Cohen et al. 1987: 375)

While they go on to point out that in a postmodern context in which stable goals and criteria for judgement are absent, individuals may move from one 'elective centre' to another or fall away when initial excitement at the discovery of a new centre of meaning fades, I think that they overestimate the degree to which this happens, or the extent to which this 'quest' leads to ultimate disillusionment. Rather, it may be better to think of this movement as a growth process, a continuous process of learning, self-discovery and new insights, the pursuit of a kind of socially relevant enlightenment, in fact a latter-day search for what Weber would classically have called 'vocation'.

But while Hetherington, successfully in my view, moves the ground on which new social movements are to be interpreted by stressing their performative and expressive nature and the spaces and occasions in and on which this identity is created, he also challenges the idea that new social movements are agents of historical change, but suggests rather that they are local, plural and situated rather than universalist. At first sight this argument would seem simply to substantiate the claim of Arrighi and colleagues that such movements simply exist in the interstices of contemporary global capitalism and have no structurally transforming power of their own. But another perspective altogether can be taken that relates the two viewpoints. All social movements are of course situated, in larger global structures as well as in their local and immediate contexts. But, as generators of new forms of knowledge, such movements also challenge the epistemological hegemony of the dominant order and create alternatives that can have very long-term effects. For, although many 'new' social movements are local in scope, and it is the case, as Arrighi et al. argue, that many of the older movements appear to have failed (they have not radically disrupted the growth or power of global capitalism), they nevertheless have had many positive effects, including that of creating new forms of discourse upon which newer forms of protest and alternatives creation have built. The whole language of protest and the whole language in which global capitalism must try to legitimate itself (a now very self-defensive language) have changed. Furthermore, it is always tempting if intellectually lazy to assume that the future will be basically a continuation of the past with some new features. In fact at the moment we face a time of unprecedented challenges and it may well be that those who are now constructing what appear to be weak alternatives to the dominant industrial/consumption system and its associated culture will in reality be those who survive and prove in the long run (or now even the relatively short run) to have been right.

For the basis of any viable and sustainable future must be a philosophical anthropology that adequately reflects the real nature of human beings and their relationship to the wider biosphere. And it is not at all evident that postmodernism has achieved this. On the contrary, as Terry Eagleton argues, postmodernism essentially converts everyone into consumers – 'mere empty receptacles of desire'. In place of those old autonomous others, who were all too stubbornly specific, there now emerges a portentously generalized Otherness, the particular bearers of which can become indifferently interchangeable: women, Jews, prisoners, gays, aboriginal peoples' (Eagleton 1996: 88). For here we must avoid two errors: one is to assume that universalism and particularism are necessarily at odds, and the other is that thought processes about society (or anything else) have to contain a highly impoverished notion of rationality or reason. Again in Eagleton's words,

> Reason at its best is related to generosity, to being able to acknowledge the truth or justice of another's claim even when it cuts against the grain of one's own interests and desires. To be reasonable in this sense involves not some desiccated calculation but courage, realism, justice, humility and largesse of spirit: there is nothing clinically disinterested about it. (Eagleton 1996: 123)

Such a critique of the basic assumptions of so much contemporary cultural theory points in some fresh and refreshing directions: away from the silliness of cultural relativism, which is clearly undermined by this expanded sense of rationality, and towards a strong sense of political agency, solidarity, cooperation, values-based behaviour. In other words, towards foundations not of the essentialist and mono-lithic kinds that postmodernism has so rightly critiqued, but based on a grasp of actual human existential realities and their location within the wider framework of nature. Indeed, in this broadened sense the distinction between reason and emotion dissolves. In practice they flow constantly into one another, and so knowledge needs to be rooted in ontology as much as in epistemology, in a complete and embodied sense of being and not solely in the head. Knowledge in fact is praxis, not simply cognition, and as such has social roots. The objective then becomes not simply to discover those roots and document them, but to nurture actively the forms of social experiment in which they grow and can positively influence the future.

This is not significant only for the study of, or the recognition of the importance of, social movements in which culture is a critical dimension. It also applies to equally vital areas (many of which involve the work of social movements), such as peace work. In his luminous book on the peace process, the scholar and activist John Paul Lederach observes:

> Transcending violence is forged by the capacity to generate, mobilize, and build the moral imagination. The kind of imagination to which I refer is mobilized when four disciplines and capacities are held together and practiced by those who find their way to rise above violence. Stated simply, the moral imagination requires the capacity to imagine ourselves in a web of relationships that includes our enemies; the ability to sustain a paradoxical curiosity that embraces complexity without reliance on dualistic polarity; the fundamental belief in and pursuit of the creative act; and the acceptance of the inherent risk of stepping into the mystery of the unknown that lies beyond the familiar landscape of violence. (Lederach 2005: 5)

And not only the familiar landscape of violence, but equally all familiar landscapes that are now changing before our eyes – economic systems, the environment, personal relationships, artistic styles. For the moral imagination, in Lederach's view, is the one thing uniquely gifted to our species, but which until now has been rarely understood or utilized. Such a view also takes us away from a purely technical view of development towards one more humanistic in its orientation, concerned with creating capacities rather than 'solving' 'problems', with creating relational spaces, and less with designing social change than allowing it to happen by freeing and acknowledging the deep creativity that abounds in every human culture, but that is honoured more in theory than in practice. The moral imagination, of course, is not simply ethics: it necessarily incorporates the artistic, creativity in general, our relationship to the sensuous and our links to the ground of our being – nature. It involves, in other words, an erotics of development every bit as much as a set of methodologies or techniques of development. The latter are the province of the technician and bureaucrat, the former is that of the total human being.

This involves, of course, the critique of culture from within itself, for by no means all culture comes even close to fulfilling the requirements of an expanded moral imagination – the consumerist trash, bad taste, gratuitous violence, poorly designed products, nutrition-free foods, junk advertising, imagination-free toys and substandard design that characterize so much contemporary popular culture are themselves in need of critique, an important role that cultural studies, under the impact of postmodernism and its own desire to establish popular or mass culture as legitimate subjects of scholarly enquiry, has mostly failed to take up. But culture that depresses or negates life and spirit should be as much subject to critique and replacement as crime, corruption or environmental pollution, which it parallels or even promotes through its generation of images. For, as Kenneth Boulding pointed out some years ago in his now classic study, our behaviour depends on the images that lie behind our actions, our causes and our social psychology. For not only is knowledge power, so is the symbol (Boulding 1975).

It is for this reason among many others that it has been a major mistake of sociology to relinquish the study of religious movements largely to religion specialists or, at the very most, to an aspect of the subdiscipline of the sociology of religion, and to relinquish the study of art movements to the art historians. For both, apart from their intrinsic interest as social movements in their own right, demonstrate clearly the significance of the image and its vital role in stimulating and sustaining social and cultural change and new forms of knowledge, and, more importantly, new modes of knowing, which in turn generate new modes of protest and struggle. It is no accident, as Martin Fuchs points out (2004), that many if not most anti-caste movements in modern India have taken the form of religious protest – the creation of new religious movements, or, as in the celebrated case of the leader of the Dalit movement, Dr B.R. Ambedkar and many of his followers and fellow 'untouchables', mass conversion to what is seen as a non-oppressive and liberatory religion already in existence – in this case Buddhism. In attempting to show how this should be so, Fuchs draws on some very significant ideas. One of these is the notion of the 'non-identity of society with itself' – the idea that society is a process, an order of becoming rather than being, and as such is always transcending itself. The sociological tendency to see society as a kind of stasis needs to be superseded by a dynamic model in which social movements, the second of Fuchs's key ideas, play a major role. He quotes Alain Touraine to support this contention: 'Social movements are not exceptional and dramatic events: they lie permanently at the heart of social life', and rather than order coming first, 'What comes first is the work society performs on itself' (Touraine 1981a: 29). The constant self-production or reproduction of society through socialization and other standard and conscious or unconscious methods is interrupted by historical moments that begin the creation of a new order, and it is social movements that act as the propellant for such developments or transformations. So far so good, but unfortunately Touraine is also committed to an oversociological view. As Fuchs summarizes his position,

> Cultural movements too, a third category which Touraine
> introduces, are ephemeral to social transformation. While concerned
> with the 'transformation of cultural values' (the 'emergence of new
> ethical values' in the case of the women's movement for example),
> they do not show stability, they 'split quickly' and remain bound
> to the social conflict which prevails. (Fuchs 2004: 42–3, referring to
> Touraine 1981a: 96; 1985: 776 ff.)

As Fuchs points out, this viewpoint 'restricts the scope of social *interpretation* and the arena of interpretive conflict. ... Culture, set up as the defining background, in the final analysis remains strangely aloof. The cultural articulations – interpretations and negotiations – do not mark the analytical starting point. All is focused on the social system's self dynamics' (Fuchs 2004: 43). Such a viewpoint not only banishes hermeneutics, but fails to articulate the linkages between social movements and cultural models, something important to do since the actors, individuals and social movements in fact act upon or arise from differing cultural orientations. This we have tried to do in the manner of a kaleidoscope – by noting the multiple linkages between culture and its social context and expressions and by showing that the imagination, while shaped by what has gone before it and by its contemporary social context, also shapes that context and endlessly remoulds, undermines and reformulates it. Social movements are the points at which imagination takes embodied social and cultural form (unlike science fiction, for example, or purely literary utopias).

Culture and development revisited

Although most sociological approaches to social movements have framed the issue in terms of the relationship between such movements and their wider social base, here we are suggesting a fundamental reformulation – from the almost inevitable oversociologizing of the sociological model to the suggestion that the key nexus is that between culture and creativity: an alternative model in which imagination is present in both and in which the emancipatory project is not only the achievement of external freedom but also liberation from the internal boundaries that trap and mischannel the creative impulse. Culture is a collective project, as are social movements, and, while the directions that imagination might take cannot be predicted, better conditions for its flourishing can indeed be socially and politically achieved. And this is perhaps a good definition of development. Speaking of the common view that culture is functional – it is something useful to the pursuit of 'development' – Ramashray Roy suggests that, to the contrary,

> In contradistinction to this, there is entirely a different perspective on culture. In this perspective, culture, even as a human artifact, acquires a trans-individual character and attains the authority of prescribing human goals and regulating the means for realizing these goals. In this sense, culture, while subject to the laws of growth and decay, rises above the vicissitudes of the phenomenal world and becomes a reliable means of coping with these vicissitudes. As a prescriptive and regulative force, it determines what development should mean and how it should be implemented. In this sense, it is culture that determines the form and substance of development. It is in this sense, too, that development becomes subservient to culture. This would be an instance of 'development at the service of culture'. (Roy 2001: 136)

For, as Roy goes on to point out,

> to expect culture to play these beneficial roles is to visualize it as qualitatively different from the one the regnant model of development creates, sustains and reinforces. Today culture means a ceaseless search for novelty and is equated with entertainment rather than enlightenment. That is to say, culture has, for all practical purposes, lost its intellectual, chiefly educational, vaguely perfective, and, above all, the evaluative significance. (Roy 2001: 144)

He goes on to suggest that if such an alternative conception of development is to work in the real world, it must be shown to be valid by way of its application to actual instances of such social change in action, which he does by examining the case of the Indian Swadhyaya movement.

The birth of cultural studies historically stemmed from two impulses. The first is the recognition of the fact that in the contemporary world the site of struggle, in particular for identity, had shifted from the conventionally political sphere to the cultural, and that this cultural politics involved a rethinking of the classical categories of gender, class and ethnicity from a more cultural perspective, including the reintroduction of the study of media and popular culture as legitimate and indeed necessary zones of enquiry. While this had the very positive effect of re-energizing sociology with a much needed cultural perspective, it also tended to freeze these perspectives as being *the* subject matter of cultural studies. This, in turn, has been challenged by the gradual broadening of the scope of cultural sociology to include the body, the self, memory and the emotions (for a sampling of examples from the literature, see Barbalet 2001; Lupton 1998; Shilling 1993), the growing realization signalled by the emergence of environmental sociology of our embeddedness in nature, and perhaps above all a movement away from the rigidities of structuralism and its parallel movements to the recognition of the essential elusiveness of human life, which can be lived but never fully grasped, least of all by the categories of the social sciences.

What the social sciences can do, however, is to move in the direction of the fuller incorporation of the existential conditions of human life into their models, to recognize that they are not 'explanations' of human social life standing outside of that life, but are part of the reflexivity that constitutes the constant dialectic of living/understanding that marks our being-in-the-world, and to honour those spaces in which new knowledges are produced and new freedoms and possibilities explored, and those collective experiments in which humans are eternally engaged to make their lives conform closer to the ideals that they have for it and the integrity with which it may be lived. Culture is the space within which these essentially imaginative exercises are conducted, the ontological space in which human beingness is worked out, and as such is the space in which human existential qualities and the demands of development must meet. There is no fixed formula for how this must be done – it is a quest or a journey, not a model, and herein lies its excitement and challenge: to bring the depths of human self-understanding and creativity together with the demands to improve our material conditions so that all might live in dignity and enjoy the conditions in which they too might explore that inherent creativity. One usually expects closure at the end of a book, but the only 'closure' here can be towards a radical openness.

References

Adger, Neil, Katrina Brown and Mike Hulme (eds) (2009) *Global Environmental Change: Human and Policy Dimensions*. Amsterday and London: Elsevier.

Appadurai, Arjun (1996) *Modernity at Large: Cultural Dimensions of Globalization*. Minneapolis: University of Minnesota Press.

Arberry, A.J. (trans.) (1994) *Discourses of Rumi*. Richmond: Curzon Press.

Arendt, Hannah (1970) *On Violence*. New York: Harcourt, Brace, Jovanovich.

Arrighi, Giovanni, Terence K. Hopkins and Immanuel Wallerstein (1989) *Anti-Systemic Movements*. London and New York: Verso.

Atkins, E. Taylor (2010) *Primitive Selves: Koreana in the Japanese Colonial Gaze*. Berkeley and London: University of California Press.

Augé, Marc (1999) *An Anthropology for Contemporaneous Worlds*. Stanford CA: Stanford University Press.

Bakshi, Rajini (2007) *An Economics for Well-Being*. Mumbai and Bangalore: Centre for Education and Documentation.

Bar On, Bat-Ami (2002) *The Subject of Violence: Arendtean Exercises in Understanding*. Lanham MD: Rowman & Littlefield.

Barbalet, J.M. (2001) *Emotion, Social Theory and Social Structure: A Macrosociological Approach*. Cambridge: Cambridge University Press.

Barenboim, Daniel, and Edward W. Said (2002) *Parallels and Paradoxes: Explorations in Music and Society*. London: Bloomsbury.

Barthes, Roland (1984) *The Fashion System*. Trans. Matthew Ward and Richard Howard. New York: Hill & Wang.

Battaglia, D. (1999) 'Towards an Ethics of the Open Subject: Writing Culture in Good Conscience'. In H.L. Moore (ed.), *Anthropological Theory Today*. Cambridge: Polity Press, pp. 114–50.

Baudrillard, Jean (1968) *Le Système des Objets*. Paris: Gallimard.

Baudrillard, Jean (1983) *In the Shadow of the Silent Majorities, or, The End of the Social*. New York: Semiotext(e).

Baudrillard, Jean (1993) *Symbolic Exchange and Death*. London: Sage.

Bauman, Zygmunt (1995) *Life in Fragments*. Oxford: Blackwell.

Bauman, Zygmunt (1999) *Modernity and the Holocaust*. Cambridge: Polity Press.

Bauman, Zygmunt (2000) *Liquid Modernity*. Cambridge: Polity Press.

Bauman, Zygmunt (2004) *Wasted Lives: Modernity and Its Outcasts*. Cambridge: Polity Press.

Bax, Mart (2004) 'Mass Graves, Stagnating Identification and War Violence in Rural Bosnia-Herzegovina'. In Oscar Salemink, Anton van Harskamp and Ananta Kumar Giri (eds), *The Development of Religion/The Religion of Development*. Delft: Eburon, pp. 179–90.

Beck, Ulrich (1992) *Risk Society: Towards a New Modernity*. London: Sage.

Becker, Ernest (1971) *The Lost Science of Man*. New York: George Braziller.

Beidler, Philip D. (1982) *American Literature and the Experience of Vietnam*. Athens: University of Georgia Press.

Bell, Michael Mayerfeld (2004) *An Invitation to Environmental Sociology*. Thousand Oaks CA, London and New Delhi: Pine Forge Press.

Berger, John (1972) *Ways of Seeing*. London: Penguin.

Berger, Peter (1976) *Pyramids of Sacrifice: Political Ethics and Social Change*. London: Allen Lane.

Berry, Philippa, and Andrew Wernick (eds) (1992) *Shadow of Spirit: Postmodernism and Religion*. London and New York: Routledge.

Berry, Thomas (1999) *The Great Work: Our Way Into the Future*. New York: Bell Tower.

Beuys, Joseph (1977) 'Admission in a Living Being'. Talk at Kassel Documenta, quoted in Ulrich Roesch (ed.), *Vision and Action for Another World*. Calcutta: Earthcare Books, 2004.

Bhaskar, Roy (2002) *From Science to Emancipation: Alienation and the Actuality of Enlightenment*. Thousand Oaks CA, New Delhi and London: Sage.

Bien, Peter (1989) *Kazantzakis: Politics of the Spirit*. Princeton NJ: Princeton University Press.

Boff, Leonardo (1997) *Cry of the Earth, Cry of the Poor*. Maryknoll NY: Orbis Books.

Bookchin, Murray (1982) *The Ecology of Freedom*. Palo Alto CA: Cheshire Books.

Booth, David (1985) 'Marxism and Development: Interpreting the Impasse'. *World Development* 13(7): 761–87.

Bornstein, David (2005) *How to Change the World: Social Entrepreneurs and the Power of New Ideas*. London: Penguin.

Boulding, Kenneth E. (1975) *The Image: Knowledge in Life and Society.* Ann Arbor: University of Michigan Press.

Bourdieu, Pierre (1979) *Outline of a Theory of Practice.* Cambridge: Cambridge University Press.

Bourdieu, Pierre, et al. (eds) (1999) *The Weight of the World: Social Suffering in Contemporary Society.* Cambridge: Polity Press.

Bowen, Elizabeth S. (1956) *Return to Laughter.* London: Gollancz.

Brah, Avtar, and Anne E. Coombes (eds) (2000) *Hybridity and Its Discontents: Politics, Science, Culture.* London and New York: Routledge.

Brush, S., and D. Stabinsky (1996) *Valuing Local Knowledge: Indigenous People and Intellectual Property Rights.* Washington DC: Island Press.

Bruun, Ole, and Arne Kalland (eds) (1995) *Asian Perceptions of Nature.* Richmond: Curzon Press.

Buck-Morss, Susan (2000) *Dreamworld and Catastrophe: The Passing of Mass Society in East and West.* Cambridge MA and London: MIT Press.

Buechler, Steven M. (2000) *Social Movements in Advanced Capitalism: The Political Economy and Cultural Construction of Social Action.* New York and Oxford: Oxford University Press.

Burroughs, William James (2005) *Climate: Into the 21st Century.* Cambridge: Cambridge University Press.

Buruma, Ian (1994) *The Wages of Guilt: Memories of War in Germany and Japan.* New York: Farrar, Straus & Giroux.

Calasso, Roberto (1995) *The Ruin of Kasch.* London: Vintage.

Callenbach, Ernest (2004) *Ecotopia.* Berkeley: Banyan Tree Books.

Camus, Albert (1979) *Selected Essays and Notebooks.* Harmondsworth: Penguin.

Canetti, Elias (1986) *The Human Province.* London: Picador.

Capra, Fritjof (1988) *The Turning Point: Science, Society and the Rising Culture.* London: Flamingo.

Capra, Fritjof (2003) *The Hidden Connections.* London: Flamingo.

Carmen, Raff (1996) *Autonomous Development: Humanizing the Landscape.* London and New York: Zed Books.

Carrier, James G., and Daniel Miller (1998) *Virtualism: A New Political Economy.* Oxford: Berg.

Carrier, James G., and Daniel Miller (2000) 'From Private Virtue to Public Vice'. In Henrietta L. Moore (ed.), *Anthropological Theory Today.* Cambridge: Polity Press, pp. 24–47.

Castoriadis, Cornelius (1987) *The Imaginary Institution of Society.* Cambridge: Polity Press.

Chanan, Michael (1972) 'Art as Experiment'. *British Journal of Aesthetics* 12(2): 133–47.

Chen, H.-K. (ed.) (1995) *Trajectories: Inter-Asia Cultural Studies.* London and New York: Routledge.

Chopp, Rebecca (1982) *The Praxis of Suffering*. Maryknoll NY: Orbis Books.

Clammer, John (ed.) (1978) *The New Economic Anthropology*. London: Macmillan and New York: St. Martin's Press.

Clammer, John (1985) *Anthropology and Political Economy: Theoretical and Asian Perspectives*. London: Macmillan and New York: St. Martin's Press.

Clammer, John (1995) *Difference and Modernity: Social Theory and Contemporary Japanese Society*. London: Kegan Paul.

Clammer, John (1996) *Values and Development in Southeast Asia*. Petaling Jaya: Pelanduk.

Clammer, John (2000) 'Received Dreams: Consumer Capitalism, Social Process and the Management of the Emotions in Contemporary Japan'. In J.S. Eades, Tom Gill and Harumi Befu (eds), *Globalization and Social Change in Contemporary Japan*. Melbourne: Trans Pacific Press, pp. 203–23.

Clammer, John (2002) 'Beyond the Cognitive Paradigm: Majority Knowledges and Local Discourses in a Non-Western Donor Society'. In Paul Sillitoe, Alan Bicker and Johan Pottier (eds), *Participating in Development: Approaches to Indigenous Knowledge*. London and New York: Routledge, pp. 43–63.

Clammer, John (2004) 'Why Social Movements Matter: Knowledge Production and Social Experiments in the NGO Sector in Southeast Asia and Beyond'. In K. Okada (ed.), *Gakunaikyoudou kenkyu Houkoksho: Global-ka to Shiminshakai, Seifu, Kigyoukann no Kyoukai no Kaikaku*. Tokyo: Jochi (Sophia) University Institute of Comparative Culture.

Clammer, John (2005) 'Beyond Power: Alternative Conceptions of Being and the (Asian) Reconstitution of Social Theory'. *Asian Journal of Social Science* 33 (1): 62–76.

Clammer, John (2009a) 'Sociology and Beyond: Towards a Deep Sociology'. *Asian Journal of Social Science* 37 (3): 332–46.

Clammer, John (2009b) *Diaspora and Belief: Globalisation, Religion and Identity in Postcolonial Asia*. Delhi: Shipra Publications.

Clammer, John (2009c) 'Beyond Power: Alternative Conceptions of Being and the Reconstitution of Social Theory'. In Ananta Kumar Giri (ed.), *The Modern Prince and the Modern Sage: Transforming Power and Freedom*. New Delhi, Thousand Oaks CA and London: Sage Publications, pp. 559–75.

Clammer, John (ed.) (2010a) *Socially Engaged Religion*. Bangalore: Books for Change.

Clammer, John (2010b) 'Nonkilling and the Body: Towards a Deep Sociology of Embodiment and Involuntary Death'. In Joam Evans Pim (ed.), *Nonkilling Societies*. Honolulu: Center for Global Nonkilling, pp. 363–82.

Clammer, John, Sylvie Poirier and Eric Schwimmer (eds) (2004) *Figured Worlds: Ontological Obstacles in Intercultural Relations*. Toronto and London: Toronto University Press.

Clayton, A. (ed.) (1996) *NGOs, Civil Society and the State*. Oxford: INTRAC.

Cohen, E., N. Ben-Yahuda and J. Aviad (1987) 'Recentering the World: The Quest for "Elective" Centers in a Secularized Universe'. *Sociological Review* 35 (2): 320–46.

Collins, Randall (1990) 'Stratification, Emotional Energy and the Transient Emotions'. In Theodore D. Kemper (ed.), *Research Agendas in the Sociology of the Emotions*. Albany: State University of New York Press.

Connerton, P. (1995) *How Societies Remember.* Cambridge: Cambridge University Press.

Cowan, Jane K., Marie-Benedict Dembour and Richard A. Wilson (eds) (2001) *Culture and Rights: Anthropological Perspectives.* Cambridge: Cambridge University Press.

Craib, Ian (1994) *The Importance of Disappointment.* London and New York: Routledge.

Cullinan, Cormac (2011) *Wild Law: A Manifesto for Earth Justice.* Totnes: Green Books.

Dallmayr, Fred (2004) *Peace Talks – Who Listens?* Notre Dame IN: Notre Dame University Press.

Daniel, Valentine E. (1997) *The Anthropology of Violence: Sri Lankans, Sinhalese and Tamils.* Delhi: Oxford University Press.

Das, Veena (1997) 'Language and Body: Transactions in the Construction of Pain'. In Arthur Kleinman, Veena Das and Margaret Lock (eds), *Social Suffering.* Berkeley: University of California Press, pp. 67–91.

de Bernières, Louis (2005) *Birds without Wings.* London: Vintage.

de Certeau, M. (1984) *The Practice of Everyday Life.* Berkeley: University of California Press.

de Sousa Santos, B. (1999) 'On Oppositional Postmodernism'. In R.O'Hearn (ed.), *Critical Development Theory.* London: Zed Books, pp. 29–43.

Derrida, Jacques (1992) 'Force of Law: The 'Mystical Foundations of Authority'. In Drucilla Cornel, Micheal Rosenfeld and David G. Carlson (eds), *Deconstruction and the Possibility of Justice.* New York: Routledge.

Des Pres, Terrence (1976) *The Survivor: An Anatomy of Life in the Death Camps.* New York: Oxford University Press.

Diamond, Jared (2005) *Collapse: How Societies Choose to Fail or Succeed.* New York: Penguin.

Dickens, Peter (2004) *Society and Nature.* Cambridge: Polity Press.

Diener, Ed, and Martin E.P. Seligman (2004) 'Beyond Money: Towards an Economy of Well-Being'. *Psychological Science in the Human Interest* 5 (1), July.

Douglas, Mary, and Baron Isherwood (1980) *The World of Goods: Towards an Anthropology of Consumption.* Harmondsworth: Penguin.

Dove, Michael (ed.) (1980) *The Real and Imagined Role of Culture in Development.* Honolulu: University of Hawai'i Press.

Dube, S.C. (1984) *Development Perspectives for the 1980s*. Kuala Lumpur: Pelanduk Publications for the United Nations Asian and Pacific Development Centre.

Dussel, Enrique (1995) *The Invention of the Americas: Eclipsing the 'Other' and the Myth of Modernity*. Trans. Michael D. Barber. New York: Continuum.

Eade, Deborah, and Suzanne Williams (1995) *The Oxfam Handbook of Development and Relief*, Volume 2. Oxford: Oxfam.

Eagleton, Terry (1996) *The Illusion of Postmodernism*. Oxford: Blackwell.

Eagleton, Terry (2003) *After Theory*. New York: Basic Books.

Eaton, Heather, and Lois Ann Lorentzen (eds) (2003) *Ecofeminism and Globalization: Exploring Culture, Context and Religion*. Lanham MD and Oxford: Rowman & Littlefield.

Eco, Umberto (1987) *Travels in Hyperreality*. London: Picador.

Elgin, Duane, and Coleen LeDrew (1997) 'Global Paradigm Report: Tracking the Shift Under Way'. *YES! A Journal of Positive Futures*, Winter 1997: 19.

Ellen, Roy (2002) 'Déjà vu, All Over Again: Reinvention and Progress in Applying Local Knowledge to Development'. In Paul Sillitoe, A. Bicker and J. Pottier (eds) (2002) *Participating in Development: Approaches to Indigenous Knowledge*. London and New York: Routledge, pp. 235–58.

Esteva, Gustavo, and Madhu Suri Prakash (1998) *Grassroots Postmodernism: Remaking the Soil of Cultures*. London and New York: Zed Books.

Etzioni, A. (1988) *The Moral Dimension; Towards a New Economics*. New York: Free Press.

Eze, Emmanuel Chukwudi (ed.) (1997) *Postcolonial African Philosophy: A Critical Reader*. Oxford: Blackwell.

Farmer, Paul (1997) 'On Suffering and Social Structural Violence'. In Arthur Kleinman, Veeda Das and Margaret Lock (eds), *Social Suffering*. Berkeley: University of California Press, pp. 261–83.

Featherstone, M. (1993) 'Global and Local Cultures'. In J. Bird, B. Curtis, T. Putnum, G. Robertson and L. Tickner (eds), *Mapping the Futures: Local Culture and Global Change*. London: Routledge, pp. 169–87.

Featherstone, Mike (1997) *Undoing Culture: Globalization, Postmodernism and Identity*. London: Sage.

Feitlowitz, Maguerite (1998) *A Lexicon of Terror: Argentina and the Legacies of Torture*. New York: Oxford University Press.

Fekete, J. (ed.) (1987) *Life after Postmodernism: Essays on Value and Culture*. New York: St. Martin's Press.

Ferber, M.A., and J.A. Nelson (eds) (1993) *Beyond Economic Man: Feminist Theory and Economics*. Chicago: Chicago University Press.

Feuerverger, Grace (2001) *Oasis of Peace: Teaching and Learning Peace in a Jewish-Palestinian Village in Israel*. London and New York: Routledge Falmer.

Finnis, John (1980) *Natural Law and Natural Rights*. Oxford: Clarendon Press.

Foucault, Michael. (1980) *Power/Knowledge: Selected Interviews and Other Writings*, ed. Colin Gordon. New York: Pantheon.

Fox, R.G., and B.J. King (eds) (2002) *Anthropology Beyond Culture*. Oxford and New York: Berg.

Frank, Andre Gunder (1998) *ReOrient: Global Economy in the Asian Age*. Berkeley: University of California Press.

Frankel, B. (1987) *The Post-Industrial Utopians*. Madison: University of Wisconsin Press.

Freeman, M. (1993) *Rewriting the Self: History, Memory, Narrative*. London and New York: Routledge.

Fretel, Alfonso Cotera (2009) 'Visions of a Responsible, Plural, Solidarity Economy in Latin America and the Caribbean'. In Marcos Arruda (ed.), *A Non-Patriarchal Economy is Possible: Looking at Solidarity Economy from Different Cultural Facets*. Rio de Janeiro: Alliance for a Responsible, Plural and Solidarity-based Economy (ALOE), pp. 87–90.

Friedland, Roger, and A.F. Robertson (eds) (1990) *Beyond the Market Place: Rethinking Economy and Society*. New York: Aldine de Gruyter.

Friedman, Jonathan (1996) *Cultural Identity and Global Process*. London: Sage.

Fromm, Erich (1982) *To Have or To Be?* New York: Bantam Books.

Fuchs, Martin (2004) 'Articulating the World: Social Movements, the Self-Transcendence of Society and the Question of Culture'. In Ananta Kumar Giri (ed.), *Creative Social Research: Rethinking Theories and Methods*. Lanham MD and Oxford: Lexington Books, pp. 37–56.

Fulbrook, Mary (2000) *Anatomy of a Dictatorship: Inside the GDR 1949–1989*. Oxford: Oxford University Press.

Gablik, Suzi (2002a) *Conversations before the End of Time*. New York: Thames & Hudson.

Gablik, Suzi (2002b) *The Reenchantment of Art*. London: Thames & Hudson.

Gardner Katy and David Lewis (1996) *Anthropology, Development and the Postmodern Challenge*. London and Chicago: Pluto Press.

Giddens, Anthony (1990) *The Consequences of Modernity*. Cambridge: Polity Press.

Giddens, Anthony (1998) *The Third Way: The Renewal of Social Democracy*. Cambridge: Polity Press.

Giri, Ananta Kumar (2005) *Reflections and Mobilizations: Dialogues with Movements and Voluntary Organizations*. New Delhi: Sage Publications.

Gladwin, Christina H. (1994) 'On the Division of Labor between Economics and Economic Anthropology'. In Stuart Plattner (ed.), *Economic Anthropology*. Stanford CA: Stanford University Press, pp. 397–425.

Glantz, Michael H., and Qian Ye (2010) *Usable Thoughts: Climate, Water and Weather in the Twenty-First Century*. Tokyo, New York and Paris: United Nations University Press.

Gottlieb, Roger, S. (ed.) (2004) *This Sacred Earth: Religion, Nature, Environment.* New York and London: Routledge.

Goulet, Denis (1995) *Development Ethics: A Guide to Theory and Practice.* New York: Apex Press/London: Zed Books.

Graeber, David (2004) *Fragments of an Anarchist Anthropology.* Chicago: Prickly Paradigm Press.

Grandin, Greg (2000) *The Blood of Guatemala.* Durham NC: Duke University Press.

Greider, William (1997) *One World, Ready or Not: The Manic Logic of Global Capitalism.* London: Penguin.

Griffin, David Ray (ed.) (1988) *Spirituality and Society: Postmodern Visions.* Albany: State University of New York Press.

Griffin, Susan (1995) *The Eros of Everyday Life.* New York: Doubleday.

Grillo, R.D., and R.L. Stirrat (eds) (1997) *Discourses of Development: Anthropological Perspectives.* Oxford and New York: Berg.

Gupta, A. (1991) 'Peasant Knowledge: Who Has Rights to Use It?' In B. Haverkort, J. van der Kamp and A. Waters-Bayer (eds), *Joining Farmer's Experiments: Experience in Paticipatory Technology Development.* London: Intermediate Technology Publications, pp. 17–20.

Gutierrez, Gustavo (1983) *The Power of the Poor in History.* Maryknoll NY: Orbis Books.

Harding, S. (1997) 'Is Modern Science an Ethnoscience? Rethinking Epistemological Assumptions'. In Emmanuel Chukwudi Eze (ed.), *Postcolonial African Philosophy: A Critical Reader.* Oxford: Blackwell, pp. 45–70.

Hartmann, Thom (2004) *The Last Hours of Ancient Sunlight: The Fate of the World and What We Can Do Before It's Too Late.* New York: Three Rivers Press.

Harvey, David (1989) *The Condition of Postmodernity.* Oxford: Basil Blackwell.

Harvey, David (2002) *Spaces of Hope.* Edinburgh: Edinburgh University Press.

Haverkort, Bertus, Katrien van t' Hooft and Wim Hiemstra (eds) (2003) *Ancient Roots, New Shoots: Endogenous Development in Practice.* London and New York: Zed Books.

Hawken, Paul (2008) *Blessed Unrest: How the Largest Social Movement in History is Restoring Grace, Justice, and Beauty to the World.* New York: Penguin.

Hay, C., and D. Marsh (eds) (2000) *Demystifying Globalization.* London: Macmillan/New York: St. Martin's Press.

Hecht, Susanna, and Alexander Cockburn (1990) *The Fate of the Forest: Developers, Destroyers and Defenders of the Amazon.* London: Penguin.

Herzfeld, Michael (1992) *The Social Production of Indifference: Exploring the Symbolic Roots of Western Bureaucracy.* Chicago: Chicago University Press.

Hesmondhalgh, David (1998) 'Globalization and Cultural Imperialism: A Case Study of the Music Industry'. In Ray Kiely and Phil Marfleet (eds), *Globalization and the Third World.* London and New York: Routledge, pp. 163–83.

Hetherington, Kevin (1998) *Expressions of Identity: Space, Performance, Politics.* London, Thousand Oaks CA and New Delhi: Sage.

Heyzer, N., J. Riker and A.B. Quizon (eds) (1995) *Government–NGO Relations in Asia: Prospects and Challenges for People-Centered Development.* London: Macmillan/New York: St. Martin's Press.

Hirschman, Albert O. (1981) *The Passions and the Interests: Political Arguments for Capitalism Before Its Trimph.* Princeton NJ: Princeton University Press.

Hobart, M. (ed.) (1993) 'Introduction: The Growth or Ignorance?' In M. Hobart (ed.), *An Anthropological Critique of Development: The Growth of Ignorance.* London: Routledge, pp. 1–20.

Hopkins, Bob (2008) *The Transition Handbook: From Oil Dependency to Local Resilience.* White River Junction VT: Chelsea Green Publishing.

Howell, S. (ed.) (1997) *The Ethnography of Moralities.* London and New York: Routledge.

Hudson, Wayne, and Steven Slaughter (eds) (2007) *Globalisation and Citizenship: The Transnational Challenge.* Abingdon and New York: Routledge.

Huizinga, Johan (1970) *Homo Ludens: A Study of the Play Element in Culture.* London: Paladin.

Hyden, Goran (2001), 'Challenges to Development Cooperation in the 21st Century'. Lecture at United Nations University, Tokyo, 21 June.

Ichikawa, Hiroya, and John Clammer (eds) (2002) *Revisiting Civil Society: Interfacing Development, Business and the International Order.* Tokyo: Sophia University Institute of Comparative Culture.

Illich, Ivan (1990) *Limits to Medicine: Medical Nemesis – the Expropriation of Health.* London: Penguin.

Ishihara, Masaie (2001) 'Memories of War and Okinawa'. In T. Fujitani, Geoffrey M. White and Lisa Yoneyama (eds), *Perilous Memories: The Asia–Pacific War(s).* Durham NC: Duke University Press.

Ivison, Duncan (ed.) (2010) *The Ashgate Research Companion to Multiculturalism.* Farnham: Ashgate.

Iyer, Pico (2004) *Sun After Dark: Flights into the Foreign.* London: Penguin.

Jackson, Michael (2005) *Existential Anthropology: Events, Exigencies and Effects.* Oxford and New York: Berghahn Books.

Jacoby, Russell (1999) *The End of Utopia: Politics and Culture in Age of Apathy.* New York: Basic Books.

Jacoby, Russell (2005) *Picture Imperfect: Utopian Thought for an Anti-Utopian Age.* New York: Colombia University Press.

Jasper, J.M. (1997) *The Art of Moral Protest: Culture, Biography and Creativity in Social Movements.* Chicago and London: University of Chicago Press.

Jomo, K.S. (1993) *Islamic Economic Alternatives.* Kuala Lumpur: Ikraq.

Jones, Ken (2003) *The New Social Face of Buddhism.* Boston MA: Wisdom Publications.

Jordon, Glenn, and Chris Weedon (1995) *Cultural Politics: Class, Gender, Race and Postmodern World*. Oxford and Cambridge MA: Blackwell.

Kanter, Rosabeth Moss (1973) *Commitment and Community: Communes and Utopias in Sociological Perspective*. Cambridge MA: Harvard University Press.

Kaplan, Allan (2002) *Development Practitioners and Social Process: Artists of the Invisible*. London: Pluto Press.

Kawada, Minoru (1993) *The Origin of Ethnography in Japan*. Trans. Toshiko Kishida-Ellis. London: Kegan Paul.

Keck, V. (ed.) (1998) *Common Worlds and Single Lives: Constituting Knowledge in Pacific Societies*. Oxford and New York: Berg.

Keown, Damien V., Charles S. Prebish and Wayne R. Husted (eds) (1998) *Buddhism and Human Rights*. Richmond: Curzon.

Khondker, H.H. (2000) 'Globalization: Against Reductionism and Linearity'. *Development and Society* 29 (1): 17–33.

Kiely, Ray (1998a) 'Introduction: Globalisation, (Post-)Modernity and the Third World'. In Ray Kiely and Philip Marfleet (eds), *Globalisation and the Third World*. London and New York: Routledge, pp. 1–22.

Kiely, Ray (1998b) 'The Crisis of Global Development.' In Ray Kiely and Philip Marfleet (eds), *Globalisation and the Third World*. London and New York: Routledge, pp. 23–43.

Kikuchi, Yasushi (ed.) (2004) *Development Anthropology: Beyond Economics*. Quezon City: New Day Publishers.

Kleinman, Arthur (1988) *The Illness Narratives: Suffering, Healing and the Human Condition*. New York: Basic Books.

Kleinman, Arthur, Veeda Das and Margaret Lock (eds) (1997) *Social Suffering*. Berkeley: University of California Press.

Kleinman, Arthur, and Joan Kleinman (1997) 'The Appeal of Experience: The Dismay of Images: Cultural Appropriation of Suffering in Our Times'. In Arthur Kleinman, Veena Das and Margaret Lock (eds), *Social Suffering*. Berkeley: University of California Press, pp. 1–23.

Korten, D. S. (1999) *The Post-Corporate World: Life after Capitalism*. West Hartford CT and New York: Kumarian.

Kovel, Joel (2002) *The Enemy of Nature: The End of Capitalism or the End of the World?* London and New York: Zed Books.

Kumar, Krishnan (1991) *Utopianism*. Minneapolis: University of Minnesota Press.

Kuper, Adam (1999) *Culture: The Anthropologist's Account*. Cambridge MA: Harvard University Press.

Kusno, Abidin (2000) *Behind the Post-Colonial: Architecture, Urban Space and Political Culture in Indonesia*. London and New York: Routledge.

Kuwayama, Takami (2004) *Native Anthropology: The Japanese Challenge to Western Hegemony*. Melbourne: Trans Pacific Press.

Lambek, M. (1993) *Knowledge and Practice in Mayotte: Local Discourses of Islam, Sorcery and Spirit Possession*. Toronto: Toronto University Press.

Langer, Lawrence, L. (1997) 'The Alarmed Vision: Social Suffering and Holocaust Atrocity'. In Arthur Kleinman, Veeda Das and Margaret Lock (eds), *Social Suffering*. Berkeley: University of California Press, pp. 47–65.

Lash, Scott, and John Urry (1994) *Economies of Signs and Space*. London and Thousand Oaks CA: Sage.

Lederach, John Paul (2005) *The Moral Imagination: The Art and Soul of Building Peace*. Oxford and New York: Oxford University Press.

Leed, Eric, J. (1979) *No Man's Land: Combat and Identity in World War I*. Cambridge and New York: Cambridge University Press.

Lefebvre, Henri (1971) *Everyday Life in the Modern World*. London: Allen Lane.

Lerner, Michael (1996) *The Politics of Meaning: Restoring Hope and Possibility in an Age of Cynicism*. New York: Addison Wesley.

Lerner, Michael (2000) *Spirit Matters*. Charlottesville VA: Hampton Roads Publishing.

Levine, Stephen (1987) *Healing into Life and Death*. New York: Doubleday.

Long, Norman (2001) *Development Sociology: Actor Perspectives*. London and New York: Routledge.

Loy, David (2003) *The Great Awakening: A Buddhist Social Theory*. Boston MA: Wisdom Publications.

Lupton, Deborah (1998) *The Emotional Self: A Sociocultural Exploration*. London, Thousand Oaks CA and New Delhi: Sage.

MacIntyre, Alastair (1981) *After Virtue*. South Bend IN: University of Notre Dame Press.

Maffesoli, Michel (1990) *Au Creux des Apparences: Pour une Ethique de l'esthetique*. Paris: Plon.

Maheshavarananda, Dada (2003) *After Capitalism: Prout's Vision for a New World*. Copenhagen and Washington DC: Proutist Universal Publications.

Manes, Christopher (1990) *Green Rage: Radical Environmentalism and the Unmaking of Civilization*. Boston MA: Little, Brown.

Marchak, Patricia(1999) *God's Assassins: State Terrorism in Argentina in the 1970s*. Montreal and London: McGill–Queens's University Press.

Marcuse, Herbert (1968) 'Philosophy and Critical Theory'. In *Negations*. London: Allen Lane.

Márquez, Gabriel García (2004) *Living to Tell the Tale*. London: Penguin.

Mato, Daniel (2001) 'Comment'. In Daniel Mato (ed.), *Estudios Latinamericanos: Sobre Cultura y Transformaciones Sociales en Tiempos de Globilizacion*. Buenos Aires: CLASCO, p. 161.

McKibben, Bill (2007) *Deep Economy: The Wealth of Communities and the Durable Future*. New York: Henry Holt.

Melkevik, Bjarne (2004) 'The Customary Law of Indigenous Peoples and Modern

Law: Rivalry or Reconciliation?' In John Clammer, Sylvie Poirier and Eric Schwimmer (eds), *Figured Worlds: Ontological Obstacles in Intercultural Relations*. Toronto and London: Toronto University Press, pp. 225–42.

Melucci, Alberto (1989) *Nomads of the Present: Social Movements and Individual Needs in Contemporary Society*. Philadelphia: Temple University Press.

Merry, S.E. (1997) 'Legal Pluralism and Transnational Culture: The Ka Ho 'Kolokolonui Kanaka Maoli Tribunal, Hawai'i 1993'. In Richard Wilson (ed.), *Human Rights, Culture and Context*. London: Pluto Press.

Mies, Maria, and Veronika Bennholdt-Thomsen (1999) *The Subsistence Perspective: Beyond the Globalized Economy*. London and New York: Zed Books.

Miles, Malcolm (2000) *Art, Space and the City: Public Art and Urban Futures*. London and New York: Routledge.

Miles, M., and V. Bennholdt-Thomsen (1999) *The Subsistence Perspective*. London and New York: Zed Books.

Miller, Daniel (1987) *Material Culture and Mass Consumption*. Oxford: Basil Blackwell.

Moore, Henrietta, L. (ed.) (2000) *Anthropological Theory Today*. Cambridge: Polity Press.

Moore, Sally Falk, and Barbara G. Myerhoff (eds) (1975) *Symbols and Politics in Communal Ideology*. Ithaca NY and London: Cornell University Press.

Morris, David, B. (1998) *Illness and Culture in the Postmodern Age*. Berkeley and London: University of California Press.

Mosse, David (2004) 'Social Analysis as Project Development: Anthropologists at Work in the World Bank'. In Oscar Salemink, Anton von Harskamp and Ananta Kumar Giri (eds), *The Development of Religion/The Religion of Development*. Delft: Eburon, pp. 77–87.

Moyo, Dambisa (2009) *Dead Aid: Why Aid is Not Working and How There is a Better Way for Africa*. New York: Farrar, Straus & Giroux.

Munck, Ronaldo, and Dervis O'Hearn (eds) (1999) *Critical Development Theory: Contributions to a New Paradigm*. London and New York: Zed Books.

Murphy, Brian K. (1999) *Transforming Ourselves, Transforming the World*. London and New York: Zed Books.

Murphy, Susan (2004) *Upside Down Zen*. Melbourne: Lothian Books.

Muzaffar, Chandra (2005) *Global Ethic or Global Hegemony? Reflections on Religion, Human Dignity and Civilizational Interaction*. London: ASEAN Academic Press.

Naess, Arne (1995) 'The Deep Ecological Movement: Some Philosophical Aspects'. In G. Sessions (ed.), *Deep Ecology for the 21st Century: Readings on the Philosophy and Practice of the New Environmentalism*. Boston MA and London: Shambhala, pp. 64–84.

Najita, Tatsuo (1989) 'On Cultural and Technology in Postmodern Japan'. In Masao Miyoshi and H.D. Harootunian (eds), *Postmodernism and Japan*. Durham

NC: Duke University Press, pp. 3–20.

Nandy, A. (1999) 'A New Cosmopolitanism: Toward a Dialogue of Asian Civilizations'. In H.-K. Chen (ed.), *Trajectories: Inter-Asia Cultural Studies*. London and New York: Routledge, pp. 142–9.

Narotzky, Susana (1997) *New Directions in Economic Anthropology*. London and Chicago: Pluto Press.

Nederveen Pieterse, J. (2001) *Development Theory: Deconstructions/Reconstructions*. London and Thousand Oaks CA: Sage.

Newman, Edward, and Albrecht Schnabel (eds) (2002) *Recovering from Civil Conflict: Reconciliation, Peace and Development*. London: Frank Cass.

Newman, Edward, and Joanne van Selm (eds) (2006) *Refugees and Forced Displacement: International Security, Human Vulnerability and the State*. Tokyo, New York, Paris: United Nations University Press.

Nyamwaya, D.O. (1997) 'Three Critical Issues in Community Health Development Projects in Kenya'. In R.D. Grillo and R.L. Stirrat (eds), *Discourses of Development: Anthropological Perspectives*. Oxford and New York: Berg, pp. 183–201.

O'Brian, Jodi, and Judith A. Howard (eds) (1998) *Everyday Inequalities: Critical Inquiries*. Oxford and Malden MA: Blackwell.

Oliver de Sardin, Jean-Pierre (2005) *Anthropology and Development: Understanding Contemporary Social Change*. London and New York: Zed Books.

Ong, A. (2000) 'Clash of Civilizations or Asian Liberalism? An Anthropology of the State and Citizenship'. In H.L. Moore (ed.), *Anthropological Theory Today*. Cambridge: Polity Press, pp. 48–72.

O'Sullivan, Edmund (1999) *Transformative Learning: Educational Vision for the 21st Century*. London and New York: Zed Books.

Owens, Craig (1994) *Beyond Recognition: Representation, Power and Culture*. Berkeley and London: University of California Press.

Panikkar, Raimon (1993) *A Dwelling Place for Wisdom*. Louisville KT: John Knox Press.

Parfitt, Trevor (2002) *The End of Development: Modernity, Postmodernity and Development*. London: Pluto Press.

Paris, Erna (2000) *Long Shadows: Truth, Lies, and History*. Toronto: Vintage.

Peet, Richard, and Michael Watts (eds) (1998) *Liberation Ecologies: Environment, Development and Social Movements*. London and New York: Routledge.

Pim, Joam Evans (ed.) (2010) *Nonkilling Societies*. Honolulu: Center for Global Nonkilling.

Polak, Fred (1973) *The Image of the Future*. Amsterdam and New York: Elsevier.

Porter, Roy (1993) 'Diseases of Civilization'. In W.F. Bynum and Roy Porter (eds), *Companion Encyclopedia of the History of Medicine*, Volume 1. New York: Routledge, pp. 585–600.

276 | CULTURE, DEVELOPMENT AND SOCIAL THEORY

Posey D. (2002) 'Upsetting the Sacred Balance: Can the Study of Indigenous
  Knowledge Reflect Cosmic Connectedness?' In Paul Sillitoe, A. Bicker and
  J. Pottier (eds), *Participating in Development: Approaches to Indigenous Knowledge*.
  London and New York: Routledge, pp. 24–42.
Pottier, J. (1997) 'Towards an Ethnography of Participatory Appraisal and
  Research'. In R.D. Grillo and R.L. Stirrat (eds), *Discourses of Development*.
  Oxford: Berg, pp. 203–27.
Preston, P.W. (1996) *Development Theory: An Introduction*. Oxford and Cambridge
  MA: Blackwell.
Quarles Van Ufford, Philip, and Ananta Kumar Giri (eds) (2003) *A Moral
  Critique of Development: In Search of Global Responsibilities*. London and New
  York: Routledge.
Quinn, D. (1999) *Beyond Civilization*. New York: Three Rivers Press.
Rahnema, Majid (1995) 'Participation'. In W. Sachs (ed.), *The Development Diction-
  ary: A Guide to Knowledge and Power*. London: Zed Books, pp. 116–31.
Rahnema, Majid, and Victoria Bawtree (eds) (2003) *The Post-Development Reader*.
  London and New York: Zed Books.
Rao, V.K.R.V. (1970) *The Gandhian Alternative to Western Socialism*. Bombay:
  Bharatiya Vidya Bhavan.
Rifkin, Jeremy (2004) 'The Age of Access'. In Jerome Binde (ed.), *The Future of
  Values*. Paris: UNESCO/Oxford: Berghahn Books, pp. 129–41.
Rigg, Jonathan (1997) *Southeast Asia: The Human Landscape of Modernization and
  Development*. London: Routledge.
Ritzer, George (1996) *The McDonaldization of Society: An Investigation into the
  Changing Character of Contemporary Social Life*. Thousand Oaks CA: Pine
  Forge Press.
Robertson, Roland (1995) 'Glocalization: Time–Space and Homogeneity'.
  In M. Featherstone, S. Lash and R. Robertson (eds), *Global Modernities*.
  London: Sage.
Roland, M. (1991) *In Search of Self in India and Japan*. Princeton NJ: Princeton
  University Press.
Roodman, David (2007) *Macro Aid Effectiveness Research: A Guide for the Perplexed*.
  Working Paper 135, Washington: Centre for Global Development.
Roy, Arundhati (2002) *The Algebra of Infinite Justice*. New Delhi: Penguin Books
  India.
Roy, Ramashray (2001) 'Culture and Development: Lessons from Swadhyaya'.
  In Ananta Kumar Giri (ed.), *Rethinking Social Transformation: Criticism and
  Creativity at the Turn of the Millennium*. New Delhi: Rawat.
Rubin, D.C. (ed.) (1996) *Remembering Our Pasts: Studies in Autobiographical Memory*.
  Cambridge: Cambridge University Press.
Sabapathy, T.K. (ed.) (1996) *Modernity and Beyond: Themes in Southeast Asian Art*.
  Singapore: Singapore Art Museum and Landmark Books.

Sachs, Wolfgang (ed.) (1995) *The Development Dictionary: A Guide to Knowledge and Power*. London and New York: Zed Books.

Sahlins, Marshall (1996) 'The Sadness of Sweetness: The Native Anthropology of Western Cosmology'. *Current Anthropology* 37 (3): 395–415.

Said, Edward W. (1985) *Orientalism*. London: Penguin.

Said, Edward W. (1993) *Culture and Imperialism*. London: Chatto & Windus.

Salamon, L. (1994) 'The Rise of the Non-Profit Sector'. *Foreign Affairs* 73 (3): 109–22.

Samson, Colin (2004) 'We Live This Experience: Ontological Insecurity and the Colonial Domination of the Innu People of Nothern Labrador'. In John Clammer, Sylvie Poirier and Eric Schwimmer (eds), *Figured Worlds: Ontological Obstacles to Intercultural Relations*. Toronto and London: University of Toronto Press, pp. 151–88.

Sassen, Saskia (1999) 'Digital Networks and Power'. In Mike Featherstone and Scott Lash (eds), *Spaces of Culture: City, Nation, World*. London: Sage Publications, pp. 49–62.

Schech, Susanne, and Jane Haggis (2000) *Culture and Development: A Critical Introduction*. Oxford and Malden MA: Blackwell.

Scheper-Hughes, Nancy (1992) *Death without Weeping: The Violence of Everyday Life in Brazil*. Berkeley: University of California Press.

Schumacher, E.F. (1979) *Small is Beautiful: A Study of Economics as if People Mattered*. London: Abacus.

Schumacher, E.F. (1980) *Good Work*. London: Abacus.

Schuurman, F.J. (1996) 'Modernity, Postmodernity and the New Social Movements'. In F.J. Schuurman (ed.), *Beyond the Impasse: New Directions in Development Theory*. London and New York: Zed Books, pp. 187–206.

Schuurman, Frans J. (ed.) (1996) *Beyond the Impasse: New Directions in Development Theory*. London and New York: Zed Books, pp. 187–206.

Schwartz, Vera (1997) 'The Pane of Sorrow: Public Uses of Private Grief in Modern China'. In Arthur Kleinman, Veeda Das and Margaret Lock (eds), *Social Suffering*. Berkeley: University of California Press, pp. 119–48.

Scott, James (1985) *Weapons of the Weak: Everyday Forms of Peasant Resistance*. New Haven CT: Yale University Press.

Scott, James C. (1998) 'Freedom and Freehold: People and State Simplification in Southeast Asia'. In D. Kelly and A. Reid (eds), *Asian Freedoms: The Idea of Freedom in East and Southeast Asia*. Cambridge: Cambridge University Press.

Scott, Sue, and David Morgan (eds) (1993) *Body Matters: Essays on the Sociology of the Body*. London and Washington DC: Falmer Press.

Sebald, W.G. (2003) *On the Natural History of Destruction*. New York: Random House.

Sen, Amartya (1999) *Development as Freedom*. New York: Knopf.

Sen, Amartya (2007) *Identity and Violence: The Illusion of Destiny*. New York and London: W.W. Norton.

Sessions, George (ed.) (1995) *Deep Ecology for the 21st Century: Readings on the Philosophy and Practice of the New Environment*. Boston MA: Shambhala.

Shilling, Chris (1993) *The Body and Social Theory*. London: Sage.

Shiva, Vandana (2005) *Earth Democracy: Justice, Sustainability and Peace*. Cambridge MA: South End Press.

Shuman, Michael H. (2000) *Going Local: Creating Self-Reliant Communities in a Global Age*. New York: Routledge.

Sicinski, Andrezej, and Monica Wemegah (eds) (1983) *Alternative Ways of Life in Contemporary Europe*. Tokyo: United Nations University.

Sillitoe, P. (1998) 'The Development of Indigenous Knowledge: A New Applied Anthropology'. *Current Anthropology* 39 (2): 223–52.

Sillitoe, P. (2002) 'Participant Observation to Participatory Development: Making Anthropology Work'. In P. Sillitoe, A. Bicker and J. Pottier, *Participating in Development: Approaches to Indigenous Knowledge*. London and New York: Routledge, pp. 1–23.

Sillitoe, P., A. Bicker and J. Pottier (eds) (2002) *Participating in Development: Approaches to Indigenous Knowledge*. London and New York: Routledge.

Sivakumar, Chitra (2001) 'Transformation in the Sri Lankan Tamil Militant Discourse: Loss of Tamil Self, Violence and the Hermeneutics of Recovery'. In Ananta Kumar Giri (ed.), *Rethinking Social Transformation*. Jaipur and Delhi: Rawat Publications, pp. 304–53.

Skelton, Tracy, and Tim Allen (eds) (1999) *Culture and Global Change*. London and New York: Routledge.

Smart, B. (1999) *Facing Modernity: Ambivalence, Reflexivity and Morality*. London and Thousand Oaks CA: Sage.

Smiers, Joost (2003) *Arts under Pressure: Promoting Cultural Diversity in the Age of Globalization*. London and New York: Zed Books.

Smith, Linda Tuhiwai (1999) *Decolonizing Methodologies: Research and Indigenous Peoples*. London and New York: Zed Books.

Smith, M.J. (2000) *Culture: Reinventing the Social Sciences*. Buckingham: Open University Press.

Soja, Edward (1996) 'Margin/Alia: Social Justice and the New Cultural Politics'. In A. Merrifield and E. Swyngedouw (eds), *The Urbanization of Injustice*. London: Lawrence & Wishart, pp. 180–99.

Soper, Kate (1995) *What is Nature?* Oxford and Cambridge MA: Blackwell.

Southall, Aidan (1992) 'Migration, Class and Post-Urban Society: The Big Apple and the Rotten Apple'. In C.W. Gailey (ed.), *Civilization in Crisis: Anthropological Perspectives*. Gainesville: University of Florida Press, pp. 293–301.

Spalding, Julian (2003) *The Eclipse of Art: Tackling the Crisis in Art Today*. Munich, London and New York: Prestel.

Srivastava, R.K. (1998) *Vital Connections: Self, Society, God: Perspectives on Swad-hyaya*. Tokyo and New York: Weatherhill.

Starr, Amory (2000) *Naming the Enemy: Anti-Corporate Movements Confront Globalization*. London and New York: Zed Books.

Steiner, Rudolf (1985) *The Renewal of the Social Organism*. London and Spring Valley NY: Anthroposophic Press.

Stevens, Wallace (1954) 'The Poems of Our Climate'. In *The Collected Poems of Wallace Stevens*. New York: Alfred A. Knopf.

Stoller, Paul (1997) *Sensuous Scholarship*. Philadelphia: University of Pennsylvania Press.

Strathern, Marilyn (1998) *The Gender of the Gift: Problems about Society and Problems About Women*. Berkeley: University of California Press.

Strydom, Piet (2002) *Risk, Environment and Society: Ongoing Debates, Current Issues and Future Prospects*. Buckingham: Open University Press.

Subramaniam, Suneetha, and Balakrishna Pisupati (eds) (2010) *Traditional Knowledge in Policy and Practice: Approaches to Development and Human Well-Being*. Tokyo, New York and Paris: United Nations University Press.

Sulak, Sivaraksa (1992) *Seeds of Peace: A Buddhist Vision for Renewing Society*. Berkeley: Parallax Press.

Tal, Kali (1996) *Worlds of Hurt: Reading the Literatures of Trauma*. Cambridge: Cambridge University Press.

Taussig, Michael (1980) *The Devil and Commodity Fetishism in South America*. Chapel Hill: University of North Carolina Press.

Tewari, Badri Narayan (2001) 'Documenting Dissent: A Study of Contesting Memory'. In Ananta Kumar Giri (ed.), *Rethinking Social Transformation*. Jaipur and New Delhi: Rawat Publications, pp. 354–91.

Theobald, Robert (1999) *We DO Have Future Choices: Strategies for Fundamentally Changing the 21st Century*. Lismore NSW: Southern Cross University Press.

Theweleit, Klaus (1987) *Male Fantasies*, Vol. I: *Women, Floods, Bodies, History*. Minneapolis: University of Minnesota Press.

Theweleit, Klaus (1989) *Male Fantasies*, Vol. II: *Male Bodies: Psychoanalyzing the White Terror*. Minneapolis: University of Minnesota Press.

Thomas, Nicholas (1994) *Colonialism's Culture: Anthropology, Travel and Government*. Cambridge: Polity Press.

Thomas, Nicholas (1997) 'Collectivity and Nationality in the Anthropology of Art'. In Marcus Banks and H. Morphy (eds), *Rethinking Visual Anthropology*. New Haven CT: Yale University Press, pp. 256–75.

Tobin, J.J. (ed.) (1992) *Remade in Japan: Everyday Life and Consumer Taste in a Changing Society*. New Haven CT: Yale University Press.

Tomlinson, John (2000) *Globalization and Culture*. Cambridge: Polity Press.

Tonkin, Elizabeth (1992) *Narrating Our Pasts: The Social Construction of Oral History*. Cambridge: Cambridge University Press.

Touraine, Alain (1981a) *The Voice and the Eye: An Analysis of Social Movements*. Cambridge: Cambridge University Press.

Touraine, Alain (1981b) 'Introduction to the Study of Social Movements'. *Social Research* 52 (4): 749–87.

Touraine, Alain (1988) *Return of the Actor: Social Theory in Postindustrial Society*. Minneapolis: University of Minnesota Press.

Vacca, Roberto (1974) *The Coming Dark Age*. London: Panther Books.

Viswanathan, Gauri (1998) *Outside the Fold: Conversion, Modernity and Belief*. Princeton NJ: Princeton University Press.

Wallman, Sandra (ed.) (1979) *The Social Anthropology of Work*. London and New York: Academic Press.

Warren, Kay (2003) 'Violence and Development Under Globalization: Case Studies from South America, South Asia and Central Africa'. Lecture delivered at Sophia University, Tokyo.

Webber, Jonathan (1992) *The Future of Auschwitz*. Oxford: Oxford Centre for Postgraduate Hebrew Studies.

Webster, Andrew (1986) *An Introduction to the Sociology of Development*. London: Macmillan.

Wielenga, Bas (1999) *Towards an Eco-Just Society*. Bangalore: Centre for Social Action.

Wilbur, Ken (2004) *A Theory of Everything: An Integral Vision for Business, Politics, Science and Spirituality*. Dublin: Gateway.

Wines, James (2008) *Green Architecture*. Cologne and Los Angeles: Taschen.

Woodiwiss, Anthony (2005) *Human Rights*. London and New York: Routledge.

Woost, M.D. (1997) 'Alternative Vocabularies of Development? "Community" and "Participation" in Development Discourses in Sri Lanka'. In R.D. Grillo and R.L. Stirrat (eds), *Discourses of Development: Anthropological Perspectives*. Oxford and New York: Berg, pp. 229–53.

World Bank (2000) *Entering the 21st Century: World Development Report 1999/2000*. New York: Oxford University Press.

World Watch Institute (2011) *State of the World 2011: Innovations that Nourish the Planet*. New York and London: W.W. Norton.

Yamashita, Shinji, and J.S. Eades (eds) (2003) *Globalization in Southeast Asia: Local, National and Transnational Perspectives*. Oxford and New York: Berghahn.

Yoneyama, Lisa (1999) *Hiroshima Traces: Time, Space and the Dialectics of Memory*. Berkeley: University of California Press.

Young, Allen (1997) 'Suffering and the Origins of Traumatic Memory'. In Arthur Kleinman, Veena Das and Margaret Lock, *Social Suffering*. Berkeley: University of California Press, pp. 245–60.

Zeldin, T. (1995) *An Intimate History of Humanity*. London: Minerva.

Zukin, Sharon (1996) 'Cultural Strategies of Economic Development and the Hegemony of Vision'. In A. Merrifield and A. Swyngedouw (eds), *The Urbanization of Injustice*. London, Lawrence & Wishart, pp. 223–43.

Zunes, Stephan, Lester R. Kurtz and Sarah Beth Asher (eds) (1999) *Nonviolent Social Movements*. Oxford and Malden MA: Blackwell.

Index

About Zed Books

Zed Books is a critical and dynamic publisher, committed to increasing awareness of important international issues and to promoting diversity, alternative voices and progressive social change. We publish on politics, development, gender, the environment and economics for a global audience of students, academics, activist and general readers. Run as a co-operative, we aim to operate in an ethical and environmentally sustainable way.

Find out more at
www.zedbooks.co.uk

For up-to-date news, articles, reviews
and events information visit
http://zed-books.blogspot.com

To subscribe to the monthly Zed Books e-newsletter
send an email headed 'subscribe' to marketing@zedbooks.net

We can also be found on Facebook, ZNet,
Twitter and Library Thing.